Forward

Ready, Aim, Hired

You already know this book meshes smoothly and powerfully into your high speed world. Just read the title.

In three words, Fred Coon gives you the edge you must have in an economy where job searches take months.

Want proof? Consider this:

What you need ...	What this book delivers ...
❑ A way to make sense of the welter of "folklore" that surrounds getting a job	❑ A straight forward, step-by-step plan to get you hired
❑ Knowledge you can apply in real job hunting situations	❑ Realistic exerc ises that reinforce learning and build confidence
❑ Insider information to make you an irresistible candidate	❑ Proven tools from Fred Coon's years as both recruiter and career coach
❑ Self-assurance to answer any interview questions—without memorizing anything	❑ Techniques that convert interrogations into collaborations, leveraging the increasingly popular behavioral questions
❑ More career stability	❑ Methods to ensure that you thrive in your new job.

For 17 years, I've read and contributed to dozens of " how -to-get-a-job" books. I post on blogs and write for trade magazines often.

This book distills the essence from all those sources. It's practical, comprehensive, and honest. Yet it's completely adaptable to any career field, any industry, and nearly any level of experience.

Congratulations on taking control of your career. You couldn't have a better guide than Fred Coon.

Donald P. Orlando, MBA, CPRW, JCTC, CCM, CCMC, CJSS

The McLean Group
One of America's first personal, professional career coaches
Former Charter Member, Board of Directors, Career Management Alliance
Monthly columnist: Professional Association of Resume Writers; regular contributor: NETSHARE.com
Published in more than 56 collections of the best resumes in the United States, Canada, and Australia
http://www.linkedin.com/in/donorlandocareercoach

Acknowledgments

I would like to thank my wife, Alcyone, for her belief in me and her steadfast and unwavering support of my career, and for her caring encouragement, every step of the way. She has always supported my dreams. Who could ask for anything more?

I would like to also thank each person on the Stewart, Cooper & Coon team who, daily, provide consistent professional and caring support to our clients. Their work ethic, their loyalty and their constant drive to see that our clients come first makes me know that my vision is supported.

I would specifically like to thank Michelle Settle, who manages the SC&C operations and has been one of the main contributors to our company success. She is the glue that keeps it all together. The other senior member of my team whom I wish to thank is Kristine Barney who manages one of our company divisions. I highly value Kristine's practical and sound advice. There isn't enough space to mention everyone in the company so I would just like to say "thank you" to all members of the SC&C team. All of you inspire me daily.

My father and mother, M. Fred and Anita Coon, taught me values and had a few sayings that I have sprinkled throughout this book in one form or another. They are: "Always work hard, be honest, have high integrity, do right by others, be creative, do your best, try hard then try harder, never give up, don't lie or cheat or steal, don't buy a pig in a poke and don't brush your teeth with your tie on." Life lessons for sure.

I would like to thank my colleagues throughout the career industry for their encouragement and support of my efforts to deliver superior services to each client we serve. To Jack Chapman because I like his reality and gritty wisdom on the do's and don'ts of interviewing. To Susan Britton Whitcomb, Chandlee Bryan and Deb Dibb for helping me understand the Twitter phenomenon and how to apply those tactics to my clients' benefit. To Louise Kursmark and Wendy Enelow, probably the most senior resume writers in the United States, for their unflagging dedication to excellence in the resume writing industry and the encouragement and expertise they have so often given to those of us in the career field. To Laura DeCarlo, President of the Career Director's International organization. She has always been there to answer questions for me and share ideas freely - a wonderful resource for me personally. In my professional job search and strategic career management efforts, I have discovered so many creative and smart people who are willing to share their knowledge freely with me. That inspires me too.

It is a great feeling to know that these resources exist and are so readily available to me and to others who need advice and council. Thanks everyone!

INFORMATION SOURCES

The Campaign Directors at Stewart, Cooper & Coon: Bill Temple, Leslie Noyes, Barbara Limmer, Jo Ann Moser and George Stecyk. What a wealth of experience and solid information!

Bill Temple – Bill authored Chapter 10, Power of Words, for this book. Bill, better known to his clients and the rest of us as "The Professor," is, in my opinion, the finest Career Management and Communication Strategist I've ever had the pleasure to work with. Bill has over 17 years of experience and has represented 1800+ clients who collectively represent more than $187 million in negotiated compensation. Bill is the author of The Principles of Effective Personal Marketing©, as well as a contributing columnist and speaker on the subject of interpersonal communications. Bill currently serves as the SVP Consulting Campaign Management for Stewart, Cooper & Coon, Inc. Bill is one of the people who inspire me daily.

Ready Aim Hired

Survival Tactics For Job & Career Transition

THIRD EDITION

Fred Coon, LEA, JCTC, CRW

GAFF Publishing
Phoenix, AZ

This book is published by:

GAFF Publishing
P.O. Box 94477
Phoenix, AZ 85070-4477

ISBN 0-9724235-0-8

SAN: 255-0504

Publisher's Cataloging-in-Publication (Provided by Quality Books, Inc.)
Coon, Fred.
   Ready Aim Hired: Survival Tactics for Job & Career
Transition / Fred Coon.
   p. cm.
1. Job hunting.   I. Title.

HF5382.7.C66 2003   650.14
           QBI02-200940

Ron Venckus - Ron and I jointly authored Chapter 9, Behavioral Competency Interviewing. Ron Venckus, is an Author, Consultant and my friend. He authored Why Shouldn't We Hire You?© His book was written for the many job seekers, who are in serious need of learning how to prepare for and manage a successful interview by reducing stress and developing their likeability factor. Ron is also a Senior Behavioral Interview Consultant with Stewart Cooper Coon. Ron and I are jointly authoring a new book on behavioral competency interviewing that will ensure better behavioral hiring tactics and emphasize reducing the cost of hire through solid behavioral interviewing practices.

Geoffrey B. Coon – Geoff authored Chapter 12, Social Media Networking Overview. Geoffrey B. Coon, MA, CPRW Geoffrey Coon is a Certified Professional Resume Writer and an expert on new media. He holds a Master's degree in New Media from DePaul University in Chicago, Illinois. His company, Resume Platform, LLC provides new media strategies and advice to individuals as it pertains to their professional careers. He is an avid user, advocate and contributor to new media and is always exploring the newest developments in the field.

Shally Steckerl and Glenn Gutmacher – contributed to Chapter 6, Internet Research, and provided the Question/Answer section of the New Media Chapter as well. The Question/Answer sections are extracts from www.Arbita.net. Arbita and the information is copyrighted and printed with Shally's permission. It is the recruiting industry's premier leader in sourcing & research since 1998. Some of the work was taken from their executive recruiter support and training subscriber-based newletter produced by Arbita.net. This online publication, The Arbita Guru Guide, is intended to facilitate the location of information on the Internet.

Shally is an Atlanta-based recruiting and sourcing consultant, strategist, and prolific writer, blogger and celebrated industry conference speaker. He is renowned for pioneering and innovating many sourcing methods, and architecting and managing centralized teams of recruitment researchers for Motorola, Cisco, Coke, Google, Microsoft and others. The founder of JobMachine and an RIT graduate, he is now EVP and Chief CyberSleuth of Arbita Inc., a leading recruitment marketing, technology, media, train- ing, workforce development and consulting firm, working with many private clients in the Fortune 500. shally@arbita.net

Glenn is VP of the Recruiter Education and Consulting Division of Arbita Inc., focused on helping corporate and third-party recruiting professionals take their talent sourcing skills and department opera- tions to the next level. He was previously a lead sourcer at Microsoft and Getronics and founder of the Boston area's first newspaper chain-owned job board. The founder of Recruiting-Online.com and a Yale graduate, he conducts many public and private client webinars, speaks at industry events, and enjoys writing and blogging about recruiting topics. glenn@arbita.net

Jason Alba - founder of JibberJobber.com, and the author of I'm in LinkedIn — Now What? www.jibberjobber.com

The Twitter Job Search Guide© – Susan Britton Whitcomb, Chandlee Bryan and Deb Dibb published by JIST Works. I can't say enough good things about this book. I highly recommend you purchase this book, if you want to develop your online brand and manage an online Twitter marketing campaign. www.amazon.com.

Susan Ireland – Susan is a prolific blogger and I pulled information on Twitter #hashtags and shortcuts from her website: http://joblounge.blogspot.com/search/label/twitter for our Chapter 12 on New Media.

Susan is the author of Susan Ireland's Ready-Made Resumes software and four job search books, including The Complete Idiot's Guide to the Perfect Resume. Her books and software are sold to individual job seekers, and licensed to government and college career centers. Trained in resume writing by the late Yana Parker (author of The Damn Good Resume Guide), Susan founded a certification program for professional resume writers in 1991. Program graduates comprise Susan Ireland's Job Search Team, which serves clients of all occupations and levels of employment. Information about Susan's products and professional services can be found on her website, www.susanireland.com.

Irina Shanaeva contributed part of Chapter 6. Irina is an executive recruiter and an expert sourcer. For the past five years she has been a partner with Brain Gain Recruiting, placing senior full-time employees in IT, ERP, strategy consulting, and finances. Irina runs a fast-growing "Boolean Strings" network at http://booleanstrings.ning.com/. Since Google seems to be the main search engine, I've chosen this piece for inclusion in the book and simplified and edited her whole piece on logic strings.

Cybel Elaine Werts - Cybel contributed part of Chapter 6 on internet research. Her passion is in emerging technologies such as webcasts, podcasts, & online surveys, and using them as a tool for collaboration and training. She believes that technology should be accessible and fun for people – not scary. You may contact Cybel at (cybelew@aol.com).

RESUME AND COVER LETTER WRITERS

I selected a few resume examples, each showing a little different approach to branding. So, in advance, I wish to apologize to my many, many friends and colleagues around the globe who are excellent writers and do a magnificent job for their clients but, because of space limitations, their work is not presented here. I selected the authors I did, because they are all TORI Award winners. The TORI award is the highest recognition that can be received by a writer who is a member of the Career Director's International. CDI provides a venue for global career professionals to access educational, networking and personal / professional development opportunities in the careers industry. CDI is one of several resume writing and career organizations.

Barbara Safani – Barbara provided the resume for Paul Bailey and the cover letter for Rhonda Lucas. Barbara Safani, owner of Career Solvers, has 15 years of experience in career management, recruiting, and executive coaching. Ms. Safani partners with both Fortune 100 companies and individuals to deliver targeted programs focusing on resume development, job search strategies, networking, interviewing, salary negotiation skills, and online identity management. She is a six-time winner in the TORI (Toast of the Resume Industry) awards competition sponsored by Career Directors International and author of Happy About My Resume: 50 Tips for Building a Better Document to Secure a Brighter Future and #JOBSEARCHtweet.

Gayle Howard, MRW, CERW, CPBS
Gayle may be one of the most certified writers on this planet. Her award list is staggering and she is a multi-award winning Master Resume Writer, published author and Certified Personal Branding Strategist, Gayle Howard is published in more than two dozen international career books, has received twenty-one industry awards, and is a specialist in creating unbeatable value propositions for senior executives. Top Margin, www.topmargin.com - Melbourne, Australia

Gayle provided both resumes and cover letters for this book. What I asked her to also do was to provide her thinking about why she structured the documents the way she did. As a job seeker, you will gain valuable insight by reading her comments and thinking yourself about how to brand yourself and develop your collateral materials. The resume for Yvette Sanderson and cover letters for Murray Maxfield, Matthew Johnson, Vasa Hallerman and Grace Maxfield were prepared by Gayle. The resume and cover letters contain an explanation of why they were structured in that specific manner. It gives the reader an insight into the branding thinking that is so necessary to distinguish oneself in today's marketplace.

Peter Hill, CPRW, CERW – Peter submitted the cover letters for Kent and Kumamoto. He also provided the resume for Brian Washington, with a supporting explanation, and the cover letters for Daivd Kent and Edward Kumamoto. Peter is an international career and job search advisor, speaker, trainer, award-winning résumé writer, and member of The Five O'Clock Club Guild of Career Coaches. He is Principal Consultant of P.H.I. Consulting, a boutique career-services firm providing coaching, résumé development, and corporate outplacement services since 1999. His clients span a wide variety of industries and global markets. Peter is visiting lecturer at China Europe International Business School and Shanghai Jiao Tong University where he teaches MBA-level classes on career development. Peter has lived and worked for an extended period in Nagoya, Japan. He now splits his professional time between his hometown of Honolulu, Hawaii and Shanghai, China. E-Mail: pjhill@phi-yourcareer.com   Website: www.phi-yourcareer.com

Michael Kranes – Michael provided the resume for Tom Tucker. Michael has an M.F.A. in writing from the University of Texas at Austin and B.A. in History from the University of Utah. Michael has over ten years of experience as a writer, editor, teacher, and produced playwright. He has a 1st Place 2009 TORI (Best Military Conversion Resume) and 2nd Place 2008 TORI (Best Technical Resume). He is a member of Career Directors International (CDI), and is a Certified Advance Resume Writer (CARW). Website: www.Resumeslayer.com

There are many fine writers both here in the United States and around the globe. Two of our contributing authors live outside the continental United States. Here are two national organizations where you can find a competent writer. I strongly recommend that you engage a professional writer to "brand" yourself properly.
Career Director's International: http://www.careerdirectors.com/
National Resume Writers Association: http://www.thenrwa.com/

Other Contributors:
Revised Cover and Page layout: QIP Printing and Brenda Wooden (Effect Media)
Printed in USA by QIP Printing, San Diego, CA
Ready Aim Hired Website Design and Interactive Web Exercises: Anita Benton and Brenda Wooden
Cartoons: Jon Jaharus Cartoons

Brenda Wooden (Effect Media - www.effectmedia.us): My very special thanks goes to Brenda Wooden for cleaning this book up, sticking with the project with diligence, and her devotion to a successful outcome. Brenda does great professional web design and has been my webmaster at SC&C for a number of years.

Richard "Dick" Bolles: Dick has been one of the people that continues to inspire me to think outside the box. In every conversation I have ever had with him, including one I had just before this book went to print, I am pleasurably forced to pause and think about whatever subject we are discussing. He inspires me so much. Dick wrote the book, What Color Is Your Parachute. His book has sold more copies than any other career book in history.

TABLE OF CONTENTS

Chapter 3 – Why Should They Hire You? Continued

Chapter 4 –The Résumé

Chapter 5 – Who Needs You?

Chapter 6 – Internet Research

Chapter 7 – Securing The Interview

Chapter 7 – Securing The Interview Continued

Chapter 8 – Controlling Your Interviews

Chapter 9 – Behavioral Interviewing

Chapter 10 – The Power of Words

Chapter 11 – Negotiating Strategies That Work

Chapter 12 – Leveraging New Media

Chapter 13 – Post Employment Rules

Chapter 14 – Thoughts About the 50+ Job Seeker

ATS (Activity Tracking System)

Index

PROLOGUE

All of you reading this book fall into at least one of the following categories:

✓	Unemployed, or about to be	✓	Underemployed
✓	Need additional income	✓	Been with the same company too long
✓	Face an acquisition or merger	✓	Bored and need a change
✓	Under-recognized	✓	Intellectually curious
✓	Career path blocked	✓	Want to change your life or situation
✓	Under-appreciated	✓	Underpaid

Regardless of your reasons, let's agree upon one clear and indisputable point from the beginning of your search. The skills you possess and experience gained thus far in your career comprise a unique product. They can be marketed. Any prospective employer will "buy" this product (YOU), depending upon situational timing, their needs and your presentation.

Therefore, like any other product, your skills must be packaged and sold. Competition is stiff; so, like the hundreds of similar "products" out there, not only must you be seen to be better, but also so much so that employers want to pay more to get you. The main reason you purchased this book is to learn more effective methods of marketing a unique product - YOU.

A job search is a difficult and grueling task. To be successful, you must make a commitment to yourself that, for the duration of this effort, most of your time will be spent toward this end. You must act deliberately, steadily, ceaselessly and, at times, swiftly. Under no circumstances are you to sit still. You must be tough, disciplined and persistent. Nothing less is acceptable.

You will also experience a wide range of emotions, at times becoming frustrated and angry and, on other occasions, elated and joyful. At no time must you allow yourself to see a half-empty glass or become depressed. If you do the former, you will position yourself as a loser. If you do the latter, you are not doing enough in your campaign to accomplish your goals.

The purpose of this book isn't a lengthy, strategic treatise written to teach you how to build an automobile. It is written as a tactical action plan, the purpose of which is to provide sufficient information to teach you how to start the car, guide you where you want to go, negotiate traffic and avoid accidents, and wind up where you dreamed you'd be in the first place.

Remember the following rules: Don't lose the keys, get scared and slam on the brakes, ignore the other drivers, run out of gas or forget where you are going.

You bought this book hoping to learn how to quickly secure the job and money you want. In today's marketplace, by the time you read all the career books and spend untold hours gleaning the best from them, someone else already has the job you were thinking about applying for anyway. This book is tactical and geared to getting you where you want to go as quickly as you and the market will allow.

This is a highly directive book. I don't spend much time explaining the "why" of each task. Instead, I try to spend our time together focusing on what to do, how do it right and when to do it. But, I promise you this: If you follow my instructions, complete all exercises, and campaign like there is no tomorrow, you will cut your search time dramatically, increase your income package significantly, stand a good chance of achieving a more pleasant working situation, develop a more rewarding career path and construct a better financial future for yourself.

After you have secured the job you want and the money you deserve, you can afford the luxury of relaxing and reading why you blindly followed my instructions. Here are some of the rules I live by. I hope they help you in this job search and later throughout your career and personal life.

- ✓ **You Either Make Dust or Eat Dust.... So Keep Focused** – It's easy to be waylaid by life's little distractions, pleasures, and depressions. DON'T! Job search time is precious. You can't afford the luxury of theses costly diversions.

- ✓ **Good Enough, Never Is** – No matter what, you can always improve something about your life, work habits, job search campaign, resume, personal appearance or your interview style.

- ✓ **Think Before You Speak or Act** – What you say and do not only causes you to succeed or fail, but also affects others around you.

- ✓ **Be Disciplined** – Make a schedule of <u>meaningful</u> things to do and DO THEM, <u>as planned and on time</u>!

- ✓ **Have Lots of Energy** – Start exercising and taking vitamins. It will keep your energy up because, before this process is through, you will need all the energy you can muster!

- ✓ **Don't Worry About Rejection** - They are not rejecting you. It is simply not the right time or place or someone more qualified than you got the job. Hey, those rules have been, and will continue to be, true throughout your life. Why should you expect a new set of rules to apply to your job search? You were a good person before this all began and you still are.

- ✓ **Don't Sweat The Small Stuff**- Remember, be concerned only over those things over which you have control, not those things you don't.

- ✓ **Develop and/or Maintain Your Sense of Humor** – the most popular and successful people in the world have good sense of humor. Something to think about isn't it?

- ✓ **Constantly Seek Support From Family and Friends** – You are not alone, even though you may think you are. Your family and friends will support you if you ask. On the other hand, don't complain to them. Nobody likes a whiner but everybody respects a winner!

- ✓ **Be Kind To and Certainly Respect Yourself** – Take comfort breaks as planned. Take your spouse or a friend to supper or lunch. Don't beat yourself up too much. You are your own best friend so treat yourself like one. Work hard, play hard!

You have undertaken a tough task. Be tough yourself. <u>You can do it!</u> Please share your success stories and let me know what worked best in your particular situation. I heartily welcome your thoughts and comments.

In closing, I want to wish you lots of luck, which you make anyway, in your search. Good hunting!

Chapter 1
<<< Getting Ready

"THE REAL JOB SEARCH PUZZLE"

ou are in a contest. The rules for your contest are exactly the same as for those of the gladiators in the days of the Roman Empire. The last person standing wins! Your competitors' main objective and yours are exactly the same. You must avoid being eliminated. They don't hire two people for the same job.

Every action you take, or fail to take, will either keep you in the running or eliminate you from consideration. Actually, there may be better candidates than you in the contest. However, if they eliminate themselves because they don't know or don't follow the rules in this book, then you win.

The main purpose of this book is threefold. First, to show you how to keep from being eliminated. Second, to describe techniques you can employ to speed your search. Third, to illustrate techniques you will use in your interview and negotiation sessions that will cause you to come away with a better package than you hoped for.

The following exercises and supporting narrative will help you understand:

■ How committed you really are

■ How long it should take

■ Your financial readiness

■ Daily/weekly tasks to be done

■ The amount of time required

■ Necessary supplies

■ How to avoid common mistakes

First, I want you to understand that no one is too good, makes too much money, or is too exalted to participate fully in these exercises. If they seem silly, or beneath you, don't be fooled. All of my clients, including those exceeding $500,000 + in annual income, do them too.

These exercises will bring focus to your job search. Focus facilitates action and **meaningful** action will cut your search time dramatically. Last, let's not forget the increased financial rewards attached to a successful search effort.

MONTHLY EXPENSES AND PROJECTED SEARCH TIME

How long should your overall search take? The U.S. Department of Labor states that, in normal economic and market conditions, one should allow about 1 month for each $10,000 in expected annual income. At that rate, if you expected to make $75,000, the search should take you about 8 months.

Don't worry. If you do exactly what you are instructed to do throughout this book (depending upon your personal circumstances and the economy at the time), you may cut up to 40% off the time it takes to land a new position, as well as increase your overall financial package.

All exercises are found at the end of each chapter.

Exercise 1.1
Monthly Expenses - Search Time **www.RAH2010.com**

The *Monthly Expenses* exercise is designed to help you understand the financial reality of your present situation and help you adjust your expenses until you land your next position.

I know this sounds elementary, but if your expenses exceed your income, you should try to figure how to reverse this formula and keep expenses as low as possible to save as much as you possibly can. Sit down and list all your expenses. See which ones you can cut and which you can't cut. If you have credit card debt, call the card company, explain your situation, and in most cases, they will negotiate a minimum payment plan with you during your search period. Remember, they want their money and don't want to chase you around the courts trying to get it. Believe me, they will work with you.

WHAT YOU NEED TO START YOUR SEARCH

Before you perform any job, you need the right tools and a place to work. For the duration of your job search, set aside a place to work where no one else will bother your materials. The actual place is not important.

The key is to select a place where you can easily start and re-start projects and follow up tasks with a minimal amount of set-up time. Keep the area neat and do your filing and posting daily. No excuses, you have the time.

Get a fax program that allows you to fax from your computer. Get a simple fax machine or locate one within easy access to your job search headquarters. A second phone or your cell phone for out-going calls or internet searches is not mandatory, but very nice to have.

Your "office" should have a quality telephone. A novelty phone might look cute, but if the sound isn't crystal clear you may eliminate yourself. Scanning and Fax capabilities are important too.

You will need an answering machine, voice mail, or answering service, with a business-like message. Save the cute, funny stuff until you have your new position. Your 5-year old daughter may be wonderful, but the president of a company calling from an airport to schedule an interview with you might not think so. Don't do anything to eliminate yourself in advance.

Whether you use a PC or a MAC doesn't matter because today word and spreadsheet programs for both are interchangeable.

Your working environment must be well-lit, have a comfortable chair, and be free from distractions. There should be one hard and fast rule - NO TV - and certainly nowhere within hearing distance. You can have a radio, but keep it on the lighter, less advertised FM stations, with easy listening music or classical music. Don't set yourself up to fail by adding to your distractions.

Not only do you need a place to work, you need proper materials as well. Take the following materials list down to your local discount office supply store and purchase those things you need.

Materials List

1. **Stationery for job-search letters**
   8.5 x 11, 24 lb, 25% cotton paper, white, linen finish.
2. **Matching envelopes (#10)**
3. **Manila envelopes (9 x 12)**
4. **Stamps**
5. **Travel and expense forms**
6. **Leather-like portfolio with notepad for interviews**
7. **3-ring binder (3" or 4") with tabs**
8. **Post-it notes**
9. **Thumb Drive**

Keep travel and expense forms. They are to be used to keep track of all job-search expenses, including long-distance phone calls, transportation costs, and meals. These expenses may be tax-deductible. Check with your accountant.

The leather-like portfolio used in the interviewing control method is critical to a successful interview. In it, you will not only carry additional resumes and reference sheets, but you will also have your core skills summaries, SHARE Story "key words" (explained in a future chapter), and other items that play a critical role in your job search.

You will need an appropriate, coordinated wardrobe when you interview. It must be planned to the last detail, from footwear to umbrella. Keep in mind that most positions require more than one interview. Therefore, make sure that you have a different outfit for the second and third interviews. For goodness sake, don't wear brown shoes and a blue suit. Get a book on dressing for success or similar reference and look at the pictures. Remember, getting hired is a process of elimination and everything you do is a potential eliminator. They look you over and decide if you fit their image.

Finally, make sure you have business cards. They must be simple. Put only your name, address, phone, fax, email and any other essential contact information. The most important thing to put on them is the list of your key skills.

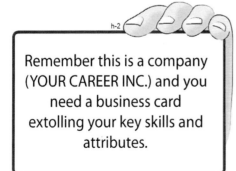

Remember this is a company (YOUR CAREER INC.) and you need a business card extolling your key skills and attributes.

DON'T GET MAD OR DEPRESSED, GET BUSY

No matter how focused, determined, positive or jovial you are, there will come a time in this search when depression will raise its ugly head. Everyone experiences it. Depression is often associated with the "dead" time between getting ready for your search and the first interview. It can also arise between interviews and certainly at the time you are told that you didn't get a position for which you applied.

Whether you are rejected from the interview selection process and really know you are the best-qualified applicant, or for dozens of reasons, legitimate or otherwise, perceived or real, it still hurts and the pain exists. Don't give in!!! Acknowledge the feeling, but take the steps to move on!!

Any number of things can work against a positive outcome over the course of your job search and knock you out of the running for that "ideal" job. What makes the difference between winners and losers is how you handle this natural phenomenon. Keeping busy is one part of the solution. An old boss of mine, Howard Tullman, always said, "Good enough never is." How true. There is always something you can do or re-do to improve your situation. Don't get mad, get busy!

As I told you earlier, this is a tough business and only the tough and smart survive. Toughness also requires intense dedication and persistence.

Below, in Exercise 1.2, I have inserted the 25 Rules I ask my personal clients to follow during the course of their work with me. If you are smart, you will develop and maintain a positive attitude and accept responsibility for your actions as called for in these rules.

Exercise 1.2

25 Rules Worksheet
www.RAH2010.com

Remember, you are in charge of this search, no one else. **MAKE SIX PRINTED COPIES OF THE RULES.** Post them in the following locations:

- On the bathroom mirror

- On the refrigerator door

- Back of your front door

- In your briefcase

- One for your search partner or significant other

- In your 3-ring binder

Posting a copy on the bathroom mirror, or so near to it that you can't miss it, ensures that you will see it at least twice daily. While brushing your teeth, read the rules to yourself. What else do you have to do anyway while you are brushing? Then *say Rule 25 out loud*. Either before or after the mouthwash is OK. When you go to the kitchen for breakfast, a meal or snack, look over the list on the refrigerator.

You and your search partner (or job search helper) are to agree, in advance, on a time each week when and where you say the rules out loud to him/her while that person listens and follows along using a separate copy. *This is one of the hardest tasks you will perform in your search.*

Why? Because very few of us like accountability and feel embarrassed when we have to present ourselves to others, especially when we

may not have done enough the previous week to live up to these rules.

Putting the document on the back of the front door reminds you that as you go out into the world, you have a mission and nothing will dissuade you from it. At lunch or wherever you spend your noon period, pull it out of your briefcase and read it to yourself. Go post these around your house, right now.

OK, now that you've printed, read, signed and posted the three in-home agreements and placed one in your 3-ring binder and one in your briefcase, I want you to give your search partner or job search helper their "rules" agreement. WHAT? You didn't post them? Go do it now!!

Exercise 1.2.1

Search Partner's Rules
www.RAH2010.com

As your job search progresses, you will find these reminders extremely helpful in maintaining both attitude and focus.

Discuss your signed agreement with your search partner and secure that person's agreement to assist you in your search. Of course, your search partner or job search helper wants to support and help you, but knowing how may be challenging. By providing a structured method for helping, you ensure the constructive support you need from that person.

If you don't have a search partner, a friend will do. Make sure it is a good friend because he/she will be receiving a telephone call from you weekly to discuss your search and to hear you repeat your commitment statement.

If you are too embarrassed to do this, or you don't have any friends, then you need to find a support group. You **will** need the support.

COMMON JOB SEARCH MISTAKES

Here are the major don'ts of your search. I have added my own thoughts to those of my colleague, Jack Chapman, author of "Negotiating Your Salary: How to Make $1000 a Minute," © 1996. Ten Speed Press, ISBN# 0-89815-890-7.

 I highly recommend you purchase Jack's book for your job search library.

b-1

I have Jack's permission to lift my favorite ideas from his book. Here's a summary of our combined thoughts.

1. Answering All the Want-Ads

Newspaper ads generally represent entry-level positions and are mostly a waste of time. Pick a select few and spend no more than 5% of your valuable job-search time on want ads. I know how comfortable it is to get a cup of coffee on Sunday morning and read the paper, cut out ads, paste them onto search sheets and then go play in the afternoon, thinking you've really made a great search effort. You haven't!

2. Avoiding Answering the Local Newspaper Help-Wanted Ads

This simply means that you must at least look them over and try to pick a few good ones and follow through. It is a resource, albeit not a good one, most of the time. However, by not scanning the ads and responding to those which appear to meet your criteria, you may deprive yourself of a few promising leads. Respond appropriately, but don't go hog wild and think that you've done your day's work.

3. Mailing Unsolicited Resumes

As Jack puts it: "They are garbage, scrap paper, wasted effort and job-search dung." I think Jack's mostly right here. There are some companies advertising on the www that can put you in the driver's seat by selling you a direct-mail campaign. If the truth were known, this can cost $2,000 - $10,000, or more. If you send out 5,000 resumes, you should experience a 1% return response, or 50 letters.

Unfortunately, most companies who respond, if they ever do, usually say, "thank you for your inquiry, but we'll call you," etc. Maybe, just maybe, you will land an interview, but it's highly unlikely that you will find your "ideal" job this way, no matter what they say in their ads. Let's see… $5,000 for 50 responses = $100.00 per letter mailed. Would I be crazy or what?

4. Looking for "Vacancies"

Job research conducted by Mark Granovetter of Harvard states that among unadvertised positions, 43.3% are created for the applicant, often at the time of the interview. Yet, job-hunters keep asking people to tell them about the openings.

5. Inept Networking

For those early in their careers, asking a friend's dad for a position probably works. When you are in the senior job market, it doesn't. Person-to-person networking is the most effective method of obtaining your next position. Bad networking can cause serious short and long-term damage.

6. Trying to Go After Too Many Types of Jobs

As Jack puts it, "Don't confuse a job market with a singles bar." Serious jobs don't land in your lap if you throw enough stuff against a wall and hope something sticks. You must pick your targets and go after them.

7. Not Planning and Scheduling Properly

The average person spends more time planning vacations than a job search.

8. The "Doing It Alone" Myths

Here are some myths going around: don't pay anyone to help you; companies should pay fees to find you; you don't need any help; be self-sufficient.

Society expects you to know how to get good jobs on your own, but nobody ever shows you how, do they? On the other hand, be careful whom you choose to help you. Confusing, isn't it?

9. Letting Motivation Take Care of Itself

Jack states this one very well: "Nothing puts your self-esteem on the line faster than a job search. You face rejection and self-doubt daily." He uses an expression I think is priceless. "A single day of beggar mentality (please, somebody, give me a job) is a whole day wasted." Amen to that!!

An old friend of mine from years ago, Kerry Russell, once told a group of new sales recruits that he wanted "No Stinkin' Thinkin". Kerry influenced me greatly in the half-full glass area and since you've signed my rules sheets, you know where I stand on this issue.

10. Letting Others Control Your Job Search

When the next associate, or person, to whom you casually mention your search, offers to pass your resume around, don't let them. When you do this, you relinquish control of your search! This is a serious mistake. Many of you secretly hope that some recruiter will mysteriously appear and whisk you away to the Elysian fields of jobdom.

Recruiters typically charge companies up to 30% of a candidate's first-year salary to find the perfect candidate. Unless they have an open job order for just your skills, you go into the computer or dead-letter file along with the thousands of others "shot gunning" their resumes around the country hoping for something to work. Don't waste your time.

11. Not Preparing Well Enough for Interviews

How many times do you think I sit and listen to prospective job seekers say to me: "Just get me in front of the decision-maker and I'll take it from there?" How self-impressed and over-confident can you be?

Many people don't have a clue as to what the interview questions mean, much less how to properly answer them. Being well-prepared is the most critical factor in claiming success.

12. Talking About Money Too Soon

Employers always ask how much you want. If you answer too high, you are too expensive. If you answer too low, you're not worth it. What to do? Focus on value, not money.

Each of these issues is discussed in the remaining chapters.

 Remember, the process of getting hired is one of elimination. He/She who is left standing wins.

b-2

Therefore, you must look good on paper, sound good on the phone and be perceived to be the best candidate in the interview. There is no second place in this game.

AVAILABLE WEEKLY SEARCH HOURS

Many people start their campaign with excuses. The primary excuse everyone gives me is that the time they can spend on the search is limited. Don't even go there. What this really means is that they don't know how to structure their search or aren't disciplined enough to manage it. You don't have the luxury of that distraction.

I tell my clients they should adjust their 168-hour weekly routines to closely parallel the following schedule during their search: 46 hours sleeping; 12 hours eating; 45-58 hours working (includes drive time); 14 hours with family or friends; 5 hours in school or in self-improvement educational advancement classes or in the library doing research on target companies; 12 hours searching the internet; 1 hour role-playing or preparing for interviews; 3 hours re-working resume(s) and developing/printing cover letters; 1 hour writing follow-up thank-you notes; 16 hours making phone calls.

No, you say? Too little time allotted for work? Then adjust your priorities, become more efficient at what you do, shift workloads as appropriate or implement another set of time management strategies.

If you are not working, you have almost unlimited time to devote to your search and I would recommend the following schedule:

Sleeping 52 hours; eating 18 Hours; family time 27 hours; web research 25 hours; networking 24 hours; telephone work and written follow-up on networking and interviews 12 hours; developing share stories and working on better cover letters and resumes 4 hours; school and self-development work 6 hours.

Exercise 1.3

Available Weekly Search

Take a moment and jot down your weekly calendar, according to your personal needs. Get started. When you've "eyeballed" your week, you will be ready to put your information on paper and "calendarize" it by breaking down each day into one hour periods that will contain your planned activities.

www.RAH2010.com

Set objectives for each day, record your efforts daily and quantify your results weekly. Set performance standards. For example, return all calls within 24 hours and get thank-you letters into the mail the day after the interview. Above all, establish a regular job-hunting routine and stick to it!

Make outgoing calls as early in the day as possible. If you are working full-time, then use your lunch hours to focus on your calling activity. Work on your mailings and be available for return calls in the afternoon, unless you are at a networking meeting or an interview.

If you work during the day, concentrate on your job search every evening and on the weekends. It is essential, however, that you find snippets of time during the business day to make outgoing calls and to return phone calls. Do so, even if you have to take breaks and step outside to make your calls.

Be sure and retain your resume in your laptop so that you can respond while in the field if you identify a great opportunity. Carry your resume on a thumbdrive or whatever the latest device available when you go out of town. You never know when you will be required to remotely email it to someone. Don't wait until you return to the office or home. Timing is everything. Also, admitting you can't manage the latest computer technology is tantamount to admitting failure before you start!

Plan each day's activities in advance. Be aggressive! Evaluate your performance daily. Don't lie to yourself and accept no excuses! You know the old expression that goes "plan your work and work your plan!"

Exercise 1.4

Daily Work Schedule
Create your daily work schedule now.
www.RAH2010.com

WHAT ARE YOUR GOALS?

Well, now that you have been through the initial test of fire, we must address the next area of our search: *What Are Your Goals?* This exercise requires you to state your goals. Please work with your search partner or job search helper in forming the answers to these questions. These are really tough questions about what your goals are for both the short and long term.

I've included a life question about finances and retirement planning that you and your search partner could discuss and work toward resolving. The thing to remember is that, whether or not you want to focus on these issues, you must do so. They will force constructive thinking and decision-making that will directly impact your future.

The decisions you make now will follow you to your retirement. What type of retirement lifestyle do you want for yourself and will your current path provide for that?

This exercise asks you to define your short- and long-term goals, both economic and personal. Some people have saved for their retirement, while others haven't. It is never too late to start and set a direction for your life. Here are the questions you must address. You owe it to yourself and your family to come up with the right answers. Please construct two sets of answers. One is financial, and the other career or life-oriented.

Exercise 1.5

What Are Your Goals?
www.RAH2010.com

1. What five things do you wish to accomplish in 30 days?

2. What five things do you wish to accomplish in the next 6 months?

3. What four things do you wish to accomplish in the next 12 months?

4. What four things do you wish to accomplish in the next 5 years?

5. What three things do you wish to accomplish in the next 10 years?

6. What three things do you wish to accomplish in the next 15 years?

7. When you retire...

   ■ You will require an income of?

   ■ Where do you want to live?

8. How will you accomplish each of the goals (1-7) listed above?

SUMMARY

You have your job search headquarters located and stocked with all the proper supplies for the search. You have agreed to some pretty tough rules. You have set your goals. You have a calendar of daily events written down and ready to implement. Now, you must focus on an attack strategy to accomplish your goals.

Monthly Expenses

Exercise 1.1

Interactive Exercise Available at www.RAH2010.com

This exercise is designed to help you understand the financial reality of your present situation and help you estimate how long it will take you to land your next position.

The first column shows an example household. List your current expenses in the second column. In the last column list what you would like your monthly expenses to be.

Be sure to include yearly costs by adding an average monthly amount.

The U.S Department of Labor states that the average search time is calculated by figuring a month for every $10,000 in annual income.

	Example Household	Your Current Expenses	Desired Levels
Home			
Rent/Mortgage	$1,575.00		
Other			
Subtotal	$1,575.00		
Utilities			
Gas, Electric and Water	$175.00		
Telephone & Cell Phone	$75.00		
Cable TV & Internet	$50.00		
Other			
Subtotal	$300.00		
Food			
Grocery and Dining Out	$450.00		
Subtotal	$450.00		
Transport			
Car Payments	$300.00		
Car Insurance	$100.00		
Fuel/Bus Fares	$100.00		
Other			
Subtotal	$500.00		
Insurance			
Health Insurance	$225.00		
Life Insurance	$75.00		
Disability Insurance	$10.00		
Other			
Subtotal	$310.00		
Legal Expenses			
Legal Expenses			
Alimony/Child Support			
Other	$20.00		
Subtotal	$20.00		
Additional Expenses			
Child Care			
Clothes	$100.00		
Medical Expenses	$25.00		
Entertainment	$100.00		
Frivilous Spending	$100.00		
Memberships			
Other	$20.00		
Subtotal	$345.00		
Total Expenses	$3,500.00		
Income	$100.00		
Net Total	-$3,400.00		
Break Even Required ??			

25 Job Search Rules
Exercise 1.2 as taken from <u>The Ready Aim Hired Series</u>[©]

Life is tough and not always fair. These rules are also tough, but fair. Before you begin your job search, think about what you must start doing to make your search meaningful. We strongly recommend you secure a "search partner". Select someone who will listen to you during your search, who will discuss, not necessarily agree, with your search strategy and who will hold you accountable for implementing these rules. You must place these rules in the following locations: ⇒Bathroom Mirror   ⇒Refrigerator Door   ⇒Back of Front Door   ⇒Computer Monitor at Home ⇒Your briefcase   ⇒Give one to your Search Partner ~~ You must also read this aloud weekly to your search partner.

1. I will only see a half-full glass and have no "stinkin' thinkin'."
2. I will not waste time and will follow my weekly search schedule.
3. I will not complain.
4. I will be disciplined.
5. I will not accept rejection as personal, just business.
6. I will exercise and maintain a balanced diet.
7. I will concern myself with those things over which I have direct control, and not those things over which I have no control.
8. I will develop or maintain my sense of humor.
9. I will involve my family and friends and keep them involved.
10. I will respect myself and be kind to my family and friends.
11. I will not expect the next job to fall into my lap. I will find it!
12. I will not daydream my way into my next job.
13. I will take consistent and meaningful actions every day.
14. I will not place blame on others, only on myself.
15. I will control my job change.
16. I will complete a minimum of 40-50 job-hunting activities weekly.
17. I will read everything I can to improve my position in this search.
18. I will complete all book exercises.
19. I will give myself permission to try.
20. I will give myself permission to fail.
21. I will give myself permission to ask for help.
22. I will give myself permission to make mistakes.
23. I will give myself permission to succeed!
24. I will do my best at whatever task I attempt.
25. I will repeat TO MYSELF EACH morning and EACH evening. "Starting today, I am in control of:

- My Goals
- My Activity Level
- My Effectiveness
- My Schedule
- My Own Research
- My Job Change Strategy
- *MY FUTURE*

Search Partner's Rules   Exercise 1.2.1

Life is tough and not always fair. These rules are also tough, but fair. Your significant other is undertaking a serious and relationship-challenging task. It will require their intense focus. It will require your cooperation. The goal of their search is to quickly find the job they want and money they deserve. This is a tough assignment for anyone. It is tougher if they aren't receiving your support. Your job is to provide feedback. That does not mean you need to always agree. Your job is to coach, discuss, encourage, motivate and help in whatever way you can. The end result makes economic sense and justifies the sacrifice on everyone's part. Each rule begins as follows: "I will":

1.   Participate in developing the weekly job search schedule.

2.   Conduct a formal discussion of the job search weekly.

3.   See only a half-full glass.

4.   Avoid complaining.

5.   Help my partner to accept rejection as "just business".

6.   Parallel the exercise and balanced diet routine of my partner.

7.   Maintain my sense of humor.

8.   See that she/he is involved with my family and friends weekly.

9.   Take consistent and meaningful actions every day to support my partner.

10.   See that my partner places blame squarely on him/her-self, never others.

11.   See that she/he completes a minimum of 40-50 job-hunting activities weekly.

12.   Read everything I can to support this search.

13.   Complete book exercises as appropriate.

14.   See that this list is posted on the bathroom mirror, home office wall, refrigerator door and the back of outside front door to our dwelling.

15.   My significant other will repeat to me at least once weekly;

"Starting today, I am in control of My:

Goals

Activity Level

Effectiveness

Schedule

Own Research

Job Change Strategy

FUTURE"

Signed _____   Date _____

Witnessed By _____   Date _____

Make 3 Copies

Available Weekly Search Hours

Exercise 1.3

	Ideal Week		Your Week	
	Hours	Hours Left	Hours	Hours Left
Total Hours Available	168		168	
Sleep	46	122		
Eat	12	110		
Work	58	52		
Family/Personal Time	14	38		
School	5	33		
Internet Research	12	21		
Interview Preparation	1	20		
Resume Work/ Cover Letters	3	17		
Follow up, thank-you notes	1	16		
Phone Calls	3	13		
Exercise	3	10		
Education	4	6		
Travel	0	6		
Miscellaneous & All Other	6	0		
Total Hours Used	168			

Extra Campaign Time	0 hours		

Dump everything into family time for all other activities you do in the week.

Daily Work Schedule   Exercise 1.4

	Planned Time	Actual Time			
SUNDAY	Total	Start	Stop	Total	Comments
Family Time					
Correspondence					
Newspaper Search					
Other Media Search					
Internet Research					
Planning of Upcoming Week					
Sub Total					
MONDAY	Total	Start	Stop	Total	Comments
References/Network					
Trade Association Contact					
Recruiter Contact					
Job Fairs Attended					
Correspondence					
Resume and Cover Letter Work					
Interview Preparation					
Interview Follow-up					
Internet Research					
Library Research					
Sub Total					
TUESDAY	Total	Start	Stop	Total	Comments
References/Network					
Trade Association Contact					
Recruiter Contact					
Job Fairs Attended					
Correspondence					
Resume and Cover Letter Work					
Interview Preparation					
Interview Follow-up					
Internet Research					
Library Research					
Sub Total					

Daily Work Schedule   Exercise 1.4

	Planned Time	Actual Time			
WEDNESDAY	Total	Start	Stop	Total	Comments
References/Network					
Trade Association Contact					
Recruiter Contact					
Job Fairs Attended					
Correspondence					
Resume and Cover Letter Work					
Interview Preparation					
Interview Follow-up					
Internet Research					
Library Research					
Sub Total					
THURSDAY	Total	Start	Stop	Total	Comments
References/Network					
Trade Association Contact					
Recruiter Contact					
Job Fairs Attended					
Correspondence					
Resume and Cover Letter Work					
Interview Preparation					
Interview Follow-up					
Internet Research					
Library Research					
Sub Total					
FRIDAY	Total	Start	Stop	Total	Comments
References/Network					
Trade Association Contact					
Recruiter Contact					
Job Fairs Attended					
Correspondence					
Resume and Cover Letter Work					
Interview Preparation					
Interview Follow-up					
Internet Research					
Library Research					
Sub Total					

Daily Work Schedule   Exercise 1.4

SATURDAY	Planned Time Total	Actual Time Start	Actual Time Stop	Actual Time Total	Comments
Correspondence					
Resume and Cover Letter Work					
Interview Preparation					
Internet Research					
Library Research					
Family Time					
Sub Total					

WEEK'S TOTALS	Planned Time Total			Actual Time Total	
Sunday					
Monday					
Tuesday					
Wednesday					
Thursday					
Friday					
Saturday					
Total					

What Are Your Goals?   Exercise 1.5

| **30** Days | What 5 things do you wish to accomplish in 30 days? |

1. _____
2. _____
3. _____
4. _____
5. _____

| **6** Months | What 5 things do you wish to accomplish in the next 6 months? |

1. _____
2. _____
3. _____
4. _____
5. _____

| **12** Months | What 4 things do you wish to accomplish in the next 12 months? |

1. _____
2. _____
3. _____
4. _____

| **5** Years | What 4 things do you wish to accomplish in the next 5 years? |

1. _____
2. _____
3. _____
4. _____

| **10** Years | What 3 things do you wish to accomplish in the next 10 years? |

1. _____
2. _____
3. _____

| **15** Years | What 3 things do you wish to accomplish in the next 15 years? |

1. _____
2. _____
3. _____

| **Retirement** | When I retire… |

I will require an income of $
I will want to live in
My goals above will accomplish this? _____

TASK LISTS

Exercise 1.6

Follow this list to ensure that you are doing all you can to move your search forward. Remember, if you are employed, you are to do 50 activities weekly. If you are unemployed, 250 weekly.

TASK LIST 1	TASK LIST 2	TASK LIST 3
Read Chapter 1	Read 25 Rules To Search Partner	Read 25 Rules To Search Partner
Identify Practice Coach	**Exercises**	Continue Target Company Research
Exercises	3.1 20-Second Quiz	Revise Resume Per Reviews
1.1 Expenses	Rewrite 20-Second Quiz Answers	Prepare ASCII - Text Resume
1.2 25 Rules Agreement	3.2 Rank Your Transferable Skills	Prepare Cover Letters - Email
1.2.1 Search Partner's Rules	3.3 Skills & Traits Exercise	Post New Resume On All Job Boards
1.3 Available Weekly Search Hours	3.4 "I AM" Exercise	Call 2nd level References (2ndLVR)
1.4 Daily Work Schedule	3.5 RESUME WORKSHEETS	Send Thank-You's to (2ndLVR)
1.5 What Are Your Goals?		Develop Recruiter List
	Read Chapter 4	Call References
Post 25 Rules	Read Chapter 5	Write Reference Thank-You's
Purchase Supplies	Reference List - Personal	Read Chapters 6 & 7
Set Up Command Post	Reference List - Business	Research Referral Provided Companies
Set Up 3-Ring Search Binder	Write Reference Inquiry Letters - Personal	Exercise 6.1 FEAR
Read Chapter 2	Write Reference Inquiry Letters - Business	Develop & Refine 5 SHARE Stories
Exercises	Write Resume Draft - Formal	Rehearse SHARE Stories w/Partner
2.1 Your Personality	Identify 3 Resume Readers	Write 5 Example Reference Letters
2.2 Complete Life Balance	Distribute Resume To Readers	Mail 5 Example Reference Letters
2.3 Your Career Health	Construct My Job Doctor™ Web Resume	Search For Upcoming Job Fairs
2.4 Job Change Readiness Quiz	Collect Print Media Ads	Collect Print Media Ads
2.5 What's Missing In Your Job?	Surf Net for Associations	Surf Net for Associations
2.6 Ideal Job Characteristics	Call Association(s) Executive	Call Association(s) Executive
2.7 Salary & Package Preferences	Identify 5 Event Opportunities	Print Business Cards
Read Chapter 3	Search for Job Fairs	Reference List - Personal
	Begin Target Company Research	Reference List - Business
Rewrite Your 20-Second Quiz Answers	Remove Your Old Resume From All Job Boards	Identify 5 Event Opportunities (EO)
Reference List - Personal	Surf Web for Job Listings	Write 5 EO Letters
Reference List – Business	Print & Put Listings in 3-Ring Binder	Call On 2 Previous EO Letters
Collect & Organize Print Media Ads		Develop 3 Association Groups
Identify Local Associations		Work 5 Network Leads
Identify 5 Event Opportunities		Set Appointments for Info/Referral Interviews
Design Business Cards		Web Search For Job Listings
Search for Job Fair		Print and Put Listings in 3-Ring Binder
Web Search For Job Listings		Call On Job Listings
Print & Put Listings in 3-Ring Binder		Send Resume To Job Listings
		Enter All Contacts Into ATS

Read 25 Rules To Search Partner	Read 25 Rules To Search Partner	Read 25 Rules To Search Partner
Read Chapters 8 & 9	Re-Read Chapter 7	Re-Read Chapter 8
Re-Read Chapter 7	Re-Read Chapter 8	Re-Read Chapter 9
Select 50 Direct Mail Target Companies	Re-Read Chapter 9	Read Chapter 10
Review Commonly Asked Questions (CAQ)	Read Chapter 10	Attend 1 Association Meeting
Prepare Your Answers To CAQ	Attend 1 Association Meeting	Attend Job Fair
Thank-You's for Info/Ref Interviews	Attend Job Fair	Call 5 New EO Companies
Look Over Offer Form Review	Call 5 Event Opportunity Companies	Send/Call 50 Direct Mail Targets
Call 5 Event Opportunity Companies	Send/Call 50 Direct Mail Targets	Telephone Follow-Up for Target Companies
Prepare 5 SHARE Stories	Telephone Follow-Up for Target Companies	Review Commonly Asked Questions (CAQ)
Rehearse SHARE Stories w/Partner	Review Commonly Asked Questions (CAQ)	Refine Answers To CAQ
Collect Print Media Ads	Refine Answers to CAQ	Rehearse SHARE Stories w/Partner
Surf Net for Associations	Prepare 3 SHARE Stories	5 Info/Referral Interviews
Set 3 New Info/Referral Appointments	Practice SHARE Stories w/Partner	Thank-Yous for Info/Ref Interviews
Schedule 5 Recruiter Interviews	Conduct 5 Info/Referral Interviews	Interview Issue Questions
Call Association(s) Executive	Thank-You's for Info/Ref Interviews	Collect Print Media Ads
Reference List - Personal	Collect Print Media Ads	Surf Net for Associations
Reference List - Business	Surf Net for Associations	Call Association(s) Executive
Identify 5 Event Opportunities	Call Association(s) Executive	Reference List - Personal
Write 5 Event Letters	Reference List - Personal	Reference List - Business
Call On 5 Previously Sent EO Letters	Reference List - Business	Identify 5 Event Opportunities
Work 5 Network Leads	Work 5 Network Leads	Write 5 Event Letters
Attend 1 Association Meeting	Set Appointments for 3 Info/Referral Interviews	Call On 5 Previous Event Letters
Attend Job Fair	Schedule 2 Recruiter Interviews	Develop 3 Association Groups
Develop 3 New Association Groups	Identify 5 New Event Opportunities	Work 5 Network Leads
Pre-Interview Worksheets	Write 5 EO Appointment Letters	Set Appointments for 3 Info/Referral Interviews
Pre-Interview Questionnaire	Call On 5 Previous EO Letters	Schedule 2 Recruiter Interviews
Have 5 Info/Referral Interviews	Develop 3 Association Groups	Surf Net for Job Listings
Interview Issue Questions	Web Search For Job Listings	Print Listings & Put In 3-Ring Binder
Web Search For Job Listings	Put Job Listings in 3-ring Binder	Call On Job Listings
Print & Put Listings in 3-Ring Binder	Call On Job Listings	Send Resume To Job Listings
Call On Job Listings	Send Resume To Job Listings	Enter All Contacts Into ATS
Send Resume To Job Listings	Enter All Contacts Into ATS	
Enter All Contacts Into ATS		

Repeat week 6 activities until you are employed.

Chapter 2
<<< Who Are You?

"Sweat Of Your Brow"

ho you are, most times, is based upon a combination of genetics, experiences, and life circumstances. Unfortunately, because most people are so busy just living, they don't take the time to find out who they are and what drives their behavior. It is important for you to understand your motivations and needs, at least enough for you to begin to make clear decisions about your career.

Achieving enough of a balance to initiate good career choices is important to your career and emotional health. You may not know exactly what you want in a job or career situation, but understanding what you don't like is sometimes equally as important as knowing what you do like.

This knowledge will help you avoid unpleasant situations you have put yourself into in the past.

h-4

My survival rule for change is that changing your situation should be achieved through knowledge and understanding, not circumstance.

LET'S FOCUS

The answer to "Who Am I?" partially lies in determining what turns you on. I promise not to spend a great deal of time on the areas that have been beaten to death in hundreds of books. However, these exercises will help you gain some focus. Focus is the purpose of this book. I can't tell you the number of people I've met who go from one seemingly "good" opportunity to another, without a clue as to how any particular job supports their career path.

These exercises are valuable and some are critical in taking charge of your long-range career path plan. You must answer each question carefully.

The "Why?" part of each question is *at least as important* as the question itself.

b-3

So many times, people come to me and state that they are "not sure what they want to be when they grow up." The changing economic forces surrounding us are forcing many to grapple with this question, often in mid-career. I have learned that life is just too short to go through it being miserable and wishing you had done something else.

Take stock now and make the changes, as appropriate. Some of the exercises are simple and just plain fun. They get progressively more difficult as you go through them. They force you to think about what you want and don't want from your next job and your career. That's enough philosophy, for now.

Exercises 2.1 and 2.2 were first provided to me courtesy of Charlene Walker, Principal with Career Focus.

YOUR PERSONALITY

Your Personality, EXERCISE 2.1, will provide a small measure of insight into this important aspect of your career planning efforts. There are hundreds of self-analysis and career assessment exercises floating around.

On the career resources page, found on the sitemap of our website www.stewartcoopercoon. com, I've listed career testing sites for your testing pleasure. By themselves, they won't do a thing to help you secure a new job. However, they are important in understanding how you relate to others, both personally and in the workplace.

Should you determine that you would like to seek additional testing or professional support, explore the resource section of our site and look at the variety of testing and counseling services available. Some of them are deadly accurate, so you might want to check them out on the website. Or you may contact us and we can recommend further services to meet your needs.

From the results of your assessments, you can make some assumptions about the work environment, management style, co-workers and type of work you would find most satisfying in the future.

Exercise 2.1

Personality test.
www.RAH2010.com

LIFE BALANCE

Life Balance, EXERCISE 2.2, is a great test. We all have family, social interactions, cultural difficulties, health and financial problems at one point or another in our careers. This test will help you understand if you might want to consider seeking counseling resources, either personal or career, at this point in your life.

Exercise 2.2

Life Balance test.
www.RAH2010.com.

YOUR CAREER HEALTH

Your Career Health, EXERCISE 2.3, is a way of determining just how healthy your current career path really is. You don't have to spend time doing the math because we've done it for you. Just answer the questions and see where you stand.

Exercise 2.3

Career Health test.
www.RAH2010.com

CHANGE READINESS

Depending upon your score in EXERCISE 2.3, *The Change Readiness Quiz,* EXERCISE 2.4, will tell you how ready you are to change careers or jobs. Again, the math is done for you so just enjoy the lighthearted, fun approach to a very serious issue.

Exercise 2.4

Change Readiness Quiz.
www.RAH2010.com

YOUR IDEAL JOB

Now, it is time to get very serious. When it comes to careers, most people are like a fishing bobber floating in a lake. They bounce from the shore to the dock to the boat and are carried adrift by whatever current drags them along, seemingly without purpose. Why did you take your last job? How did you secure it? Was it more happenstance than planned? Look at your career so far. Would you say that you actually calculated and planned each move? Most job seekers answer no, so you're not alone.

We go to work each day and do our jobs and try to get the most from that experience. Also, most sane people like to be happy. If you fall into that category, then you are normal and healthy. But that's a fairly utopian view of the "real" world of work. Daily pressures, pay cuts, mergers and acquisitions, bad bosses, market shifts and thousands of other reasons taint our work environment experiences.

Don't worry. They taint **every** work environment, not just yours. You will never find the "perfect" job, because it doesn't exist. I repeat, there is no perfect job. There are, however, nearly "ideal" environments. They are ideal because they meet your definition of ideal. What you must now do is define your "ideal."

What's Missing In Your Job, EXERCISE 2.5, begins that process. Look over each of the items and assign them a number, according to instructions on the exercise page. Then rank them in order of your personal priority.

Exercise 2.5

What's Missing In Your Job exercise.
www.RAH2010.com

Where you choose to live is also an important consideration. List the geographical locations in which you wish to reside and then describe the reasons for wanting to live there. Ask your search partner to complete the geographical selection exercise as well. You may want to live in Chicago, but maybe he/she wants New Orleans.

These are basic issues underlying the definitions for "ideal." Spend a day or two discussing your answers together and then rank the geographical locations by mutual agreement.

Characteristics of My Ideal Job, EXERCISE 2.6, brings focus to answering the questions surrounding "ideal" job characteristics. It also brings into play the "soft" issues of feelings about recognition and self-worth on the job. Don't discount these. Most of my clients tell me they used to do this and were miserable for years.

This is a slightly harder exercise because you must rank your preferences. Take your time and think about why you rank each item the way you do. In each exercise in this book, the why is almost equal in importance to the what (perhaps, more).

Exercise 2.6

Characteristics of My Ideal Job.
www.RAH2010.com

Salary and Package Preferences, EXERCISE 2.7, asks you to define the difference between what you "must have," "would like to have," are "neutral" about and what you "don't need." These cover a multitude of options in considering a compensation package for yourself and your family.

For those of you who are married or have a significant other, make two copies of the page because your partner (if you have one) will need to fill out the answers and complete the ranking exercises on the second copy.

Once again, take a day or two and discuss and compare your answers and make sure you are in agreement on the rankings. This list will become a reference during your new offer negotiations.

Exercise 2.7

You and your search partner need to separately rank your Salary and Package Preferences. Compare your results. www.RAH2010.com

Well, now what do you know? You've completed a series of exercises. You should know the following: What you like and don't like about your workplace and fellow workers. An idea of what you think the ideal job is. Where in the country you want to work. A good description of what your short- and long-range career goals are. When you think about it, this is a lot of information.

From Exercise 2.7 you began to define the ideal company. As you later identify and research target companies, it will be valuable to have these criteria available during your considerations.

Write down your preferences for where you want to live and why. Prioritize these. Do your homework on salary levels in these areas. Again, this is useful data in developing your search criteria and company selection. Your spouse or search partner should do this exercise independently and you should compare notes. You should now have the ability to state, "Who You Are."

SUMMARY

New York, Pittsburgh, Phoenix, LA, or Grass Lick, West Virginia. You now know the place where you want to move, that you're ready, that your life needs a change, what you want and don't want and what appears ideal to you. That's a lot of information. Your next challenge is to continue participating in the self-discovery process and move to the next step in the process which is covered in Chapter 3, *Why They Should Hire You?*

Your Personality

Interactive version available online

1. When do you feel the best?
   a. in the morning   c. late at night
   b. during the afternoon and early evening
2. You usually walk
   a. fairly fast, with long steps
   b. fairly fast, with short, quick steps
   c. less fast, head up, looking the world in the face
   d. less fast, head down
   e. very slowly
3. When talking to people you
   a. stand with your arms folded
   b. have your arms clasped
   c. have one or both of your hands on your hips
   d. touch or push the person to whom you are talking
   e. play with your ear, touch your chin, or smooth your hair
4. When relaxing, you sit with
   a. your knees bent with your legs neatly side by side
   b. your legs crossed
   c. your legs stretched out or straight
   d. one leg curled under you
5. When something really amuses you, you react with
   a. a big, appreciative laugh
   b. a laugh, but not a loud one
   c. a quiet chuckle
   d. a sheepish smile
6. When you go to a party or social gathering you..
   a. make a loud entrance so everyone notices you
   b. make a quiet entrance, looking around for someone you know
   c. make the quietest entrance, trying to stay unnoticed
7. You're working very hard, concentrating hard, and you're interrupted. Do you..
   a. welcome the break   b. feel extremely irritated
   c. vary between these two extremes
8. Which of the following colors do you like the most?
   a. red or orange   b. black
   c. yellow or light blue   d. green
   e. dark blue or purple   f. white
   g. brown or gray
9. When you are in bed at night, in those last few moments before going to sleep, you lie:
   a. stretched out on your back
   b. stretched out face down on your stomach
   c. on your side, slightly curled
   d. with your head on one arm
   e. with your head under the covers
10. You often dream that you are
    a. falling
    b. fighting or struggling
    c. searching for something or somebody
    d. flying or floating
    e. you usually have dreamless sleep
    f. your dreams are always pleasant

Score Key
1. (a) 2 (b) 4 (c) 6   **2.** (a) 6 (b) 4 (c) 7 (d) 2 (e) 1
3. (a) 4 (b) 2 (c) 5 (d) 7 (e) 6   **4.** (a) 4 (b) 6 (c) 2 (d) 1
5. (a) 6 (b) 4 (c) 3 (d) 5   **6.** (a) 6 (b) 4 (c) 2
7. (a) 6 (b) 2 (c) 4
8. (a) 6 (b) 7 (c) 5 (d) 4 (e) 3 (f) 2 (g) 1
9. (a) 7 (b) 6 (c) 4 (d) 2 (e) 1
10. (a) 4 (b) 2 (c) 3 (d) 5 (e) 6 (f) 1
Add up the total number of points and read score.

Over 60 Points
Others see you as someone they should "handle with care." You're seen as vain, self-centered, and one who is extremely dominant. Others may admire you, wishing they could be more like you, but don't always trust you, hesitating to become too deeply involved with you.

51 to 60 Points
Others see you as an exciting, highly volatile, rather impulsive personality; a natural leader, who's quick to make decisions, though not always the right ones. They see you as bold and adventuresome, someone who will try anything once; someone who takes chances and enjoys an adventure. They enjoy being in your company because of the excitement you radiate.

41 to 50 Points
Others see you as fresh, lively, charming, amusing, practical, and always interesting; someone who's constantly in the center of attention, but sufficiently well-balanced not to let it go to their head. They also see you as kind, considerate, and understanding; someone who'll always cheer them up and help them out.

31 to 40 Points
Others see you as sensible, cautious, careful & practical, clever, gifted, or talented, but modest. Not a person who makes friends too quickly or easily, but someone who's extremely loyal to friends you do make and who expect the same loyalty in return. Those who really get to know you realize it takes a lot to shake your trust in your friends, but equally that it takes you a long time to get over it if that trust is ever broken.

21 to 30 Points
Your friends see you as painstaking, fussy, very cautious, extremely careful, a slow and steady plodder. It'd really surprise them if you ever did something impulsively or on the spur of the moment, expecting you to examine everything carefully from every angle and then, usually decide against it. They think this reaction is caused partly by your cautious nature.

Under 21 Points
People think you are shy, nervous, indecisive, someone who needs looking after, who always wants someone else to make the decisions and who doesn't want to get involved with anyone or anything. They see you as a worrier who always sees problems that don't exist. Some people think you're boring. Only those who know you well know that you aren't.

Life Balance

Exercise 2.2

Interactive version available online

Directions

For eveything you have experienced in all parts of your life in the last year, check the box to the left.

Count up the total number of changes.

5 or Less Changes

You are having an easy year. Congratulations!

6 through 10 Changes

This year has been challenging; you might want to reassess your priorities

11 or More Changes

Get help! You can't do this alone. If you're experiencing major changes in your career, slow down; don't react immediately.

A. Professional and Career

- [ ] Bored
- [ ] Unrecognized
- [ ] Passed over
- [ ] Laid off or fired
- [ ] Company has re-engineered or is experiencing re-engineering
- [ ] Feel stuck
- [ ] Changed work hours or conditions

B. Family

- [ ] Suffered death of spouse, family member or friend
- [ ] Family changes: adoption, birth, children moving in or out, newly married, divorced or separated
- [ ] Spouse's employment has changed

C. Social Difficulties

- [ ] Changed social activity, dropped or added volunteering
- [ ] Had a falling-out with close personal relationship
- [ ] Experienced loss, theft or damage to personal property
- [ ] Involved in an accident

D. Emotional and Mental Difficulties

- [ ] Increased Stress
- [ ] Procrastination in making decisions
- [ ] Losing interest in others
- [ ] Self-critical
- [ ] Underachieving

E. Intellectual and Cultural Difficulties

- [ ] Started or stopped college
- [ ] Stopped reading or don't read books in your field
- [ ] Not involved in or not overly involved in outside activities
- [ ] Started or stopped a hobby
- [ ] Haven't taken a vacation this year
- [ ] Laughs are few and far between

F. Financial and Economic Difficulties

- [ ] Major purchase
- [ ] Experienced business reversal or financial loss
- [ ] Change in personal finances

G. Health

- [ ] Experienced illness or injury
- [ ] Stopped exercising
- [ ] Experienced weight gain or loss
- [ ] Experienced change in sleeping habits

Your Career Health

Exercise 2.3

Interactive version available online

This test is designed to give you a better understanding of your career health. First rate your overall career health, then answer questions 2 - 48. Aftwards, compare your original career health estimate with the results of this test.

Circle the appropriate number	Low										High
1. Your overall career health.	0	1	2	3	4	5	6	7	8	9	10

Mark the appropriate box	Never	Rarely	Some-times	Fre-quently	Mostly	Always
2. I like the kinds of people who are attracted to my field.	O	O	O	O	O	O
3. I am honest and accurate in assessing my skills.	O	O	O	O	O	O
4. I am honest and accurate in assessing my interests.	O	O	O	O	O	O
5. I am honest and accurate in assessing my values.	O	O	O	O	O	O
6. These assessments confirm my career or job choices.	O	O	O	O	O	O
7. Decisions I made at important turning points in my career were beneficial to my career.	O	O	O	O	O	O
8. In retrospect, these decisions seemed inevitable.	O	O	O	O	O	O
9. I am energetic and optimistic about my career and my life.	O	O	O	O	O	O
10. Professional colleagues, mentors, advisors, and role models were important in my life.	O	O	O	O	O	O
11. These people have been helpful in my career.	O	O	O	O	O	O
12. Excellent job opportunities and offers well suited to me have come my way as if by chance or serendipity.	O	O	O	O	O	O
13. In my professional & social life, I present my truest and best self.	O	O	O	O	O	O
14. I'm honest and positive in assertions about myself and others.	O	O	O	O	O	O
15. I strive to lead a balanced life.	O	O	O	O	O	O
16. I work hard and play hard.	O	O	O	O	O	O
17. I don't mind (I even enjoy) necessary drudgery in my job or career.	O	O	O	O	O	O
18. My work and I seem uniquely suited or well matched to each other.	O	O	O	O	O	O
19. During career transitions, "imperfect movement is better than perfect paralysis."	O	O	O	O	O	O
20. I am well regarded professionally.	O	O	O	O	O	O
21. I am well regarded socially.	O	O	O	O	O	O
22. I intuitively develop abiding relationships with my friends and colleagues.	O	O	O	O	O	O
23. These later on prove to be helpful in my career.	O	O	O	O	O	O
24. I seem to have many social and professional acquaintances and contacts who keep me up to date on what's happening.	O	O	O	O	O	O
25. I gain energy, pleasure, and renewal from my work or career.	O	O	O	O	O	O
26. I have a realistic view of trends in my field and how they fit into the larger picture.	O	O	O	O	O	O

Your Career Health   Exercise 2.3

Interactive version available online

Career Health Continued...	Never	Rarely	Some-times	Fre-quently	Mostly	Always
27. I know what I can change, what I can't change, and the difference between them.	O	O	O	O	O	O
28. I can't control the wind, but I can adjust the sails.	O	O	O	O	O	O
29. I make things happen because I work hard.	O	O	O	O	O	O
30. The harder I work, the luckier I get.	O	O	O	O	O	O
31. When I add valuable contributions to my field, I feel personal satisfaction.	O	O	O	O	O	O
32. No matter what work I do, I am fully and constantly aware of the fact that I must generate more income or value than I receive.	O	O	O	O	O	O
33. Logical, systematic, scientific thinking is useful in many venues.	O	O	O	O	O	O
34. I redirect my energies, instinct, and desires into useful pursuits.	O	O	O	O	O	O
35. I defer pleasures and problem solving.	O	O	O	O	O	O
36. I strive to be self-reliant.	O	O	O	O	O	O
37. When I help others, I feel satisfaction.	O	O	O	O	O	O
38. In order to achieve my goals and avoid pitfalls, I plan systematically.	O	O	O	O	O	O
39. The people I work with are people I like or admire.	O	O	O	O	O	O
40. I respect my colleagues at work.	O	O	O	O	O	O
41. I try to maximize my utility and usefulness in my work.	O	O	O	O	O	O
42. I am intense about my work, my family and my friends.	O	O	O	O	O	O
43. I try to be adaptable and to accept compromise.	O	O	O	O	O	O
44. I have no career regrets.	O	O	O	O	O	O
45. Life is full of random events that I attempt to convert to adventures.	O	O	O	O	O	O
46. Humility is a great virtue.	O	O	O	O	O	O
47. I believe in action rather than drift.	O	O	O	O	O	O
48. I take things as they come, with equanimity and humor.	O	O	O	O	O	O

Total the number of marks in each column here.

x 0	x 1	x 2	x 3	x 4	x 5

Multiply the column totals by the numbers in each column.

0					

Sum the final totals and divide by 23.5.

[   ] / [23.5] = [   ]

Compare this final number with the estimate you made for question 1.

Job Change Readiness

Interactive version available online

Exercise 2.4

Circle the letter that best describes your situation.

1. The last time you got a promotion was
   a. In your current position at your last review
   b. In your current company within the last two years
   c. In the last five years
   d. In your dreams

2. If you were asked to describe your current boss, which of the following words most closely capture him/her?
   a. Best boss ever
   b. OK
   c. Difficult, little direction
   d. Has the charisma of a wet noodle

3. How clear are your responsibilities in your current position?
   a. Very clear outline of responsibilities and expectations
   b. Some responsibilities and expectations are clear
   c. No boundaries at all; make things up along the way
   d. Are you kidding?

4. Everyone tries his/her best to be polite and civil at work. Are you the same cooperative self when you get home from work or are you tired, irritable and hard to live with?
   a. I am rarely irritable, considering we all have good and bad days
   b. Some irritability recently
   c. Tired, irritable and hard to live with
   d. I love to be irritable and don't mind irritating my family

5. Does your contribution at work make a difference in the company?
   a. Absolutely, My job is important
   b. My work contributes at some level
   c. Not really
   d. I think my position could be eliminated

6. Do you know what you would like to be doing in your career?
   a. I am doing exactly what I want to be doing
   b. I have many ideas but can't seem to narrow them down
   c. Yes, and this isn't it
   d. I've never known what I've wanted to do

7. It's Sunday evening. How do you feel about going to work tomorrow?
   a. I really enjoy most of what I do and like the people I work with
   b. I can take it or leave it
   c. I have the bottle of Tylenol out already in anticipation of another week of insanity
   d. Hate, loathe, despise and abominate

8. In the past year, have you been having thoughts of leaving the company? Have you perhaps sent out some resumes?
   a. No
   b. I've just started thinking of a change but haven't done
   c. Yes
      I should have left the company a week after I got the

9. When you think of leaving your current position, do you get fearful because you are too old to change, don't have the right education or experience, or feel there isn't the right
   a. No. I am confident I can make a successful career change
   b. I may experience some fear but will eventually make the move
   c. Yes. Fear has kept me from trying to leave
   d. Reality is reality. No one else will hire me. I'm a loser.

10. When I suggest a new approach to a project or a current
    a. Management is receptive to my ideas and encourages them
    b. Management listens to some of my ideas but hasn't implemented any
    c. I have learned to keep it to myself. No one pays any attention
    d. The management philosophy of this company is simple: Do it their way. Period!

Scoring
For all questions the point value is a=6, b=3, c=1, d=0. Sum up the points.

Below 27 Points
You are dissatisfied. Examine your options. It might be time to move. Develop a plan to change your position within the company and for seeking a position elsewhere.

30 to 43 Points
You are coping (for now). Clarify your goals and reassess your priorities.

45 to 50 Points
High job satisfaction. Congratulations!

What is Missing in Your Job?   Exercise 2.5

Interactive version available online

In my job current or previous position:	Always Missing	Usually Missing	Sometimes Missing	Rarely Missing
1. social well-being	O	O	O	O
2. autonomy	O	O	O	O
3. creativity	O	O	O	O
4. family time	O	O	O	O
5. financial status	O	O	O	O
6. learning envirnoment	O	O	O	O
7. physical well-being	O	O	O	O
8. recognition	O	O	O	O
9. stability	O	O	O	O
10. workplace environment	O	O	O	O
11. fun	O	O	O	O
12. teamwork	O	O	O	O
13. job status	O	O	O	O
14. intellectual challenge	O	O	O	O
15. promotion potential	O	O	O	O
16. realistic goals	O	O	O	O
17. performance standards	O	O	O	O
18. realistic expectations	O	O	O	O
19. defined career path	O	O	O	O
20. feeling good about work you're doing	O	O	O	O
21. dependable co-workers	O	O	O	O
22. diligent co-workers	O	O	O	O
23. smart co-workers	O	O	O	O
24. trustworthy co-workers	O	O	O	O
25. considerate co-workers	O	O	O	O
26. management quality	O	O	O	O

Now you must rank them in order of importance for both "Always Missing" and "Usually Missing."

Always Missing

1.	
2.	
3.	
4.	
5.	
6.	
7.	
8.	

Usually Missing

1.	
2.	
3.	
4.	
5.	
6.	
7.	
8.	

Now you can focus on finding companies and jobs that meet your needs.

Characteristics Of My Ideal Job

Exercise 2.6

Interactive version available online

My ideal job should …	Strongly Agree	Agree	Disagree	Strongly Disagree
1. have autonomy to make decisions.	O	O	O	O
2. be physically challenging.	O	O	O	O
3. have a creative work environment.	O	O	O	O
4. need precision work.	O	O	O	O
5. have a fast paced environment.	O	O	O	O
6. have a flexible schedule.	O	O	O	O
7. have customer contact.	O	O	O	O
8. be mentally challenging.	O	O	O	O
9. have an office location.	O	O	O	O
10. have a prestigious office location.	O	O	O	O
11. have recognition for my work.	O	O	O	O
12. be in a large company.	O	O	O	O
13. be in a small company.	O	O	O	O
14. have a structured environment.	O	O	O	O
15. have varied workspace.	O	O	O	O
16. be in a company that is a good corporate citizen.	O	O	O	O
17. be in a profitable company.	O	O	O	O
18. be in a good community.	O	O	O	O
19. be in a stable environment.	O	O	O	O
20. be in a team environment.	O	O	O	O
21. be independent.	O	O	O	O
22. be indoors.	O	O	O	O
23. be outdoors.	O	O	O	O
24. include analyzing data.	O	O	O	O
25. be budgeting and analysis work.	O	O	O	O
26. have customer contact.	O	O	O	O
27. have detailed work.	O	O	O	O
28. have educational reimbursement.	O	O	O	O
29. have management responsibilities.	O	O	O	O
30. manage money and budgets.	O	O	O	O
31. should have deadlines.	O	O	O	O
32. include negotiating.	O	O	O	O
33. require organizing and managing projects.	O	O	O	O
34. include people contact.	O	O	O	O
35. require project management.	O	O	O	O
36. include public speaking.	O	O	O	O
37. have a risk-taking environment.	O	O	O	O
38. have a solid benefit package.	O	O	O	O
39. include strategic planning.	O	O	O	O
40. include teaching others.	O	O	O	O
41. have a bonus award system.	O	O	O	O
42. have a good boss.	O	O	O	O
43. have steady paced work.	O	O	O	O
44. have a pressured environment.	O	O	O	O
45. include writing reports.	O	O	O	O

On separate sheet of paper, rank the statements that you strongly agreed with. These statements summarize what is important to you when seeking a new position. Don't settle for less!

Salary and Package Preferences

Exercise 2.7

Interactive version available online

		Must Have	Should Have	Could Have	Don't Need
1.	Base Salary Stock options	O	O	O	O
2.	Long-term disability insurance	O	O	O	O
3.	Vacations, free travel for spouse	O	O	O	O
4.	Continued benefits after termination	O	O	O	O
5.	Group auto insurance	O	O	O	O
6.	Matching investment programs	O	O	O	O
7.	Annual physical exam	O	O	O	O
8.	Pension plan	O	O	O	O
9.	Deferred Compensation	O	O	O	O
10.	Financial planning assistance	O	O	O	O
11.	Overseas travel	O	O	O	O
12.	CPA and tax assistance	O	O	O	O
13.	Medical Insurance	O	O	O	O
14.	Install appliances/drapes/carpets	O	O	O	O
15.	Short-term loans	O	O	O	O
16.	Continuing education	O	O	O	O
17.	Consumer product discounts	O	O	O	O
18.	Severance pay	O	O	O	O
19.	Athletic club membership	O	O	O	O
20.	Country club membership	O	O	O	O
21.	Luncheon club membership	O	O	O	O
22.	Legal assistance	O	O	O	O
23.	Outplacement	O	O	O	O
24.	Shipping of boats and pets	O	O	O	O
25.	Life Insurance	O	O	O	O
26.	Mortgage prepayment penalty	O	O	O	O
27.	Closing costs, bridge loan	O	O	O	O
28.	Lodging fees while between homes	O	O	O	O
29.	Installation	O	O	O	O
30.	Sales Commission	O	O	O	O
31.	Bonus	O	O	O	O
32.	Profit Sharing	O	O	O	O
33.	Expense Accounts	O	O	O	O
34.	Company car or car allowance	O	O	O	O
35.	Use of vehicle in off/after hours	O	O	O	O
36.	Company sponsored vanpool	O	O	O	O
37.	AD&D Insurance	O	O	O	O
38.	Real estate brokerage fee	O	O	O	O
39.	House hunting trips	O	O	O	O
40.	Moving expense	O	O	O	O
41.	Mortgage rate differential	O	O	O	O
42.	Early stock option vesting	O	O	O	O
43.	Company purchase of your home	O	O	O	O

On a separate piece of paper, rank your "Must Have" and "Should Have" salary and package preferences in order of importance to you.

Let your significant other complete this exercise also. Spend the next day or two discussing the items and why you ranked them the way each of you did.

The results of this exercise and discussions with your significant other will form a foundation of healthy understanding of your common goals and make the evaluation of your next job offer easier.

Chapter 3
<<< Why Should They Hire You

"WHY THEY CALL"

To become employed, you must identify and satisfy an unfulfilled company need. Each interviewer is wondering if they are receiving a full measure of worth and talent for each dollar they are paying you. Moreover, they want to know that even though you are a wonderful person, they can make money off the sweat of your brow.

Can they track your performance to the bottom line? If so, you are the one. If not, they will hire someone else who seemingly has the ability to make them money. Why they hire you becomes an exercise in being able to effectively communicate your self-awareness and talents, both verbally and in writing, to the satisfaction and comprehension of your potential employer. When you have done this, they will employ you.

20-SECOND QUIZ

The 20-Second Quiz asks you to describe both what you like and don't like and what you want and don't want. Then it asks you to include why or how. You must answer both parts of the question in 20-seconds or less. They will be used in target company selection, interviewing, negotiating and evaluating offers received. Their other purpose is to start you thinking about your answers to the stressful behavioral and job-specific questions you will face in various interview situations.

Sit in a quiet place, look the list over once and then answer to yourself a simple "yes" or "no" to each question. Then sit with a friend or search partner and actually have the person ask you each question with a stop or wristwatch handy, in order to time your answers.

Just so you know, very few job seekers have made it through the entire exercise with fluid, succinct answers. Many try to bluff their way through and, when asked follow-up questions to support their 20-second responses, they stumble.

All get some, none get all, and many ramble or pause, or say to their chosen listener, "I can do that one," or "that's not important," or "let's go on" when in fact, they can't really provide the answer. This exercise is one of the many building blocks in this book. You are now beginning the preparation process for your resume work and interviews. Don't skip this exercise. And for your own sake, don't fake it! Don't say "ummmm" or "uhhhhh" or pause or hesitate in any way. If you can't answer any of these questions, or are uncertain about differentiation between terms, don't worry. You will be able to answer before you are finished.

Exercise 3.1

20-Second Quiz. How did you do? "Perfect," you say - "Baloney," says I.
www.RAH2010.com

YOU ARE A PROBLEM SOLVER

Let's be clear on this one point. The hiring authority employs you because you are affordable, you fall within budget parameters, can harmoniously fit in and they know they can make money off the sweat of your brow. The major reason they hire you is because you can solve problems they either can't or don't want to solve.

The following are the essential questions you must address in this job search: What kind of problem solver are you? How many mountains can you move? What size mountains are they? Can they find someone they can pay less who can do the same thing? Will you fit into their company and not disrupt the natural flow of harmony (assuming there is really such an animal out there)?

Can they track your work results to the bottom line and justify their investment and faith in your abilities? All the exercises you have completed so far, and every one you will do from this point forward, will address these absolutely critical issue areas.

TRANSFERABLE SKILLS

An important aspect of developing who you are is found in The Transferable Skills Worksheet, EXERCISE 3.2. The purpose of this exercise is to identify your transferable skills. So many times I hear recruiters say that a candidate (you) isn't employable because they haven't worked in that specific industry, employing a specifically defined set of skills. Poppycock!

I recently had a candidate who worked for a Fortune 50 company in their mechanical and electrical controls systems division. Basically, he was responsible for selling HVAC (heating, ventilation and air conditioning) controls to larger corporations and public institutions.

I coached him for less than one month. Near the end of that time he secured employment at an IT company and is now happily working as their VP of Sales, selling sophisticated networking and software solutions. By the way, this was not a dot.com. They've been in business over 7

years and are highly successful. So don't tell me that it can't be done. Just Do It!

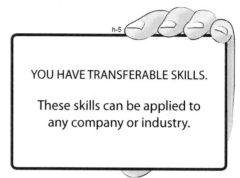

YOU HAVE TRANSFERABLE SKILLS.

These skills can be applied to any company or industry.

This exercise will help you identify your transferable skills. Once identified, you may apply them to the process of developing your resume and interviewing.

Exercise 3.2

Transferable Skills.
www.RAH2010.com

GENERAL SKILLS AND TRAITS

Adaptive Traits, EXERCISE 3.3, asks you to review a list of skills and traits and assign them a number between 1-4, with 1 being most like you and 4 being not like you. For the most part, these are action-oriented. Please assign your personal value to each one. You will now have a list of your top 15 skills and traits. Print this page now.

Now take these top 15 skills and traits that you just printed and transfer them into the form, I Am, EXERCISE 3.4. Begin each sentence in this exercise with the words, "I am." You must put into each sentence a reason why (i.e., what demonstrates) you are this way. These will be used later in your interview preparation process.

This is a tough exercise.

We all have transferable skills and abilities. They may be transferred into a variety of industries and jobs.

Exercise 3.3

Adaptive Traits.
www.RAH2010.com

Exercise 3.4

Using your top skills and traits from your Skills and Traits exercise, write a sentence for each. Begin each sentence with "I am" and explain what indicates you are this way.
www.RAH2010.com

RESUME PREPARATION HISTORY AND JOB WORKSHEETS

The next two worksheet exercises will take hours of thinking and preparation on your part. They are the basic bricks and mortar of your resume and also form the building blocks for your interview and negotiation sessions. You will need to fill out the forms below, so you might as well take a stab at putting together your own resume. If you don't like it when you're finished, there are national resume writing associations that will provide lists of writers from which you may choose.

"Resume Preparation History," EXERCISE 3.5, is one used by my clients to frame an overview of their work history. It also identifies job skills and is used by my staff recruiters to code each candidate for placement on one or more of the national recruiter consortiums to which we belong.

As you prepare answers to the questions, go back and review your exercises completed so far. You will find that certain ideas and words will jump out at you and you can use these to complete this form.

RESUME WORKSHEETS

"Resume Worksheet," EXERCISE 3.5, is used to develop your resume, identify terms specific to your field of work, summarize your strengths and quantify your performance results in each position.

When you get to the "Job History" section be sure that if you occupied more than one position in a single company, **fill one out for each such position**.

What we are looking for here is differentiation among similar things. Don't redo the information about the same company multiple times. What we are trying to establish are unique and distinguishing items that will set you apart from all the other gladiators competing in the arena.

If you have only had one job, that's fine. If you've had too many jobs within this period of time, then you might be seen as a job jumper and have an entirely different set of problems.

Exercise 3.5

Resume Worksheets, taking into consideration the last 15 years of your career history.
www.RAH2010.com

"SHARE" STORIES

Over the years, various companies have developed a myriad of approaches to the problem of describing and communicating value.

My method is called SHARE. A SHARE story is a way of describing a problem, what you did to solve it, how well you solved it, and what it is about you that allowed this solution to take place.

My <u>Ready Aim Hired System</u>™ was primarily directed at quantitative issues in describing a problem faced and its solution. However, in November, 2000, I attended the International Career Development Conference in San Francisco. There I met Laurie Collins, on staff with Howard Community College in Maryland. She had some great thoughts on behavioral interviewing that she shared in a workshop we attended together. After her presentation at the conference, I incorporated one more dimension to my existing system. I now term it the Ready Aim Hired System™ SHARE response.

Adding a newly defined dimension, "E," allowed for a more comprehensive picture to be formed of a client's decision-making capability. This new aspect asks you to evaluate your past decision and describe future actions you might take to improve your problem-solving ability in this particular issue area. It also allowed for a description of emotion expressed as a Behavioral Competency.

By adding this, you should get really close to describing the real essence of your work, why they would want to hire you and who you really are.

Will you modify your handling of this type of problem in the future and why? If not, why not? In the behavioral interview setting, being able to communicate your decision-making coupled with an understanding of yourself or your decisions will drive the nail home and ensure success over your competition.

S The Situation is just that. State a problem you faced in your last position. Do not exceed the number of lines provided for in the space on the form. As you can see, this requires you to really boil it down and be succinct in your description.

H The Hindrance is the main thing standing in the way of your solving this specific problem. Of course, there were probably many things in concert with each other hindering your problem-solving ability. They range from lack of resources (manpower or money) to product faults, seasonal timing, uncooperative vendors or suppliers, etc. Whatever the problem, be brief and be specific and don't exceed the number of lines provided. Remember, they hire you to move mountains. They want to know what stood in the way of your moving the mountain. It is the statement that begins to establish your capability and benchmark your added value.

A The Action(s) you took can list no more than three things you did to address the problem and remove the hindrances. I would prefer you focus, not ramble, in this part of your story.

R The Results you achieved MUST BE QUANTIFIABLE or MEASURABLE. This is the second most important aspect of this exercise. When there are anywhere from 100-1000 resumes submitted for a given position, you must be able to dramatically distinguish yourself from all the others. If you can move numbers, change things for the better or improve things so as to make an impact, then this is the place to put that information. Take your time and think, think, think!

The quantifiable results stated in the "R" section of the SHARE story can also be lifted as bullet points into both your cover letters and into your resume.

E The "emotional" component of who you are is as critical as the R (result) component. It is only through other people that one accomplishes anything. Therefore, your ability to manage people to achieve results is the lynchpin for your success or failure.

Your ability to communicate what it is about you that enables you to "play well with others" is the spice to each of your SHARE stories. Remember, they are hiring you for ALL of your abilities, not just those that you do alone to move numbers and achieve results. When in doubt, read the second sentence of this E section again. The SHARE descriptions must include the *E*motional component. For more on this, read and practice the exercises in Chapter 9, Behavioral Interviewing.

Pay particular attention to the Problem Sheets section. I am only asking for six, but you may have more that are important. Complete as many as you need to tell your story. Go for it! Remember the two things I told you earlier. First, they hire you to solve problems. Second, getting hired is a process of elimination.

The best way to describe the use of these stories is to use the example of a cube. A cube is multi-dimensional because it has six sides. You

too, are multi-dimensional in both your personal and work life.

In the Resume Worksheets, we ask you to describe multiple SHARE stories for each position you've held. When the hiring authority turns the cube around and inspects each side, they will see different aspects of your work skills and qualifications. When you demonstrate enough of these, you begin to set yourself apart from the competition and eliminate them one by one.

Like it or not, you are a product to be sold. How you market and sell yourself will determine your income and, possibly, your career path.

When any new product is introduced to market, you must consider both the obvious and "hidden" benefits of said product. The exercises you just went through are directed toward determining these benefits. You must number your SHARE stories and you must give them a two or three word name such as, "Learning Curve," "People Skills," "Crisis Management," "P&L Management," "Terminating Personnel," "New Sales Territory," etc. How you use the names will be made very clear as you move through the Interviewing Unit.

Now, you must be creative in your marketing approach. You must determine what will motivate the customer (hiring authority) to buy this product (you). You must also clearly demonstrate to the buyer what benefits are to be derived from purchasing the product. The materials developed to this point in the search process will be pulled together in the chapter on developing your resume.

The more SHARE stories you have, the better off you will be when faced with multiple interviews at the same company. Each of your SHARE stories must not duplicate the skills expressed in any other SHARE story. This may sound tough, but try to think of all the things you do in a given day and all the projects you manage and the interactions you have with other workers. Each of these represents a particular problem with measurable outcomes. Start writing and don't stop until you have exhausted your entire work day, week, month and year. You can't have enough SHARE stories. ALSO, it is critical that you research and inspect your weaknesses, define them in terms that WILL arise in the course of your interviews and develop SHARE stories to address each and every weakness.

SHARE stories that focus on your weak points must conclude by turning a negative into a positive and demonstrating how you overcame another similar problem and managed the problem to a positive outcome. **Failure to have at least three such stories will jeopardize your job search campaign.**

SUMMARY

Well, you've been through some deep soul searching and career analysis. You have effectively described your talents and your problem-solving abilities. You can now describe what kind of problem solver you are. You can tell them how many mountains you can move, how far you can move them, and what resources you will use. You can tell them why they should hire you. These reasons are documented in the SHARE stories you've written. Your next step is to learn how to communicate this to the hiring authority.

20 Second Quiz   Exercise 3.1

What you need:

An assistant to read you the questions.
A watch with a second-hand for the assistant to time your responses.

Instructions to assistant:

Read each question out loud to the job seeker. Time how long it takes him/her to answer. They must also answer the Why? portion of the question within the same 20-seconds.

Read these instructions

Can you answer the following questions in 20 seconds with fluid and succinct responses? No uhms, pauses, throat clearing, looking at the ceiling or hot air.

		Was the question answered?		
		No	**Yes**	**Time**
1.	What kind of company do you want to work for?	☐	☐	
2.	What type of boss do you want and why?			
3.	What type of work do you want and why?			
4.	What type of office surroundings do you want to have and why?	☐	☐	
5.	What type of fellow workers do you want and why?	☐	☐	
6.	What are your abilities?	☐	☐	
7.	What are your transferable skills?	☐	☐	
8.	What are your adaptive skills?	☐	☐	
9.	What are your personal traits?	☐	☐	
10.	What personality traits do you dislike in fellow workers and why?	☐	☐	
11.	What is you ideal compensation package and why?	☐	☐	
12.	Where do you want to be in your career in 5 years and how are you going to get there?	☐	☐	
13.	Where do you want to be in your career in 10 years and how are you going to get there?	☐	☐	
14.	Where do you want to be in your career in 15 years and how are you going to get there?	☐	☐	

For those upon which you stumbled, now write the answers to each, and practice saying them out loud.

Rank Your Transferable Skills

Exercise 3.2

Interactive version available on CD

I can	Strongly Agree	Agree	Disagree	Strongly Disagree
1. sort data.	O	O	O	O
2. use organization skills.	O	O	O	O
3. apply information to solve problems.	O	O	O	O
4. make and keep a schedule.	O	O	O	O
5. work with facts and figures to solve problems.	O	O	O	O
6. predict future trends.	O	O	O	O
7. use multiple sources of information.	O	O	O	O
8. set priorities.	O	O	O	O
9. keep a set schedule.	O	O	O	O
10. evaluate information.	O	O	O	O
11. gather information.	O	O	O	O
12. sort objects against preset instructions.	O	O	O	O
13. manage time effectively.	O	O	O	O
14. apply standard methods to analyze data.	O	O	O	O
15. design experimental models or plans.	O	O	O	O
16. identify problems.	O	O	O	O
17. objectively listen.	O	O	O	O
18. manage group activities toward a goal.	O	O	O	O
19. work under pressure.	O	O	O	O
20. take risks.	O	O	O	O
21. delegate tasks and responsibilities.	O	O	O	O
22. monitor responsibilities delegated.	O	O	O	O
23. be empathetic to the needs of others.	O	O	O	O
24. follow through on commitments.	O	O	O	O
25. communicate effectively with others.	O	O	O	O
26. place value judgments on others.	O	O	O	O
27. describe events with minimal errors.	O	O	O	O
28. identify critical decision making issues.	O	O	O	O
29. analyze tasks.	O	O	O	O
30. maintain positive self image under fire.	O	O	O	O
31. work well with peers.	O	O	O	O
32. work well with subordinates.	O	O	O	O
33. work well with superiors.	O	O	O	O
34. teach others willingly.	O	O	O	O
35. adapt to surrounding environments.	O	O	O	O
36. follow through with assignments.	O	O	O	O
37. delegate well.	O	O	O	O
38. organize people and tasks.	O	O	O	O
39. write well.	O	O	O	O
40. effectively communicate.	O	O	O	O
41. manage a course of action.	O	O	O	O
42. express company values to others.	O	O	O	O
43. foster trust in others.	O	O	O	O
44. accept critics.	O	O	O	O
45. learn from my mistakes.	O	O	O	O
46. "own" my mistakes as mine alone.	O	O	O	O
47. persist no matter what.	O	O	O	O
48. effectively communicate my wants and needs.	O	O	O	O

On separate sheet of paper, rank the transferable skills you Strongly Agree you have and write a share story for each skill you have.

Skills and Traits

Exercise 3.3

Interactive version available on CD

I am	Always	Usually	Some-times	Never
accurate	O	O	O	O
an achiever	O	O	O	O
adaptable	O	O	O	O
adept	O	O	O	O
adventuresome	O	O	O	O
alert	O	O	O	O
appreciative	O	O	O	O
an analyzer	O	O	O	O
articulate	O	O	O	O
artistic	O	O	O	O
assertive	O	O	O	O
astute	O	O	O	O
authoritative	O	O	O	O
calm	O	O	O	O
cautious	O	O	O	O
charismatic	O	O	O	O
competent	O	O	O	O
consistent	O	O	O	O
contagiously enthusiastic	O	O	O	O
cooperative	O	O	O	O
courageous	O	O	O	O
creative	O	O	O	O
caring for others	O	O	O	O
decisive	O	O	O	O
deliberate	O	O	O	O
dependable	O	O	O	O
diligent	O	O	O	O
directive	O	O	O	O
diplomatic	O	O	O	O
discreet	O	O	O	O
driving	O	O	O	O
dynamic	O	O	O	O
economical	O	O	O	O
effective	O	O	O	O
energetic	O	O	O	O
enthusiastic	O	O	O	O
exceptional	O	O	O	O
exhaustive	O	O	O	O
experienced	O	O	O	O
expert	O	O	O	O
firm	O	O	O	O
flexible	O	O	O	O
a good mentor	O	O	O	O

I am	Always	Usually	Some-times	Never
human orientated	O	O	O	O
impulsive	O	O	O	O
ingenious	O	O	O	O
independent	O	O	O	O
innovative	O	O	O	O
inventive	O	O	O	O
an initiator	O	O	O	O
insightful	O	O	O	O
knowledgeable	O	O	O	O
loyal	O	O	O	O
methodical	O	O	O	O
a motivator	O	O	O	O
objective	O	O	O	O
perceptive	O	O	O	O
persevering	O	O	O	O
persistent	O	O	O	O
pioneering	O	O	O	O
persuasive	O	O	O	O
pleasant	O	O	O	O
practical	O	O	O	O
punctual	O	O	O	O
quick, mentally	O	O	O	O
a quick worker	O	O	O	O
quick on the uptake	O	O	O	O
rational	O	O	O	O
realistic	O	O	O	O
reliable	O	O	O	O
resourceful	O	O	O	O
responsible	O	O	O	O
responsive	O	O	O	O
self-motivated	O	O	O	O
self-reliant	O	O	O	O
sensitive	O	O	O	O
sophisticated	O	O	O	O
strong	O	O	O	O
supportive	O	O	O	O
tactful	O	O	O	O
thorough	O	O	O	O
tough	O	O	O	O
unique	O	O	O	O
unusual	O	O	O	O
versatile	O	O	O	O
vigorous	O	O	O	O
a risk taker	O	O	O	O

1. Divide a separate sheet of paper into four columns.
2. Label each as "Always", "Usually", "Sometimes" and "Never".
3. Under the appropriate label, rank your skills and traits.

I am ...   Exercise 3.4

Instructions

Complete Exercise 3.3, *What Are Your Skills and Traits?* List one top skill and/or trait at each number below. Write a sentence for each explaining why you have this skill or trait. These sentences will be used later in your cover letters and resumes.

1. I am
_____
_____

2. I am
_____
_____

3. I am
_____
_____

4.   I am
_____
_____

5. I am
_____
_____

6. I am
_____
_____

7. I am
_____
_____

8. I am
_____
_____

9. I am
_____
_____

10. I am
_____
_____

RESUME WORKSHEETS   Exercise 3.5

How to Build Your Resume

GENERAL BIO INFO
Full Name:
Address #1:
Address #2
PO Box:
City: State: Zip:
Phone Number: Fax Number: Email Address:
Do you wish to travel?
Do you have a military security clearance?   Describe:
Where would you be willing to relocate:
Languages:

CAREER GOALS
Current Job Title:
List at least two job titles you seek:

What qualifies you for this line of work?

• My 15 years of sales and supervisory experience in the field of equipment sales and capital goods items, coupled with my success in managing a sales force that has exceeded all sales quotas for the past 7 consecutive years, qualifies me to assume the role of VP Sales.

• Having taught school at the senior-high level and served in the capacity of acting principal on numerous occasions, matched with the fact that I now have achieved my Masters in Educational Administration, allows me to pursue the position of Vice Principal at Rogers High School.

Describe your career up to now: Below are some examples to follow.

• I have spent the past 15 years in sales associated with the manufacturing of specific widgets and other non-capital goods items.

• For the past 7 years, I have been a science teacher in the middle school system, teaching General Science and Biology.

• As a multi-skilled Manufacturing Industry Executive I have been successful in building corporate value through my contributions in engineering and production management, quality, performance reengineering, cost control and profit improvement.

• I have spent the past 12 years working in the Human Resources field with specialties SAP. I have focused on analyzing existing processes and developing effective manual/automatic procedures. I have also managed development and production support functions, financial planning, corporate service contracts, and IT budgets.

RESUME WORKSHEETS   Exercise 3.5

Where would you like to be in 5-10 years?

- In 5 years I want to be at the Director level in my company or in a new company.

- In 3 years I want to be my own boss or own my own company.

- In 10 years I want to retire.

- In 7 Years I want to be able to manage my own department.

- In 5 years I want to have my Masters Degree.

What is the main purpose of this resume?
- The purpose of this resume is to position me for a change of careers.
- The purpose of this resume is to better position me for my next promotion.
- I want a job with XYZ Company and this resume is necessary for the application process.
- I want to update my resume in case a great opportunity comes along and I need one quickly.
- This resume will be a brief portfolio for potential clients.

IDEAL JOBS
Spend a few minutes and search major job boards such as Career-Builder, Dice.com and Monster and find three jobs that you would consider your dream job. Print the ads out and put on separate pieces of paper.

Take a careful look and see what things these jobs have in common. How are they different? What do you really like about each? How many things they are looking for are a match? If your selections match 85% or more, then they are describing the key skills and core competencies in your resume.

CERTIFICATIONS / LICENSES

Certification Name:

Certifying Organization:

Month/Year Obtained:

OTHER EDUCATION / TRAINING
List any other training you have received relevant to your career choice, such as certification courses, classes, or workshops.

Training Type:
Description:

Training Type:
Description:

MILITARY SERVICE

Branch of Service:
Locations Served:
Final Rank:
Month/Year Entered
Month/Year Left
Medals or Acknowledgements:
Discharge Status:

AFFILIATIONS / MEMBERSHIPS

Name of Organization

RESUME WORKSHEETS   Exercise 3.5

Membership Status (Officer?)

PUBLICATIONS AND OTHER WRITINGS

Type of Work:

Title of work:

Date Presented or Published:

Publisher, Periodical or Location:

PREVIOUS EMPLOYMENT
On a separate piece of paper for each job held in the past 10-15 years relevant to the career you are looking for now, develop the following information for each job. If you held multiple positions within a single company, don't repeat company data. The data here will also be used in applications, interviews, etc. Take your time. Don't hurry through this.

Company Name:

City, State:

Your Title:

Salary:

Additional Bonuses:

Start Month/Year

End Month/Year

Reason for leaving:

Brief description of the firm: no more than 4-5 lines AT MOST.

Main product/service/dept you were part of:

Description of your work there:

Number of direct/indirect reports, who/what you were responsible for:

S. H. A. R. E. STORIES
As I stated in the book in Chapter 7, S.H.A.R.E. stories are absolutely critical for resume development and enabling you to control the interview process. They provide solid, quantifiable evidence of your skills and accomplishments. I cannot emphasize enough how important it is to develop short, powerful, hard-hitting, informative stories that can be told conversationally in 45 seconds or LESS.

Initially, they will be long when you first write them. You MUST edit them down or have your search partner do it for you. In either case, they cannot exceed 9 lines when all is said and done. They are used in your interviews, in your reference letters, letters of follow-up and a dozen other places.

The first list below consists of memory triggers for you to use in remembering things you've done that warrant S.H.A.R.E. story development:
- **Projects you worked on**
- **Projects you took on outside of your normal duties**
- **Asked to lead a project or team and its results**
- **Developing new or more effective techniques**
- **Increasing personal, team, or company-wide productivity**
- **Saving the company money**
- **New responsibilities you were asked to assume**
- **Created a new product or bettered an existing one**
- **Sales increases**
- **Company or industry awards you received and why**
- **Demonstrated independent initiative**
- **The biggest challenges you faced in this position**
- **Knowledge gained while in this position**

RESUME WORKSHEETS   Exercise 3.5

Example Share Story #1:

- **Situation**
  Outsource manufacturing requirements, Internal manufacturing costs - labor/overhead expenses were rising faster than product cost relief or retail pricing would allow for product.
- **Hindrances: What Major**
  The need for outsource manufacturing was restricted by the knowledge individuals would be reassigned or terminated. These individuals were long-term employees of the company. Additionally, there were several external organizations willing to provide outsourcing capacity at significant cost savings
- **Actions**
  Interviewed several offshore manufacturers with site visits to review manufacturing capacity, product handling, cost containment programs and capability to current product offering. Reviewed manpower requirements without internal manufacturing; possible transfer to technical services, telemarketing or termination. Developed and implemented 2-year sales forecast with subsequent profit margin and inventory turns profile.
- **Results**
  Manufacturing outsourcing resulted in a 20% drop in product cost, 15% in transportation costs and additional 5% drop in overhead costs. 2 year sales forecast was underscored by 15% resulting in an additional margin and overhead savings. Manpower was reassigned to Technical Services and Telemarketing. On time delivery remained at 99%
- **Evaluation**
  Cost containment with outsource manufacturing was constant; realized 20% in product cost savings Continuously reviewed product offering consistent with outsource manufacturing.

Example Share Story #2
- **Situation**
  Employment was increasing without commensurate increase to Sales forecast or other department requirements. Administrative spending was neither budgeted nor consistent with 2-year sales forecast. Discretionary spending was not planned nor was there an ROI performed prior to dispensing of funds.
- **Hindrance**
  Company was not familiar with internal cost controls. Their focus was primarily on product cost. President was hesitant to realize internal cost controls would in fact contribute to the "bottom line".
- **Actions**
  Placed on hold all spending not relevant to product cost. Initialized a 2-year sales forecast with spending accounts for all departments (Admin., Engineering, Manufacturing and Technical Services).
- **Results**
  Overhead cost dropped by 5%. Transportation costs dropped by 15%. 2-year sales were 15% higher than projected, and costs were lowered by 3%.
- **Evaluation**
  President changed his way of viewing costs internally and procedures were installed as a permanent part of the system.

ACHIEVEMENTS
Please enter 3 to 5 of your greatest achievements in your career that you do NOT have share stories for. Please quantify by using hard numbers or results. See the examples for ideas and suggestions. Specify the position and job title you were in when you completed this achievement so you won't get confused later. Also, if you decide to redo the resume, these might be put at the top of the resume in your career achievements section.

- 19% per project average revenue increase and doubling of profit through development of new strategic direction/pricing methodology. New model led to 45% decline in direct labor costs, doubling of productivity, 25% reduction in overhead and a 225% increase in profit margin.

- Launched a suite of investment products attracting over $700 Million in Canadian assets in a start-up company.

RESUME WORKSHEETS   Exercise 3.5

- Using FOCUS, designed and implemented a database and over a dozen reports that stored and reported on phone taps and traces for use by field agents and prosecutors in criminal court cases in multi-state jurisdictions and groups.

- Turned net operating cash flow positive for only the second time in 5 years (from $1.7 million negative to $35,000 positive), through revamping of credit practices, pricing methodologies, cost restructure, and staff productivity.

- $2.5 million in write-offs prevented through hard-line negotiating and use of leverage with several large delinquent clients.

- $20 M annual incremental profit through reallocation of funds from declining business to an alternative investment opportunity. Thoroughly researched, analyzed, and compared opportunity costs, resulting in proposal being accepted.

SOFT SKILLS

Soft skills are the personality traits that cannot be measured, but rather observed. These help clarify who you are and what type of person you are to the writer and potential employers. Please list 10 attributes that you feel make up your personality. We've listed a few for you to use. Also, in Chapter 3, exercises 3.2 and 3.3, you developed your transferable skills and traits. Use these as well. Achievement-Oriented Strong Interpersonal Skills Ambitious / Energetic Results-Driven Strong Provable Achievements Goal-Focused Trainer of Others Resourceful Motivated / Motivator Commitment to Excellence Leadership through example	Results-Oriented Honesty / Integrity Dedicated / Diligent Analytically-Oriented Persistent actions Problem Solve Multi-Tasked Assignments Respected by Others Strong follow-up/follow-through Resolving client concerns Creative Responsible - can be counted on Patience in dealing with people Adaptability / Flexibility Desire to lead projects or people Planning / Thinking Ahead Conceptual Skills Loyalty Entrepreneurally Minded Innovative Clear Communications Skills Committed to Excellence	Precise / Detailed Aggressive in completing work Positive attitude towards life Meeting Aggressive Schedules Works well under stress Education/learning driven Relationship building Clearly explaining concepts Delegating authority Inventory / Office management Verbal/written skills Efficient Reliable - the "go to" person Experienced / Seasoned Organizational Ability Facilitator of ideas Project-Oriented Dynamic - energizes the group Team Player Clear / Rapid Reactions

TOP SKILLS

Think about your top skills. List at least 10-20 of your top skills relating to your career choice. Some skills you might enter are specific hardware/software technologies, sales and marketing techniques, management, etc. These skills are going to help the writer build some of the main highlights of your resume and cover letter and should be your most valuable skills.

Examples of Top Skills:

Strategic Business Planning/Modeling Consolidations/Restructurings Debt/Equity management IT/HR/Facilities Management	Contract Negotiation/Maintenance Customer Relationship Management System Design/Conversion	Business Development Support Accounting/Administration Client/Server Applications Software Development Quality Assurance/Testing Computer Hardware/Maintenance

DETAILED SKILLS

This section is where you enter everything you know that you think would be valuable to an employer. For technical and engineering individuals, this section can be as long as an entire page of your resume; for some it may be only a short paragraph. This section is also an _excellent source of keywords_ when posting your resume on job boards and sending to recruiters.

RESUME WORKSHEETS   Exercise 3.5

If you have more than 20 skills, sort your skills into groups. Choose a heading for the group and enter a comma-separated list of words, phrases, or products that you know under that heading. If your skills are brief, you may use "Skill Summary" for the heading. Non high-tech individuals should include an entry for computer and software skills.

SYSTEMS ADMINISTRATOR
Operating Systems
Linux (Slackware, RedHat, Debian), other Unix (OpenBSD, Solaris 7/8), MacOS 9/10, Microsoft Windows (9x, NT, 2kpro/server)

Network Protocols
TCP/IP v4, IPX, NetBEUI

Service Protocols
ftp, telnet, ssh, http, ssl, nis, syslog, smb, imap, smtp, pop3, dns, traceroute and others.

Connectivity Analog Modem, ISDN, xDSL, Cable modem, Frame Relay, T1/T3, DS0/DS3, ethernet, token ring, FDDI/CDDI, RS232

Security
Network and host IDS (Intrusion Detection Systems), Proxy/cache services, host and network firewalls, anti-spam practices, Win2k and UNIX host hardening, auditing, security policy development, system and log monitoring.

Desktop Software
MS Office 97, FrontPage98, Outlook, IE 5.x, Netscape 4.x/6.x, PhotoShop 6.x, StarOffice, and most Linux distributions and software apps.

Server Software
Q-mail, Apache 1.3.x, Perl5x, MySQL, PgSql, Bind, djbdns Radius, Freeswan IPSec, Vpopmail/SQWebmail/CourierIMAP, OpenSSL, wuftpd/NcFTPd, radius, dhcp, ntpd, NetSaint monitoring. Linux Virtual Server clustering, Linux QoS, MS SQL Server 2000, IIS5, Active Directory, MS network services in 2k Server.

Development
Perl 5.x programming for SQL database and web-driven administration and E-Commerce applications, ASP, SQL database/query design and normalization, bash/sh shell scripting.

Hardware
Design, installation, and repair of workstations and servers. Extensive knowledge of matching server hardware to task specifications. RAID array configuration and management, SAN implementation, clustered and high-end services. Certified for repair of most HP printers/computers/monitors with broad knowledge of all PC and server hardware.

Networking
Skilled with network equipment including routers (Cisco/3Com), switches (Cisco/3Com/Foundry), hubs, and LIU/CSU/DSU. Well-versed in category 3/5/6 cabling for Ethernet and telephone, RJ11/12/45 crimp, 66- & 110-block cross-connect and phone closet cabling. Extensive knowledge of network topology and design for ISP and enterprise networks. Skilled at troubleshooting and monitoring all network traffic.

NON-TECHNICAL
- Project Design and Management, Engineering Management, Client Presentations and Negotiations, Sales, Marketing and Global Partnerships Finance and Budget Analysis
- Strategic Business Planning/Modeling Consolidations/Restructurings Debt/Equity management Finance/IT/HR/Facilities Management Contract Negotiation/Maintenance Senior Client/Account Relations System Design/Conversion Business Development Support Non-Profit Accounting/Administration
- Management/Supervision, Budgeting/Forecasting, Planning/Scheduling, Customer Service, Conflict Resolution

RESUME WORKSHEETS   Exercise 3.5

- **Photolithography**
  Etch Rates, Epitaxial Layer, Yellow Room, Chemical Vapor Disposition, Telecentricity, Resistivity, Wafer Handling, Recticle

OTHER KEY WORDS AND JARGON
List other few keywords, key phrases, and industry jargon that you would like the reader to understand about your core competencies. These words should be the words you want used to find your resume on job board searches and recruiter database searches.

Chapter 4
<<< The Résumé

"TO GET THE INTERVIEW"

The purpose of a resume is to secure an interview. It is not to conduct one with yourself or the reader. Therefore, it should contain enough information to entice the reader to call you instead of the 50-1000+ other applicants seeking the same position. Your resume and cover letter are the first two documents they see and it is really the first impression of you they form.

You can use one of the example resumes in the workbook section of this book, substitute your information into the pre-formatted resumes and wind up with a pretty decent end product. By doing this, however, you will miss a critical component of the learning and understanding process.

Exercise 4.1

**4000+ Key Action Words and Phrases.
www.RAH2010.com.**

If you don't use the word list, it is a shame, because you now have at your fingertips what is probably one of the most comprehensive resume word lists ever compiled in a single book - over 4000+ actionable words and phrases. If that fails, you can revert to the pre-formatted example resumes in the workbook section.

Why don't you completely read the chapter and *then* decide what you need to do to produce a resume that will set you apart from the other 100-1000+ applicants who are also applying for a particular position?

There are enough books on writing resumes to fill a small town library. On the world-wide-web, you will find sites with page after page devoted to resume writing. In this book I have provided, in concise form, the rules I use in preparing resumes for my clients.

You are in competition with lots of other people and securing the job is achieved through a process of elimination. Like the gladiators competing in the Coliseum in the ~~glory~~ gory days of the Roman Empire, the last person alive and standing, won. They don't hire two people for the same job. In over 2000 years the same rule still applies.

You must be able to demonstrate clearly and concisely what you bring to the table AND, it must be deemed more valuable than that of your competitors. Otherwise, you are just another piece of paper with lots of words and no compelling reason for them to hire you.

Throughout life, most people select what works versus what doesn't. In this book, I will guide you through the process of designing and constructing resumes that have been successful for my clients.

Please notice, resumes is plural. You may wind up with two or three, depending upon your background and the number of jobs for which you apply.

> Each resume must reflect the specific nature of the job for which you are applying. This is the same for cover letters you send.

Don't fool yourself and think that you can

just change a few items and that will be enough to make a difference.

If you are like most people, you will print a stack of "standard" resumes and cover letters for immediate distribution and revise them only for special purposes or jobs.

To secure an interview, your resume must not only be seen, but it must also communicate why they should hire you. This is a much less daunting task when you have completed the Career Summary and Resume Worksheets discussed in the last chapter.

The other, and similarly important document, is your cover letter. As in your resume, your cover letter must be fashioned specifically to the job for which you are applying. Changing a few words and making minor changes won't draw the attention you require or emphasize your power enough to cause you to wind up being the last one standing. Both resumes and cover letters will be addressed in this chapter with clear instructions on the do's and don'ts of each.

THE RESUME

I want to preface this section by telling you that my friends who are professional resume writers use many different formats and rules. They are numerous and varied. If you don't like my instructions, it is perfectly OK with me. Choose whatever makes you comfortable. At the end of this chapter in Exercise 4.6, I've listed my recommended books on resumes.

1. Mechanics & Technical Issues

Size: Use only 8.5" x 11" paper.

Type of Paper: 20-24-lb, **white** linen paper, with up to a 25% Cotton fiber content is preferred. No copy machine paper is to be used. Cheap paper looks like cheap paper. However, too thick a paper will jam your printer. Too much cotton content, even with a good laser-jet, will cause uneven edges, possible smears and lack of visual clarity. It is a balancing act between clarity and looks.

Color Papers: No color papers - green, speckled, blue, gray, severe off-white to yellowish-brown, or otherwise annoying colors or patterns. Cute doesn't count on paper. If you want to be cute, then don't blame me when you get no results.

Margins: All margins are to be no less than 1 inch and a 1.25" left margin is preferred. Let's get real. Sometimes, you may have to go to a .5" margin but do not go below a .5" margin. I see so many resumes that look like the writer is trying to shovel 10 pounds of dirt into a 5-pound bag.

Type Sizes and Styles: Use **no less** than a Times New Roman 10 point type size. Don't use little-used or little-known fonts. Some studies indicate, however, that tips and curls on the serif-type fonts (Times New Roman) actually improve readability. So it's your choice. Readability can also be improved with line spacing increased to 13 or 14 point and paragraph spacing at 4-7 point.

If you must, use no more than two typestyles. I prefer one only. *Italics* and CAPITALIZATION are to be used consistently and conservatively on your formal resume but not on ones to be scanned.

Type of Printer: Use only a laser printer or have them printed by a professional printer.

Avoid laser-jet or ink-jet. Laser jets are too fuzzy on the edges, especially when your ink cartridge is running low or scanning in .pdf format and then putting it on the web. Remember that you get what you pay for and usually the results reflect what you've spent.

2. Length & Look

■ There is no magic formula for the number of pages you need. The rule is that one is better than two, but only if you can adequately tell your story.

■ Never more than two. If you can't pack the last 15-20 years into two pages, you haven't done a very good job of clarifying who you are and why they should hire you. I will tell you that I use the 15-20-year rule in most cases. You may have worked 25-30 years but the last 15-20 really tell what you can do now. How many times have I seen resumes begin with: "For the past 27 years blah, blah, blah."

Guess what? The young MBA, engineer, accountant, HR person or whomever is looking at your application is probably thinking (remember it isn't illegal to think - yet) that you might appear too old, too expensive and probably too inflexible in your business approach with that many years behind you. You have spent the past 20 years getting cushy increases and cost-of-living raises that are not performance-based and now you are too expensive for the marketplace.

That is why, for you more senior managers (20 + years) out there, the market is flooded with 35-year old MBA's who are willing

to work for nearly half of what you cost. Why would you automatically start the process of elimination by telling the reader you are too old, too experienced and too costly? Wait until you are in the arena (remember you are a gladiator now) and work yourself through the interview process. The Baby Boomers, at this printing, are also beginning to impact the marketplace so the full story keeps changing. Stay Tuned.

For those of you young Turks or Turkettes under 35, just remember that someday you will be over 45 and these same rules will apply to you then, as they now apply to your older competitors in today's marketplace.

■ Go back and rethink and rework your credentials. The exception to this rule is for academic resumes (curriculum vitae) or goverment applications that can run up to seven, or more, pages in length. In the business world, unless you are a CEO, COO, President or other very senior-level manager with international experience in a multi-national corporation, more than two pages is certain death.

■ Readers want to see lots of white space on the paper. Crowded line spacing, narrow margins and the other word processing tricks really work against you in the long run. Under the Microsoft Word Format tab there is a sub-tab called paragraph. With this button you can control line height and other important features. Use these to your advantage and create the appearance of greater white space, while adding more copy to the resume at the same time.

- For those using Word by Microsoft, go to the Format, Paragraph section and put a 3 to 6-point space between paragraphs. This avoids page hogging created by 1.5 or 2X line spacing choices. Line spacing looks really good between 13 to15 pts., depending upon the font type selected.

TYPES OF RESUMES
Reverse Chronological

This resume format is the most common and most accepted by recruiters and companies. Because it is the form preferred by recruiters and HR people, it is probably the one you should use, with certain exceptions.

It starts with your work life by listing all of the jobs you've had in your working career in reverse order from most recent through the 15-20 year period.

It can also show the fact that you don't have certain experiences or significant gaps in employment. Since you are not going past the last 15-20 years in your work history, it most likely won't give away your age for those of you over 40.

 Beware of including dates that will identify your date of college graduation.

b-25

Combination (Our personal preference)

A reverse chronologically ordered document placing your achievements in one section and your chronological experiences in another. It combines the strengths of both the chronological

and functional resume types. We add key words and generally a statement about you as well. A variety of resume examples appear at the end of this chapter.

Functional

Your accomplishments are grouped according to specific skill groups or sets. Generally, employment information is listed separately from skills. The functional format is good to use for those over age 50, but recruiters hate this format (many employers as well) because it doesn't show whether or not you have the experiences they might be seeking. It causes them to have to spend more time on finding out about you than they want to spend. See the example in the workbook.

Curriculum Vitae

A very detailed and lengthy document listing all aspects of your education, publications, awards, and work history. Nobody outside the academic systems of this country would even consider reading such a document because they are too wordy and most often don't tell the hiring authority how well you do your work, only what you did or do.

Creative

If you are in the graphic arts, desktop publishing or other industries where being creative counts, this is the format for you. It is highly effective in fields demanding creativity and visual pizzazz. Putting together your own website with flash treatments and other talent-revealing and demonstrated skills is also helpful.

Keyword

Least used and probably the least effective. It does show specific skills but does not elaborate on them and, therefore, does not provide a basis for answering the question "Why should they hire me?"

Webfolio and Online Resources

A web profile should be much more than a resume online. Such a simple document looks amateurish and presents you that way as well. Oh, you can gussie it up with fancy colors and typefont and insertions of pictures, but the real bottom line is that the document should take your candidacy well beyond that of a resume and beyond accomplishments that appear in your resume. Your web profile should also cast you as a problem solver and not only describe the types of problems you solved and how well you solved them, but it should also present your approach to solving them and your behavioral style in getting business done. I have examples on our website. When you land on the page, scroll down the page and click on several and explore. Enjoy!

Examples: http://www.stewartcoopercoon.com/executive_placement/successes/successes_webfolios.htm

! Remember, they hire you because you can solve problems.

b-4

CONTENT AND FORMAT

Corporations are there to make money or, in

the case of governmental work, provide services. Either way, the only way you can be an integral part in that process, is to get the job.

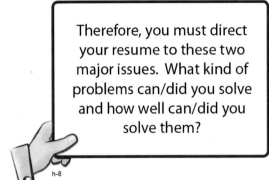
Therefore, you must direct your resume to these two major issues. What kind of problems can/did you solve and how well can/did you solve them?

h-8

Example resumes are found at the end of this chapter. We also have provided additional examples, both before and after versions, on our web site. By comparing these, you can gain an insight as to what they should look like. They are not copy-protected, so please feel free to select one you like and use the format for your own.

Regardless of your level (entry to CEO), the same rules apply to anyone. Follow the same rules and you will achieve the same results. We've included examples of both levels in the workbook. I use WORD by Microsoft and use their instructions and font styles throughout this document because most people have this program.

Here are a few thoughts on the resumes we write:

Name

At the top and on the left side of the paper is my personal preference. Put your name in bold font and in at least a **14-point type-size.**

Address

Under that, in 11-point type size, put your address, phone and email address. If you have one of those obnoxious, "cutesy" email addresses, dump it and get another immediately. There are FREE sites available on the www. Split the address across the page from the phone number so that you take up less space on the page.

Position

In **14-point bold type**, put the title of the type of position you are applying for and center it on the page (i.e.: Project Manager, Sales Manager, General Manager, etc.).

Objective

I personally don't recommend an objective. However, if you feel compelled to put one in your resume, then no more than one to four sentences in length. Preferably one to two lines long. Just remember, even if it is done very well, it makes a neutral contribution. If done wrong, you stand the possibility of eliminating yourself from consideration. Your choice.

Skills Summary

Below the position title, write a three to four (no more) line statement summarizing your skills. See sample resumes.

Key Word

Put in a table. Two or three columns with no more than four rows. Go to your Resume Worksheets and pull out 6-12 key words that do **NOT** contain the same words used in your skills summary above and insert them into the

boxes. If you can't think of any, use the 4000+ word phrase list at www.readyaimhired.com/protected.

Educational Achievment

List educational achievements, starting with your highest academic achievement and working backwards. PhD first, MBA second, etc. Each on a separate line. If you are only partially through a Masters Degree, list it.

Do NOT make it look like you have a degree when you don't. This will kill you when references and vitals are checked. Don't list high school if you've graduated from college. If you are more than five years out of college, then put your education at the end of your resume.

Line Formatting: I like a 13pt. line spacing, with anywhere from a 2 to 9 point space between paragraphs.

Your Title

State your title in the last position you held or in the one you are seeking. I like to put it into bold typeface. Put a 2-6-point space between the line above this section and your title. If you italicize this, please remove the italics for acceptance by scanners used in large corporations and recruiting firms.

Company Name

Put the name of the company in small letters on the first line of the job description.

Title and Years Employed

In CAPITAL LETTERS put your title followed by the years employed there (1986-2000). This is in bold typeface. Remove the bold for the scannable format.

Company Description

Under your title line, put a three to four (no more) line description of the company and include what they make or provide, their size (people or sales or both), and their position in their particular marketplace.

Accomplishments

These are very important. I always encourage my clients to see if they can get an accomplishment into 21 words or less. Less is actually better. The challenge is 15 words. Remember, accomplishments are designed to say in the barest and most simple terms how well you did what you did. They should always contain one or more of the following: number, percentage, dollars.

Exercise 4.2

Action Phrases
www.RAH2010.com

KEY ACTION VERBS, WORK PHRASES

Now list the key points of what you did for that company. Indicate each with an 11 to 12 point <u>bullet.</u> The words and phrases you will use come directly from Exercise 3.5., Resume Worksheets. These will help you form the proper structure and Exercise 4.1 (4000+ words and phrases) will help you if you need alternative words or phrases to avoid repetition!

For each job you've had, begin each statement in the <u>past tense</u> using an action verb (i.e.: implemented, managed, organized, etc). However, if you are still employed, then by all means use the present tense (i.e.: implement, manage, organize, etc.).

Exercise 4.3

Personal Trait Words
www.RAH2010.com

Simplicity

You must keep your resume simple and easy to read. Make sure your job title is easily understandable, don't use obscure vocabulary and try to pick words that are familiar to a variety of readers. Whenever possible, use bullet points and short phrases that are easily readable and "eye scannable" by any reader.

Overall Form

Use short, action-oriented, high-impact phrases when running out of space on a line. Do not repeat the same action verb. When describing your current position, make sure that you use the current tense and in past positions, the past tense.

Watermarks

You would be amazed at the number of people who don't check the watermarks on the paper. By placing the paper incorrectly into the printer the document is produced with the watermark upside down. Old fogeys like me look at this and might conclude that you are careless. Why would I want to hire a careless person?

Sending

I would recommend using a 9" x 12" enve-lope rather than a regular letter envelope. In this way, your resume arrives unfolded, easily scan-nable and clear. Another small consideration for not being eliminated.

Inaccuracies

Whatever you do, <u>get the spelling right</u>. If you haven't shown the courtesy and attention to detail sufficiently enough to spell correctly in your resume, you will most likely be eliminated up front!

> Don't list hobbies, personal salary information, race, age, political affiliation, sexual preferences or anything else that can potentially eliminate you.
>
> h-9

> **!** Careless proofing indicates careless work habits and poor attention to detail.
>
> b-5

These are not the characteristics they have identified when they say they want a problem solver and good communicator who can get the job done. You may very well be able to get the job done, but at what level of performance and what level of quality? Enough said. Find at least three other people to critique and proof your resume and cover letters before they are sent.

Don't use a telephone number that has been disconnected. Don't use false information or dates in your resume. They can be grounds for termination. They may not terminate you now, but the first storm that comes along, it becomes a convenient excuse to overlook your severance package. They save money and you lose!

use acronyms unless your targeted reader is in your field, will completely be comfortable with them and no one else will be seeing the resume who doesn't understand the terms. Engineers, software and hardware applicants should appro-priately put them in a section that is designated as "technical competencies." Safer this way.

Termination Reasons

Are you kidding? I spoke with an applicant the other day who presented a long diatribe about her termination.

There are many reasons not to tell, but the main one is that you don't have to. Read the unit on interviewing and learn how to answer this question.

Patents

I prefer to list them at the end under an accom-plishments section. They should be written in such a way as to stand out, but not dominate, the section into which they are placed, unless you are applying for a position where these are considered a requirement for acceptance.

OTHER POINTS TO CONSIDER

Be concise. Use no more than two or three lines for each point. One is best; two is OK; three if necessary; and four if you absolutely must. *You'd better have moved Mount Everest if you use four.* Try to use no more than five, but certainly no more than eight, items per job. If you have more, great, but some of them can be combined to make the items shorter on the page.

I like to put numbers first in the sentence wherever possible. However, using numbers first in every sentence is boring and looks contrived. Mix it up.

 Never put numbers at the end of a sentence, if you can help it. They get lost.

b-6

People read numbers first. A number will cause the resume reader to stop and think. This is what you want to achieve. You want them to stop and consider why it is they should hire you! How much, how many, by what degree, how much ahead of schedule, etc., is what is needed here. Remember, the reader is giving you less than 20 seconds in the first visual resume scan. Put your most important accomplishment first and your second most important accomplishment last. People scan. They do not read anymore. Also, wherever possible use decimal points in your numbers. Decimal point stop the eye just a fraction of a second longer. The decimal point also enhances the credibility the numbers represent. If you don't have something to catch their eye, you're dead in the water.

In your **Résumé Worksheets** forms, you used action phrases describing how you handled certain tasks. Review these and see if there are any you can use in developing the sentences used in your resume.

NEVER repeat one! There are enough for you to choose from without doing this. Any good college writing instructor will tell you never repeat a word in the same paragraph unless it is impossible not to do so. I'm telling you never to repeat one, period!

Moreover, don't repeat one in the entire document, unless there is no alternative. The reader wants to view as many facets of your work initiative as possible.

The more you repeat, the fewer facets you present. If you appear the same as the 100-1,000+ other applicants, why should they hire you? If you want to see more phrases and ideas, go to the public library and see if they use a software program called "Job Scribe." This program contains over 3,000 job descriptions and surely you can find matching phrases in these that parallel your job or at least portions of it.

You may also go to public agencies, recruiters and as many other sources as possible to secure job descriptions. All is fair in the job-securing war, so use every source available to you. Remember the number two rule from Fred's Rules: *Good Enough, Never Is!*

REFERENCES

Do not put the phrase, "Excellent references available upon request," at the bottom of the resume. It goes without saying that you will list good references anyway.

However, you must prepare your list. No less than three, no more than six. No personal, only business-related. See my interview in Chapter 8.

Technical Training

I mean, what are you going to give them anyway, bad references?

b-7

At the end of the resume, list specific technical training. This is not to be confused with education, so don't mix the two. List any computer languages, courses, programs, or seminars in which you have received licenses, earned accreditation or been credentialed.

Finally, if you have room, you may list other internships, volunteer activities, and organizations to which you belong or in which you participate. Other awards are shown here as well.

ASCII-Text Resumes

You might wish to have an ASCII-text version of your resume in your arsenal. The purpose of a text resume is to submit it to a text reader or enter it into a database for scanning and sort purposes, nothing more. What is a plain text or ASCII resume? Plain text or ASCII is a very simple form of text that almost all computers can scan, read and understand.

h-10

Unless specifically directed to do so, don't ever send a test version of your resume to a company. However, when asked to do so, do it!

Here are the basics of developing an ASCII text resume:

- After you have created your resume in Word, save it using the dropdown at the bottom of the "save as" screen "Save as Type."

  Drop down to "Text" and assign the file a name, NAME RESUME-TEXT (or whatever file name you choose) and then close the file.

- Pull up the file you just saved and you should see that it is in text format and all your beautiful WORD work is destroyed.

- Set the right-hand margins at no more than 68 characters wide.

- Make a hard return when reaching 68 characters.

- In place of Word bullets, use an asterisk (*) or the equals (=) sign.

- Watch your spacing between paragraphs.

- Don't use ALL CAPS at any time.

- Save the file as Word-TEXT.

- Now, you have a document you can copy onto your email response along with your cover letter specific to that position.

Always attach your word version to the email any time you send an ASCII text. Tell them in your email that you have attached a Word version (whatever version you have) and that if they can't open it, please email you and let you know immediately.

You may want to attach a Word version of both the resume and cover letter, but remember, the reader may have a different set-up from you and things might be missed in the translation.

Most word processing software programs allow you to easily convert your formatted resume to an ASCII or plain-text resume. If you want to make sure that everything in your ASCII resume looks good and has the correct spacing, etc., just paste it into an email and send it to yourself.

Sign up, fill in the data and post your resume. Follow the directions and paste your resume into the database. You can quickly see what you need to correct.

Other Rules

- Use black text printed by a laser printer on plain white paper. Use 12-point type.

- Be sure to leave white space around paragraphs and a minimum of ½ inch of white space on the top, bottom and each side. Be sure to use page numbers.

- Folding your resume before you submit it can also cause scanning problems. So it is best to snail mail your unstapled resume in a flat envelope.

Exercise 4.4

Instructions for Electronic Resumes
www.RAH2010.com

ELECTRONIC COVER LETTER CHECKLIST

- Have I spell-checked my email message?

- Is this message worded as though I were talking face-to-face with the recipient?

- Are my paragraphs short?

- Do my lines exceed 65 characters long?

- Have I been concise and to the points?

- Have I included my name and contact information at the bottom of the email address?

- Do I have all my key words listed in the front of the document?

The key words are really important when your resume is scanned. Most large employers put scanned resumes into their databases and these are sorted by key words and then associated with your name. When a manager gives a job description to HR at the company, the first thing they do is access their computers and enter in the key words for that job. Bingo, your name is associated with those, and that is why you should always incorporate key words into your resume. Key word examples: C++, sales, finance and a thousand others. The point here is that your key words should be specific to your industry and your function

PULLING IT ALL TOGETHER

You now know size, shape, font, look, length and the basic do's and don'ts of the document. Now we focus on the content.

From the *Resume Worksheet*, exercise 3.5, extract the data on education, training, licenses, languages spoken, computer skills, and publications and place them in the aforementioned locations on the resume.

For each job listed, import from the Resume Worksheet a description of the company. No more than four lines, at most.

From the *Resume Worksheet*, go to Achievements, and pull your prioritized achievements into the resume under this particular job title.

Continue to do this for each job. You will invariably have to work these over to get them to one line, (two at most), and be sure each line has a quantifiable number in it so you can finally answer the question, "Why should they hire you?"

Use the example resume in the workbook as your guide or just copy your data into it and be on your way.

Exercise 4.5

Example Resumes are at the end of this chapter. www.RAH2010.com

YOUR COVER LETTER

This is one of the most critical items you will prepare. Do yourself a big favor: Don't make the same mistake most people make and simply restate what is already contained in your resume. If you do, you will definitely harm your candidacy.

The purpose of the cover letter is to tell the hiring authority *why* you should be the only candidate for consideration for this position. What is the answer to this question? The answer is simple: You are a problem solver! What problems have you solved and how well?

Mechanical To Do's

Here is a brief list of the mechanical requirements for your cover letter:

- 8.5" x 11", 25% cotton content, bond and watermarked, white paper. I prefer linen style.

- Block your letter left side of page.

- Print the letter with the watermark right side up.

- No more than two lines between date and addressee name and title.

- Always use the middle initial of the person to whom you are writing. If you have to call someone to get it, then do so. It is a proper professional touch.

- Dear Mr. or Ms. is the appropriate salutation, never Mrs., unless you are specifically asked to do so. Always use the salutation, "Honorable" or "Doctor," where appropriate. People take great stock in their titles. They spent years achieving it and you should respect it by getting it right.

- Never less than 1" left and right margins.

- No more than four paragraphs.

- Each paragraph has no more than seven

lines.

- 11- to 12-point Times New Roman typeface.

- Your name and address centered at the top unless you already have pre-printed stationary.

- Under the name goes the address and phone number. The phone number should be clear and stand out. Hey, they WILL want to call you!

- Your email address must be on all correspondence.

- The "close" will depend upon the situation and whether or not you know the person being addressed. Hopefully, you will. If you don't, then a "sincerely" will suffice. Always allow three line spaces between the closing and your name/title for your signature.

- State the title of the position you seek in the first paragraph. Often the letter is separated from the resume due to scanning.

  Also, recruiters many times have multiple positions they are recruiting for and they will not waste their time trying to figure you out. There are too many other fish in the pond.

- You must show enthusiasm in your opening paragraph and a **brief** statement of why you want this particular job.

- Under no circumstances are you to mention or even allude to the fact that you may not be qualified. Go to the church of your choice and do confession, never in your cover letter.

- I have seen so many letters written with humor. Don't! Humor is great after you have the job or in the interview, maybe. But never, ever, in a cover letter!

- For Pete's sake, don't use trite clichés, such as:

  " I'm confident my skills and abilities will be beneficial to your company, blah, blah and blah." They are useless and waste precious space. Stop and think for a moment. EVERYONE applying for this position says the same thing. Your job is to set yourself above the crowd.

- Be assertive, not pretentious.

- Avoid obsolete phrases such as:

  This letter is written in response to…

  Enclosed please find…

  Per your request…

  Please consider this my application for …

- Begin your letter with a statement saying something about your skills and experiences. For example: "My specialty is managing dramatic sales increases using consultative selling techniques working with multi-disciplinary groups."

- In the closing paragraph, always tell the reader what your next action step is going to be. Will you send a follow up letter, email, or other form of correspondence? Will you make a telephone call or a visit to see them? Whatever you say you will do, you better do it when you tell them you will do it!

- The worst two sins you can commit are grammar and spelling mistakes. I guarantee you that, if either your resume or cover letter contains mistakes, it will be cast aside, regardless of how well-qualified you may be!

 Proofread everything and don't rely solely upon spell check!

b-8

Remember, "tin" and "ten" will both pass muster in Microsoft spell check programs.

Reread everything at least three times, once backwards. Read your resume out loud to yourself, make your changes, and then read it out loud to your search partner.

At this point, give it to someone who can write well. Let them review it and see if you can improve what you've done so far. Remember GOOD ENOUGH, NEVER IS! If not, go back and reread it now. You cannot afford to make a mistake.

■ The real secret to getting the interview is to take the ad (whether from the net or a paper or wherever) and break it down into its component parts to determine what they want from a candidate.

■ If they want "tall," and one of your job overview statements says how well you did "tall," then use that story in your cover letter to tell them why you are the right person. But for goodness sake, don't repeat what's in your resume!

■ You should make two to four points in your letter.

It should be only one page long and should follow the same mechanical guidelines listed above. If you can use only two paragraphs to communicate your skills, then use two.

■ Fewer are better! Never use more than four paragraphs under any circumstances and NO paragraph should EVER be more than SEVEN lines long.

Content To Do's

■ The first sentence of your cover letter is probably the most important. This sentence must be a high-impact, carefully constructed item that will compel the reader to want to read the next paragraph and ultimately the attached resume. The same holds true for the first paragraph. Keep it simple and state your business or reason for contacting them. This is your sales pitch. What sizzle are you selling?

■ If you can favorably mention their product or service in the first paragraph, it will bode well for you. Also, there is nothing wrong with letting them know you want to work for their particular company and why. If you can't come up with a sales pitch, use a question or a quote. Maybe you can state a fact that impressed you about the company.

■ The next three paragraphs of the letter focus on selling yourself. The second paragraph should be no more than four or five lines at the most in length and specifically addressing your best skills and accomplishments. Please use simple sentences that don't run on forever and always use action verbs. Read the letter over and over and see if it flows well.

If not, rewrite it until it does. Flow is very important. We don't want disjointed thoughts or sentences.

■ The third paragraph should address client issues found in the job description and other documents. Also in this paragraph, take one or two points from your background, and show the client how your particular sets of skills will benefit them. These points are to be taken from your SHARE stories.

■ The closing paragraph is your chance to tell them what you are asking for. It is also a chance to express what you want in order to move the process along. Examples might be an interview, meeting, follow-up phone call, etc.

■ Here is a neat trick. Add a P.S. to the bottom of your letter. I assure you that even if they have scanned the letter, their eyes will be drawn to the P.S. at the bottom.

Make sure this is a killer statement about your skills and what you bring to the table that will contribute to their goals and why they should hire you.

BRIEF THOUGHTS ABOUT RESUME SUBMISSION

■ The important thing to remember is that you must not try to shovel 10-lbs of dirt into a 5-lb bag! It is much better to prepare two resumes. Also, don't get lazy and just change the title on your resume from one job application to the next.

■ Repeat the process above or rethink your strategy and then direct the words and results to support the particular job you are going after.

■ Only send your cover letter and resume in response to an ad for which you are truly qualified.

■ Send it to the decision-maker. Don't know who that is? Then find out by phone or homework, and send it to them.

■ Make your ability statement razor sharp in the cover letter.

■ Make sure you've used my 4000+ Action Words and Phrases List throughout your resume and cover letter. When scanned, they will definitely be picked up in search/sort routines.

■ Use multiple key word phrases so you have the possibility of being perceived as having multiple utility (i.e., Provided a variety of management functions including hiring, benefits administration, budgeting, forecasting and marketing). Now, your chances for consideration are considerably better.

■ When you send your resume via email, put the job title or number and your name in the "Subject" line.

Put a short 3 - 4 line note in the email. You are more likely to get to this person using the email method. People don't take the time to scroll down anymore.

■ At some point in your campaign, a secretary or "gatekeeper" will screen you out. Whatever you do, try to secure the email address of the decision-maker or, at least, the HR director and you will be more likely to receive a call or an audience.

■ Beware of giving away your age by putting too many dates in the resume. I again remind you to only go back 15 years. If they want more information, provide it, but only when asked. Stress your accomplishments and skills, not your age!

■ Don't give names of references in your letters or resume. However, have a nicely printed copy ready if they do request them or for your interview situations.

■ Don't try to be everything to everybody. Target and focus.

■ Don't leave a few words on a line. Rewrite if necessary and don't dawdle or dangle words or phrases.

■ Avoid trite phrases or terms: "insofar as" or "insomuch as."

If you are not getting "hits" on a particular letter type, change styles and redo, redo and redo. **"Good Enough, Never Is!"** You are now ready to begin piecing your resume together. Good luck, and remember you can always use the examples provided in this book.

■ ANOTHER TRICK: Redo your resume to be more of a summary packed with key accomplishments. Then, make your left margins 2.5" and write the following note in this margin in your most legible handwriting: (name of your new boss) "Bob, thought you would find this interesting." Do NOT sign your name. When the gatekeeper gets this, she will likely pass it on.

On the outside of the envelope (bottom left side) write the following: Personal/Confidental.

SUMMARY

You've played around with my pre-formatted resume, plugged in your information and now have a document that tells why they should hire you and no one else. You should also stock your search larder with a career summary, a text version of your resume and a scannable resume.

Exercise 4.6

Recommended Resume Books
Books I recommend are found on a page at the end of this chapter.
www.RAH2010.com

READ THIS READ THIS READ THIS READ THIS

Both exercises 4.1 and 4.2 may be found on the website:
www.RAH2010.com

Exercise 4.3

Personal Trait Words

Achieve	Energetic	Professional Protective
Achievement-Oriented	Enthusiastic	Punctual
Adaptable	Exceptional	Quick witted
Adept	Exhaustive	Rational
Adventuresome	Experienced	Realistic
Alert	Expert	Reliable
Appreciative	Firm	Repeatedly
Assertive	Flexible	Resourceful
Astute	Helpful to others	Responsible
Authoritative	Human	Responsive
Calm	Impulsive	Self-motivated
Caring towards others	Independent	Self-reliant
Cautious	Innovative	Sensitive
Charismatic	Kind	Sociable
Competent	Knowledgeable	Sophisticated
Confrontational style	Loyal	Very Sophisticated
Consistent	Good listener	Strong
Contagious enthusiasm	Methodical	Supportive
Cooperative	Mentoring style	Tactful
Counseling style	Negotiator	Thorough
Courageous	Objective	Tolerant
Creative	Open-minded	Trusting
Decisive	Outgoing	Understanding
Deliberate	Outstanding	Unique
Dependable	Patient	Unusual
Diligent	Penetrative	Versatile
Diplomatic	Perceptive	Vigorous
Discreet	Persuading style	
Driving	Pleasant	
Driven	Persevering	
Dynamic	Persistent	
Extremely economical	Pioneering	
Effective	Practical	

PDF & ASCII - TEXT RESUMES

Here's a news flash. No matter how much you work at it, or how much time you spend on it, your resume will look funky on some browsers. It doesn't matter which word processing program you use. The best laid plans of mice and men often go awry. Browsers are also different. So here are some quick rules to follow that might get you through this quagmire.

1.   After you have typed your resume save it in Microsoft Word. Do not use the latest Word version. The reason we do not do this is that some people are still using older versions of Word and cannot open your resume if it's saved in the latest version.

2.   Now save your resume in ASCII-text, which is a universal word file that can be read by Mac, Apple, or other systems. When you save in text format it will automatically remove your bullet points and other fancy stuff and what you see is a bunch of funny looking characters going down the page. Use the following symbols for bullet points and other differentiating characters: = + ' --

3.   Save both Word and text versions of your resume on a separate thumb drive as well as your hard drive.

4.   Save your resume in a PDF format. Having your resume in PDF assures you that it will be seen exactly as you have typed it and can be read universally by anyone anywhere in the world. Unfortunately, most search engines want you to cut and paste your resume and cover letter in text format, so refer to number two above.

THEODORE A. BLACKWELL, MCSE, CNE, CCNA
7945 Brownfield Drive
Chicago, IL 55555
Phone: (555) 555-0903 * Email: email@emailaddress.com

INFORMATION SYSTEMS DIRECTOR/NETWORK SERVICES MANAGER
Proven Technical & Management Expertise in a Career Spanning 15+ Years

Technically sophisticated and business savvy management professional with a pioneering career reflecting strong leadership qualifications coupled with "hands-on" IS and networking expertise. Maintain focus on achieving bottom-line results while formulating and implementing advanced technology and business solutions to meet a diversity of needs. Superior record of delivering simultaneous large-scale, mission-critical projects on time and under budget. Team-based management style and excellent interpersonal communication skills.

**IT Strategic Planning / Business Solutions / Team Leadership / Budgeting / Project Management
Capital Expenditure Planning / Contract Negotiations / Vendor Relations**

Professional Experience

INFORMATION SYSTEMS MANAGER Medical Health Systems, Chicago, IL   **1993 – Present**

Recruited to upgrade and replace obsolete technologies at this world-class health care organization with more than 2000 users in 15 remote locations. Hire, train, develop, and lead a 20-person technical team. Manage a $2 million capital budget and $1.2 million operating budget. Scope of position is expansive and includes departmental direction and full design, installation, engineering, implementation, support, training, administration, and management authority for:

- LAN/WAN Network Services	- PC Desktop Systems
- 24x7 Data Center Computer Operations	- UNIX Systems Administration
- Applications Systems	- Database Administration
- Web/Internet Design & Operations	- Help Desk Operations

Spearheaded transition from outdated organization-wide and departmental technologies to highly functional, streamlined, and cost-effective client-server technologies and business solutions that have dramatically improved efficiency, decreased expenses, and optimized data integrity and safety.

Key Projects and Achievements:

- Directed design and installation of the complete $8 million LAN/WAN infrastructure. Utilized state-of-the-art technologies to provide network connectivity of disparate Mainframe, AS400, UNIX, Windows NT, Novell, and PC systems.

- Completed, in just 8 months – 22 months ahead of schedule – a complex $15 million project forecasted to take 2.5 years involving replacement of more than 30 systems.

- Delivered $2 million in cost savings through aggressive negotiation of contracts and pricing on a budgeted $10 million for hardware/software purchases and consulting services.

- Saved more than $1.2 million in technical consulting fees by negotiating complementary network design services from vendors.

- Performed the work of 3 full-time equivalents, slashing labor expenses substantially by expanding personal responsibility to include UNIX, network, and database administration.

- Decreased inventory, application pricing, and licensing expenses $750K by establishing standardization for applications, PC desktops, and networking systems.

THEODORE A. BLACKWELL – Page 2

INFORMATION SYSTEMS MANAGER 1993 – Present, continued

- Defused and resolved long-standing conflicts and department problems, elevated morale and decreased high employee turnover rates, achieving the best retention rate in the company.

- Managed from planning through completion, a $2.4 million Windows NT workstation and network printer implementation project. Delivered on time and $600K under budget.

- Attained consistent 99% up time by implementing disaster recovery and fault tolerance plans. Instituted the first highly reliable corporate-wide centralized back-up system.

- Championed introduction of Internet/Web technology, corporate-wide email, shared calendaring, and online meetings. Set up and managed a TCP&P environment, installed a Novell network, and implemented a data warehouse database.

- Collaborated on numerous management committees including the Systems Application Selection Team, Chair of the Network, Operations, and Security Team, and the Y2K Implementation Team.

NETWORK MANAGER, Goodman, Inc., Canton, OH   **1993**

Managed and delivered ahead of schedule, a nationwide $10 million+ network project, involving development of a fully-redundant credit verification system. Administered a multi-server LAN supporting Novell, UNIX, and Unisys systems and supported 2000 users in 850 remote sites.

DIRECTOR OF TECHNICAL SERVICES, Compunet International, Inc., Parma, OH   **1990 –1992**

Built and managed Information Systems, Technical Support, Production, and Repair Departments for this start up Novell Reseller and PC manufacturing firm. Supervised staff, oversaw computer operations, and managed budgets. Saved $2 million the first year by renegotiating manufacturing contracts and relocating production to reduce costs and improve shipping schedules. Developed and trained a team to provide support to a culturally diverse international customer base.

COMPUTER TECHNICIAN, FEC Systems, Lima, OH   **1989 – 1990**
SENIOR SYSTEMS SUPPORT SPECIALIST, Multitech Inc., Dublin, OH   **1985 – 1989**

Education $ Credentials

AMERICAN INSTITUTE OF COMPUTER SCIENCE – Chicago, IL
B.S. Candidate in Computer Science, completed three years of study

TOTAL TECHNICAL INSTITUTE – Chicago, IL
Computer Systems Support Certification – Intensive 2 year program

Technical Certifications:

- **MCSE** – Microsoft Certified Systems Engineer
- **CNE** – Novell Certified NetWare Engineer
- **CCNA** – Cisco Certified Networking Associate
- **CNA** – Novell Certified Netware Administrator

Recent Training:

- Cisco Router Programming & Internetworking
- Network Administration for UNIX Systems
- ATM – Asynchronous Transfer Mode
- Windows NT 4.0 Network Administration
- AIX UNIX Advanced System Administration
- Cisco Enterprise Management Solutions

- Bay Networks – TCP&P, SNMP, FDDI
- EDI – Electronics Data Interchange
- Windows 95 Support
- Windows NT 4.0 Technical Support
- Internet Information Server
- SQL Server 6.5 Database Administration

The Résumé   **81**

SNAPSHOT

Senior human resources executive, change agent and partner to business; expert in driving strategic change and consensus through sound corporate principles backed by vision and innovation. Adept at managing multiple tasks, isolating and resolving issues, and transforming unproductive or erroneous processes into models of best practice.

Credible and transparent leadership underpins intuitive business sense and an uncompromising commitment towards employee retention and premier support services. Reputed for clear ideals, standards and integrity, and as an energetic promoter and champion of new ideas and initiatives for greater perspective.

Inspired by finding new ways, influencing change, and uncovering new avenues to deliver people-centric organizations.

YVETTE SANDERSON

33 Plum Road, Florida, NY 10990
Cell: (845) 922-6666
Email: yvettes@hotmail.com
Residence: (201) 555-6200

EXECUTIVE ~ HUMAN RESOURCES
FELLOW, HUMAN RESOURCES INSTITUTE

FACTS. RECOGNITION. RESULTS.

- Cut employee turnover from 35% to just 9.5%—against an industry average of 25%, via the implementation of a best practice remuneration and employee benefits scheme.

- Delivered a $50M strategic HR plan well received by the Board of Directors, featuring inbuilt flexibility to provide for unresolved intangibles.

- Spearheaded a recruitment strategy that successfully attracted and retained more than 40 high caliber employees including the Project Director, Corporate Affairs Director, senior engineers and other key professionals

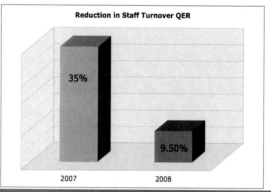

VALUE OFFERED

- HR Resource Systems Planning and Implementation
- Change Management
- Employee Assistant and Wellness Programs
- Employee Benefit Programs
- Executive Development
- Settlement Negotiations

- Benefits and Risk Management
- Executive Motivation/Coaching
- Dispute Resolution
- Employee Contracts
- Training & Development Plans
- Labor Laws and Policies
- Personnel Recruitment
- Policy Formulation

- Budget Development and Management
- Compensation Management
- Employee Marketing Programs
- Employee Incentive Programs
- Forecasting and Planning
- Strategic Planning
- Productivity Improvements

CAREER SUMMARY

QER TYE INCORPORATED, NY, **VP Human Resources**   1/2007–Present
STATE APPRENTICESHIP SERVICE, Florida NY, **Human Resources Executive**   12/2004–7/2006

PRIOR ENGAGEMENTS
- **HR Consultant,** Department of Veterans' Affairs, NY (2002–2004)
- **Policy and Programs Manager,** Department of Finance and Administration, NY (1999–2002)
- **HR Manager,** Glebe Pharmaceuticals, MN (1994–1998)

EXPERIENCE NARRATIVE

QER TYE INCORPORATED, NY   1/2007–2/2008
VP Human Resources

SNAPSHOT:
Reported to: Director, Human Resources.
Direct Reports: 3 Human Resources Coordinators and Recruitment Officer.
Employer: Engineering and resources company developing multi-billion dollar shale-to-liquids.
Summary: Strategically planned HR and recruitment initiatives; project managed payroll outsourcing, introduced best practice remuneration/benefits, created leadership development program, improved HR budget, managed workplace health and safety, and developed relationships across the business.

Injected a sense of stability by introducing formal standards and predictable outcomes in an organization transitioning through significant change. Introduced strong, definitive strategies for the organization to become an employer of choice for quality talent and cut employee turnover from 35% to 9.5%.

Confronted upon commencement with high levels of employee stress following a turbulent period of downsizing and office relocation. Complicating the HR structure was a lack of formal frameworks surrounding processes and decision-making. Recruitment was lagging with some roles remaining unfilled for 18+ months—prompting overworked employees and dissatisfaction.

- Developed a series of "quick wins" that established credibility and build confidence in initiatives to develop HR plans and strategies. Met with key stakeholders to identify issues, define expectations, and create solutions.

- Delivered a $50M strategic HR plan well received by the Board of Directors, and featuring inbuilt flexibility to provide for unresolved intangibles including unknown timeframes and vague plant sizes. Despite changing "goal posts" and the need to exercise influence with key stakeholders, delivered the four-week project in just three weeks, well under budget without compromise on quality.

- Assumed control of the recruitment function. Developed a strategy designed to cut timeframes, better manage vacant positions, target top-tier candidates and sustain quality recruitment methodologies.

- Spearheaded a recruitment strategy that successfully attracted and retained more than 40 high-caliber employees including the Project Director, Corporate Affairs Director, senior engineers and other key professionals.

- Won broad based support for initiative to produce a second-tier HR information system and outsourced payroll function that would eliminate erroneous spreadsheet-based reporting. Lobbied management successfully to phase in the *Aurion* system across six months—an idea that gained traction for having limited impact on daily operations. The financially sound system provided immediate value creating quality reports with no additional costs, and completed within budget.

- Cut employee turnover from 35% to just 9.5%—against an industry average of 25%, via the implementation of a best practice remuneration and employee benefits scheme.

- Kick-started and contributed to a new leadership development program aiming to reinforce a continuous improvement culture, succession planning, and high performing teams.

- Costed and developed the human resources budget forecasts, cash flows, and payroll—boosting accuracy and the integrity of data and setting the stage for cost savings.

- Sustained zero lost time injury rate throughout tenure—introducing several initiatives in the management and promotion of workplace health and safety.

- Counseled employees in career development, job opportunities and educational advancement. Prepared and delivered "Development Centers" to identify areas for personal career development aligned with the organization's identified business direction and areas of expertise

"It's not everyday that someone like Yvette comes along. I hesitate to use the words 'human dynamo' but it seems most apt. The way she identified problems that had plagued us for years and solved them in months, is testament to strengths in bringing all parties together and achieving agreement"—CEO

EXPERIENCE NARRATIVE

STATE APPRENTICESHIP SERVICE, Florida NY   12/2004–1/2007
Human Resources Executive

SNAPSHOT:
Reported to: Chief Executive Officer.
Direct Reports: 2 HR Coordinators
Budget: $15M payroll for 200 employees and HR budget of $150K.
Employer: Not-for-profit organization providing support services to apprentices on behalf of the federal government. Services include promotion of apprenticeships and traineeships, incentive payments, follow-up, and government paperwork assistance.

In just 18 months transformed perceptions of the HR function being "just another department"—by strategically elevating the business of HR as an acknowledged driver of high performance, dynamic employees enriched by an equitable culture rewarding talent and commitment

With 47% employee retention and an HR function unrecognized as a key strategic and value-added business driver, it was immediately clear that change was an immediate priority.

Won executive praise for devising a dynamic, multi-pronged strategy designed to reverse morale declines and attrition and instead, attract the right candidates and retain employees through a revamp of the remuneration framework, a revitalized training and development program, and new career development and succession planning paths. Promotion to the Senior Management team rapidly followed.

Key Leadership Initiatives and Results

- Launched an orientation program that for the first time offered new recruits an understanding of the organization, the legislative environment, key performance indicators and culture.

- Jumpstarted three-year strategic goal to pay employees at the median of external market surveys via the development and implementation of a recruitment framework. Initiative served to attract experienced, well-qualified staff and elevate employee retention rates.

- Secured buy-in from CEO and the senior executive team to green light the *Employer of Choice* plan—a strategic initiative aligned with business objectives and designed to attract and retain top-flight staff through reward-based recognition. Despite limited resources, built compelling argument that cited the costs of poor morale and declining reputation on the workforce and customers.

- Took charge following the unexpected non-renewal of five government contracts leaving 170 staff without jobs. Pulled together a team of professionals from the employment services industry to provide an outplacement service providing assistance in résumé development and job seeking advice. Hosted lunchtime sessions on job seeking, stress management and government/community programs. Within just two months all redundant employees had been placed with other organizations.

- Handpicked by Board Chairman to terminate the services of a senior executive—a sensitive assignment with potential to negatively impact the business. Diplomatic, respectful negotiations and settlement offer ensured a quick exit without negative media attention.

- Launched *ConnX*—an employee self-service system that saved up 10 working hours per pay cycle. New technology served to process leave applications and pay advisories, reminded managers of approval requests, and allowed employees to monitor and manage personal information.

- Pioneered a leadership development program that elevated employee satisfaction and cut turnover.

EDUCATION AND TRAINING

Postgraduate Certificate in Business Administration, Syracuse University, Syracuse, NY
Postgraduate Diploma of Applied Psychology, Syracuse University, Syracuse, NY
Bachelor of Arts (Applied Psychology), San Diego State University, San Diego, CA

Training includes: Kepner-Tregoe Problem-Solving & Decision Analysis | Accelerated Case Management | Group and Team Facilitation Skills | Remuneration Benchmarking| Mercer Human Resource Consulting | Competitive Tendering and Contracting | Recruitment and Retention | Using Salary Surveys

Explanation Summary

Yvette Sanderson is an HR executive with a really strong and dynamic personality. Consequently to represent her brand, I opted for an "in your face" opening page that screams achievement. From the selected achievements, strong business focused headings and an eye catching graph visually representing one of her greatest accomplishments, page one is intended to compel the reader to sit up and take notice. Equally, the first page is self-contained, so could be used as a one-page snap off résumé if required.

I continued this strong and dynamic theme, by electing to create a striking table next to each job.

On the left, the job basics. On the right, a bold summary of her achievements during that time.

Following, I created the text based on the CAR concept, offering the challenge that she met when she started, the actions she took to overcome those problems, and the results of her actions.

I capitalized on the opportunity of a small gap on page two to quote her CEO who described her as a human dynamo.

The clear, sans serif font, is sharp and clear on the page and provides a wonderful contrast between the bold olive green strips. Burgundy bullet points provide a "look at this" contrast.

BRIAN WASHINGTON, CPA

CHIEF FINANCIAL OFFICER • CONTROLLER

8784 Main Street
Dallas, Texas 75201
(214) 848-1234
brian_wash@cpa.com

PROVIDING BEST-IN-CLASS FINANCIAL MANAGEMENT
ACROSS MULTIPLE BUSINESS ENVIRONMENTS

An innovative senior leader with a 20-year track record of improving profitability. Successfully merge strategic, operational, and tactical financial expertise with demonstrated capabilities in business development, capital acquisition, financial planning and analysis, and P&L management. Build high-performance teams by aligning the finance function with core business segments. Drive for tangible accomplishments is counterbalanced by an equal drive for correctness. Keen to challenge the status quo when necessary.

CORE COMPETENCIES

- Strategic and Tactical Business Planning
- Financial Analysis and Modeling
- Business Process Design
- Management Reporting
- Cost Containment & Profit Management
- Building & Maintaining Relationships
- Developing Highly Productive Teams
- Information Technology
- Public Speaking and Presentations

- **Value added:** 4 years of auditing experience.
- **Value added:** 8 years of IT experience. Allows highly successful financial software implementation.

> *"Brian raises the bar when it comes to the caliber of work accomplished and managing people. His exceptional leadership, work ethic, and professional competence allow him to succeed in any task laid before him."*
>
> **— Susan Williams, VP of International Steel**

SELECT PERFORMANCE HIGHLIGHTS

- Helped a capital-poor environmental services firm go public, and develop and execute a domestic and international growth strategy. The company is now actively traded with $41M market capitalization.

- Led a critical IT, finance, and accounting systems integration for a $30B privately held company. The initiative saved $1M+ per year, improved reporting and decision support systems, and facilitated the launch of new product lines.

- Helped a start-up obtain $4.75M in private equity funding, secure multiple contracts totaling $17M, and realize domestic and international growth.

- Played a key role in boosting revenues three-fold for a homebuilding and land development company. Turned around profitability in three years—net loss of $100K to net profit of $8.5M. Secured $125M in new funding by establishing collaborative financial institution relationships.

CAREER CHRONOLOGY

Interim CFO/Controller, PROJECT BASED—Dallas, Texas	2007 – Present
CFO, CROSSBORDER COMMUNICATIONS, INC.—Austin, Texas	2005 – 2007
COO, ACME CONSTRUCTION, INC.—San Antonio, Texas	2004 – 2005
Interim CFO, INTERNATIONAL CONSULTING—Dallas, Texas	2004
Executive VP & CFO, THE HILLSIDE GROUP—Austin, Texas	1999 – 2004
Principal, INTEGRATED SOLUTIONS—Amarillo, Texas	1996 – 1999
Senior Financial Analyst, GLOBAL TELECOM SERVICES—Amarillo, Texas	1994 – 1996
Senior Auditor, YOUNG CABLE—Amarillo, Texas	1992 – 1994
Staff Auditor, YOUNG CABLE—Amarillo, Texas	1990 – 1992

EDUCATION

Bachelor of Science
Finance and Accounting (double major), 1990
University of Texas

> *"(Brian) was a trusted senior executive who provided thoughtful analysis and leadership in many areas of the company. His peers respected him and valued his positive attitude, honesty and integrity, which proved to be invaluable when difficult decisions were required."*
>
> **— Michael Rose, CEO of The Hillside Group**

Brian Washington, CPA—Critical Leadership Initiatives

~ As Interim CFO/Controller: Independent Consulting Successes ~

OVERVIEW: Project #1
A capital-poor environmental services firm and its investors wanted to go public and execute domestic and international expansion plans.

Challenge	To establish financial and accounting systems in support of their vision.
Actions	☑ Cleaned up 3 years of accounting records. Created a 5-year financial pro forma.
	☑ Established finance and accounting systems and reporting capabilities.
	☑ Redefined business processes and decision support systems.
	☑ Established asset safeguards and information controls.
	☑ Secured external auditor's opinion on financials.
Impact	**Secured initial $3M investment.** Company now actively traded with **$41M market capitalization.**

OVERVIEW: Project #2
A $30B privately held metals processing company was not realizing the benefits of a $70M manufacturing and distribution acquisition due to lack of IT systems integration.

Challenges	To assume all finance, accounting, budgeting, forecasting, and management reporting duties with no interruptions in related deliverables. To lead and manage the accounting team and assume the duties of the existing CFO who was promoted to president.
Actions	☑ Built rapport with the existing controller, created a team atmosphere, and won the respect of all senior executives and subordinates.
	☑ Created a strategic game plan and earned the CFO's buy-in.
	☑ Improved processes and procedures.
	☑ Partnered with Global Governance Solutions in a critical external audit.
	☑ Provided timely and reliable management reporting to senior executives at both the subsidiary and parent companies.
	☑ Restructured and recreated a budgeting model to improve processes, allow for easy modification, provide superior reporting analytics, and integrate with the existing software system.
Impact	**Successfully migrated the financial and accounting systems** to the parent company, which resulted in the desired business transformation. **Saved the parent company $1M+ per year, improved reporting and decision support systems, and facilitated the launch of new product lines.**

~ As CFO of Crossborder Communications: A Start-Up Victory ~

OVERVIEW
The company had no in-house financial expertise—it had all been outsourced. Still, it had managed to land a large contract in Mexico, and similar deals were in the works in both the U.S. and Mexico. It also managed to secure $10M+ from a private investor. There were no IT systems to handle many aspects of the business including inventory, accounts receivable and payable, accounting, purchasing, sales orders, and customer relationship management (CRM).

Challenge #1	To secure growth capital and implement new accounting, finance, financial modeling, IT, and business process systems to allow the company to expand domestically and internationally.
Actions	☑ Created a 5-year pro forma to paint the picture of long-term revenues, costs, and profitability.
	☑ Brought accounting in-house and established internal controls. Designed new JV deal models.
	☑ Hired, trained, and managed finance and accounting staff in the U.S. and Mexico.
	☑ Selected ABCD as independent auditors to develop domestic and international tax strategies.
	☑ Researched, selected, and collaborated with an investment banking firm to market Crossborder Communications in search of capital. Identified the investor target market; conceptualized, created, and refined the investor presentation; and wrote and finalized the "deal book."
Impact	**Company received $4.75M in private equity funding** and landed **3 new contracts worth $17M** in cash flow using new financial models. New finance and accounting infrastructure enhanced the ability to understand revenues, costs, profitability, and joint venture options.

BRIAN WASHINGTON, CPA—CRITICAL LEADERSHIP INITIATIVES

AS CFO OF CROSSBORDER COMMUNICATIONS (CONTINUED)

Challenge #2 To build an IT platform and systems that allowed the company to operate domestically and internationally with limited resources, time, and money.

Actions
- ☑ Identified and documented critical IT requirements.
- ☑ Researched and selected an online ERP/CRM system capable of multinational operations.
- ☑ Negotiated favorable pricing for system implementation, support, and ongoing service.
- ☑ Hired, developed, and managed the project implementation team.
- ☑ Directed the migration of existing records to the new system.
- ☑ Conceptualized and designed the system operation training program.

Impact New ERP/CRM system was successfully implemented in the U.S. and Mexico. **Saved approximately $50K in implementation expenses** versus a more standard approach. **Saved an estimated $85K in annual operating costs**. Significantly improved the company's ability to handle all aspects of operating a multinational business.

~ AS EVP & CFO OF THE HILLSIDE GROUP: BUILDING A COMPANY ~

OVERVIEW
This young homebuilding and land development company was experiencing significant growth and had been through three CFOs. There were no business processes in place and accounting records were in disarray.

Challenge To assume the role of CFO and build the finance, accounting, and IT functions while managing fast-paced growth. This included developing and implementing policies, procedures, internal controls, and management reporting systems.

Actions
- ☑ Implemented a workflow automation and management reporting system.
- ☑ Created pro formas and a variety of financial models for budgeting, cash management, profitability analysis, deal structure analysis, and operational metric analysis.
- ☑ Spearheaded efforts to develop automated budgeting, forecasting, and performance tracking systems.
- ☑ Redefined the organizational structure, clearly defined product line goals and business segment objectives, and explicitly linked budgets to business objectives.

Impact Significantly improved operations and productivity. **Reduced overpayments, change orders, and cost overruns.** Enhanced decision-making support systems.

Hillside's **revenues more than tripled** from $11M to $45.5M within three years. Also **increased net profit from a loss of $100K to a net profit of $8.5M.**

~ AS COO OF ACME CONSTRUCTION: AVOIDING A PARTNERSHIP MISTAKE ~

OVERVIEW
This well-established commercial construction company decided to pursue a new growth and profitability strategy: to construct the buildings <u>and</u> acquire and develop the land beneath them. Having acquired two parcels of land, the company quickly learned that land development requires unique expertise. I was hired to bring that know-how to ACME.

In addition, the company was in discussions with multiple investors to acquire a commercial property to convert to condominiums and retail space.

Challenges To create a strategy to enhance the company's ability to analyze commercial building economics. To make appropriate financial and JV decisions.

Action
- ☑ Defined JV requirements, issues, and objectives. Established critical operating and financial criteria.
- ☑ Analyzed potential financial and operating software—selected Argus and negotiated terms with the vendor. Implemented the software and developed a technology training plan.

Impact **An informed decision was made <u>not</u> to move forward with the JV** based on the enhanced understanding of commercial building economics.

Explanation Summary

Brian is a senior financial and accounting executive who is seeking a CFO or Controller position.

Page 1 of this personal marketing piece can be used as a stand-alone networking resume that provides a snapshot of his qualifications. Its purpose is to intrigue the reader by bringing concrete results to the forefront, by showcasing Brian's core competencies, by listing his career history, and by marketing his value with a few solid testimonials from a CEO and a VP.

Pages 2 and 3 are titled "Critical Leadership Initiatives." They contain select CAR stories that illustrate the positive impact Brian has made in recent consulting engagements, in helping a start-up secure additional capital, in helping a growing company optimize operations and become profitable, and in helping an established company determine that a JV project was not in its best interest. Pages 2 and 3 can be circulated with page 1 for a more narrative, comprehensive picture of Brian's performance.

Page 1 alone, or all three pages as a whole, set Brian apart as a high-performance, solution-oriented financial executive who solves problems and contributes to organizational growth.

TOM TUCKER

Seeking position as...
* DIRECTOR OF OPERATIONS *

5555 55th Street / Portland, OR 55555
tuckerman@email.net / 555.555.5555

Eight years of top-level strategic leadership, analysis, and planning in situations and cultures of rapid change.

ORGANIZATIONAL LEADERSHIP / STRATEGIC COMMUNICATIONS / PROCESS IMPROVEMENT

IMMEDIATE VALUE OFFERED

Staff Training & Development: Develop and direct teams through participatory management style that spurs 110% contribution. Understand secret to great teams is casting by individual strengths. *Achievements include...*

☑ **Received City of Newport Award for outstanding leadership**, United States Navy Department Head School.

Organizational Development: Consistently deliver mission-critical results to reengineer company processes for increased efficiencies and decreased costs. *Achievements include...*

☑ **Selected as Conrad Scholar for analysis of Sea Enterprise**, a Navy-wide initiative to implement process change and free resources for investment, recapitalization, and organizational culture transformation.

Operations / Project Management: Knowledge of complete project lifecycle—able to direct projects, programs, operations, and businesses from initial analysis through quality outcomes. *Achievements include...*

☑ **Received the Navy and Marine Corps Commendation Medal** for overcoming logistical challenges of transit of eight surface ships and ten submarines through the Suez Canal.

Transferable Skills:

High-Level Management
Program Development
Performance Metrics & Analysis
Crisis Communications
Consensus Building
Tactical Planning
Strategic Vision & Mission
Cross-Cultural & Crisis Communications
Cross-Functional Team Leadership
Logistics & Timelines
Executive Presentations
Financial Management
Long-Range Planning
Organizational Effectiveness
Relationship Building

RELEVANT EXPERIENCE & EMPLOYMENT SUMMARY

Weapons Officer, USS BAKER (DDG 55)	2006 – Present
United States Navy Department Head School	2005 – 2006
Naval Postgraduate School	2004 – 2005
Training Officer, DESTROYER SQUADRON FIVE FIVE	2002 – 2003
Damage Control Assistant, USS TITANIC (FFG 36)	2000 – 2002

EDUCATION

MBA, Financial Management, (3.9 GPA), 2005
Naval Postgraduate School, Oceanside, CA

- Norton Scholar Award in Financial Management
- Beta Gamma Sigma Honors Society Member

B.S., English, 1999
United States Naval Academy, Annapolis, MD

- Varsity basketball player for two seasons

Top Secret / SCI Security Clearance

"Tom is hands down the best Lieutenant I have ever worked with ... **the best of the best** and my go to officer for difficult tasks"

Commanding Officer

TOM TUCKER — tuckerman@email.net / 555.555.5555 RÉSUMÉ CONTINUED

RELATED AREAS OF ABILITY	

DETAIL OF KEY PROJECTS AND CHALLENGES

RELATED AREAS OF ABILITY

Program Development

Management

Program Feasibility Analysis

Operations Analysis

Strategic Planning

Management & Training

Organizational Change

Weapons Officer, USS BAKER (DDG 55)

Directed training of 330-person crew in all aspects of antiterrorism and force protection.

Results & Performance
- **Developed highly reputable ship-wide mentorship program**, which enhanced retention and maximized career opportunities and professional growth.

Led department of 65; oversaw maintenance / operation of advanced weapons technology.

Results & Performance
- Managed on-load and off-load supply chain processes of **$130 million** ammunition / weapons enterprise.
- Ranked FIRST among all exceptional department heads.

Naval Postgraduate School

Analyzed critical Navy-wide initiative Sea Enterprise with goal to modernize / recapitalize US Navy—interviewed executives, analyzed financial documents, and tracked project's progress.

Results & Performance
- Selected as Conrad Scholar for exceptional research in financial management—**award-winning thesis paved way for two new Navy-wide initiatives.**
- Hand-picked to brief the assistant secretary of the Navy at the Pentagon.

Training Officer at DESTROYER SQUADRON FIVE FIVE

Assessed readiness of six surface ships and **1,500+ personnel** for wartime deployment through astute metrics and performance measures analysis.

Results & Performance
- Fulfilled **150+ certifications** (100% completion) in less than four months, resulting in most effective training timeline in modern Navy history.
- Ranked FIRST among all exceptional division officers.

Planned / directed movement of multi-organizational strike force for Operation Iraqi Freedom.

Results & Performance
- Orchestrated successful transit of eight surface ships and ten submarines through the Suez Canal in preparation for **555 successful Tomahawk launches.**
- Communicated first-rate strategic plan to direct and overcome extensive logistical challenges in supply chain alignment.
- Received **Navy and Marine Corps Commendation Medal** for topmost performance.

Damage Control Assistant at USS TITANIC (FFG 55)

Managed and trained diverse 300-person crew in lifesaving skills to defend ship in battle.

Results & Performance
- Executed highly complex DC trouble-call system, managing performance of entire crew and organic assets to successfully deter, combat, and recover from damages.
- Motivated crewmembers to excel in strict annual certification and follow-on deployment.
- **Ranked FIRST among all exceptional division officers.**

Created more dynamic / flexible framework that greatly enhanced ship's wartime readiness.

Results & Performance
- Achieved Navy-wide recognition for new plans since multiple ships adopted framework.
- Trained entire crew in new processes, breaking down barriers to organizational change.

Explanation Summary

Tom was seeking a position as director of operations for a fitness club, and he had already had an interview for this position. The recruiter had told him that before the next interview, he really needed a résumé that pointed out his transferable skills—directly aligned with that position.

Tom's initial résumé was a one-pager with some strong accomplishments listed, but this strict chronological approach was not showing his transferable skills for a civilian transition to operations director for the fitness club. Since Tom had a specific job target—even a specific job—we were able to pull out a clear list of transferable skills to show the reader HOW his military experience matched the position.

On page one, I expanded his career summary to include accomplishments listed within functional headings: organizational development, staff training, and operations / project management. On page two, I created a "Related Areas of Ability" sidebar to directly point out his transferable skills. This was the first time I had created this dynamic visual guide—and both the client and I were highly pleased by the results.

Paul Bailey

prepared by Barbara Safani

60 FLEET STREET ▪ RALEIGH, NC 27601 ▪ C: 919-288-6772 ▪ PBAILEY@COMCAST.NET

Technology Executive ▪ *start up divisions* ▪ *business turnarounds* ▪ *high-growth* ▪ *shared services models* ▪ *off-shoring*

STRATEGIC BUSINESS DEVELOPMENT...20 years of experience implementing business plans that establish strategic direction and forecast revenue growth and profitability for public, private, small cap, and Fortune 100 companies; have managed technology function as internal resource and external vendor in multiple verticals.

TRANSFORMATIONAL LEADERSHIP... Adept at communicating the business case to achieve buy-in from all stakeholders to re-brand technology offerings, expand solution footprint, and penetrate new markets.

Core Competencies

- Business Process Reengineering
- Infrastructure Development
- Post M&A Technology Integrations
- Strategic Partnerships

- Consultative Sales
- Pipeline Development
- Vendor Management
- Client Servicing

- Staff Management
- Talent Acquisition/Retention
- Contract Negotiations
- P&L Management

Professional Experience

TECH SYSTEMS, INC. / INVUS DESIGN (previously MicroBox Inc.), Raleigh, NC, 2004 to Present

DIRECTOR, PROFESSIONAL SERVICES
TECH SYSTEMS, INC., 2006 TO PRESENT

SVP, SALES AND OPERATIONS
MICROBOX INC., 2004 TO 2006

Originally recruited to MicroBox to launch professional services practices. These practices were acquired by Invus Design who was later bought by Tech Systems, Inc. Tapped by Tech Systems to expand and manage their technology solutions group services organization. Build service delivery practices that align with technology sales and develop IT infrastructure solutions that address clients' unique information technology and business challenges. Initiated partnerships with leading IT vendors including Sun, IBM, and HDS. *P&L: $22M; Staff: 62; Vendor Management: 75 relationships*

MicroBox Account Shift

BUSINESS DEVELOPMENT

Tech Systems

- Propelled professional services sales from $1M to $10M in just 2 years by developing the business strategy and execution plans to transform a hardware-focused business model into a consultative solutions-oriented company.

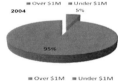

MicroBox Inc.

- Surpassed 2-year sales goal by 62% and achieved a 112% increase to $7.2M in sales; transformed a small, privately owned IT services firm with a pure staff augmentation business model into a solutions-oriented firm.

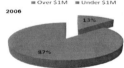

- Transitioned business development focus from small (accounts under $1M) to mid and large cap ($1.5B to $250B accounts) and added a dozen new accounts in less than 2 years.

INFRASTRUCTURE OPTIMIZATION

Tech Systems

- Following Tech Systems' acquisition of a non-profitable business, created the business case and infrastructure reengineering that enabled a $25M acquisition write-off while retaining 75%+ of professional services revenues and trimming headcount by 85% (from 60 to 10).

- Successfully scaled company that had rocketed from zero to $300M in revenue in 8 years by spearheading creation of firm's leadership council. Streamlined processes exponentially and created a forum for sharing company best-practices.

- Garnered discounts that translated into millions of dollars in savings by ensuring sales team maintained highest levels of certifications on vendor products.

Paul Bailey

MicroBox

- In 15 months, created the data management and storage and infrastructure services (Linux, Grid Computing, and Enterprise Windows) practices. Built the infrastructure to support the transition; hired staff, forged technology partnerships, created sales pipeline, developed marketing collateral, and fostered credibility in the market.

- Boosted operational efficiencies substantially by implementing new systems and technologies to streamline accounting and recruiting functions; developed design and content for a new corporate website.

SJS SYSTEMS, Raleigh, NC, 2000 to 2004

PRACTICE MANAGER, 2003 TO 2004   ENGAGEMENT MANAGER, 2001 TO 2003

Oversaw professional services sales and delivery organization for the southeast communications market area. Carried a $19M goal in support of Bel-Tel, Verizon, and Lucent accounts. Supported entertainment and media accounts including Sony, Time Inc, Time Warner Cable, and McGraw Hill. Led team of 7 sales managers, 6 architects, and 2 administrators.

CONSULTATIVE SALES

- Gained buy-in to transition from a hardware sales organization to a more strategic and lucrative solutions-based consulting model. Repositioned brand to encompass new services and successfully sell into Fortune 100 companies. Initiated numerous partnerships with hardware/software vendors, consulting firms, and resellers.

- Accelerated revenues from $1M to $8M annually and exceeded revenue goals by 200% annually; formally recognized for achieving the highest services sales revenue in the Americas for a single account.

> **KEY SALES**
>
> $4M MULTI-YEAR CRM PLATFORM
> **LUCENT**
>
> 350-SEAT CLIENT CALL CENTER
> **RCN CABLE**
>
> $3M E-COMMERCE SITE OVERHAUL
> **SAMSUNG**

OPERATIONAL HIGHLIGHTS

- Achieved more than 98% forecasting accuracy by improving processes for tracking opportunities and revenue.

- Part of a task force charged with developing several management development initiatives including competitive benchmarking, goal setting, and career planning.

TEL-BEL, Raleigh, NC, 1990 to 2000

Progressed through a series of management positions supporting software development and overseeing operations for mission-critical systems. Proposed, procured, and delivered complex IT solutions to the business and internal operations. Managed vendor relationships with Oracle, Sun Microsystems, Hewlett-Packard, EMC Corporation, and Andersen Consulting. Managed staff of 150.

HIGHLIGHTS

- Following Tel-Bel's divestiture, realigned business processes and time-to-market goals to achieve best practices and cut cycle delivery time in half (from 12 weeks to 6 weeks).

- Named Tel-Bel's technical ambassador to Oracle Corporation following the success of a ground-breaking large-scale enterprise database solution that consolidated operational data for business customers.

- Developed/executed plan to off-shore Tel-Bel customer account data management applications to India following outsourcing initiative in 2000.

> **CAREER PROGRESSION**
>
> PROMOTED 6 TIMES DURING 10-YEAR TENURE AND BECAME ONE OF THE YOUNGEST EMPLOYEES TO ATTAIN THE DIVISIONAL MANAGER TITLE.

Between 1986 and 1990, held technology support positions at UBS and IBM.

Education

BACHELOR OF SCIENCE IN COMPUTER SCIENCE, DUKE UNIVERSITY, Durham, NC, 1986

Susan J. Brooks

1427 S. Broad St. • Phoenix, AZ 85041 • Home 480-555-5555 sbrooks@msnx.com

Teacher – Business & Computer Applications

Skilled business professional choosing to devote her life to teaching. Brings valuable, practical, real-world experience to the classroom in both large and small organizations. Effective communicator and enjoys teaching ideas and concepts while working in a team environment.

BUSINESS EXPERTISE
Management/Supervision
Budgeting/Forecasting
Planning/Scheduling
Customer Service
Conflict Resolution

PERSONAL TRAITS
Patient * Honest *Reliable
Loyal * Self-Reliant
Excellent Communicator

COMPUTER PROFICIENCIES
MICROSOFT:
Windows 98 * 2000 *Excel * Word
* PowerPoint * Access * Publisher *
Project Management
OTHER PROGRAMS:
Schedule Plus * SASSY * People
Power * Quicken * Dreamweaver *
Adobe Acrobat * Bookstore
Automated Systems (ABC)

SPECIALIZED TRAINING
Six-Sigma Management Training
People Power * Crystal Reporting
TQM, TQL * Life Management
Anger Management & Conflict
Shared Services for HR
Wilson Learning Systems

EDUCATION / CERTIFICATIONS
B.S. Management – Western
International University – 1999
Arizona Teacher Certification – 2001

MEMBERSHIPS
Mujer Corporation
Hispanic Women
Vesta Club – Bd. Of Directors
Shared Services For Human
Resources (HRMS)

SUMMARY OF QUALIFICATIONS
- Experienced with computer technology, automated systems and software applications encompassing word processing, spreadsheets, graphics, database. electronic mail, Internet activity and peoplesoft.
- Solid understanding of business operations and administrative skills
- Outstanding organizational and training abilities
- Recognized for creative problem solving and solutions that work
- Functions well in multi-departmental team situations

ACCOMPLISHMENTS & CONTRIBUTIONS

AWARDS AND HONORS
- Alliance Systems – Most Valuable Employee among 6000 in division
- Recognition Awards twice for excellence on complex HR projects
- Assigned to U.S.-wide Corporate Aerospace Team Project with results impacting over 40,000 people

PROFESSIONAL EXPERIENCE
- Phoenix High School – Student Teacher - 8/2001-12/2001
- Phoenix District 1 – Substitute Teacher – 2001
- Phoenix High School District - 1999 – 2000
    Bookstore Manager – Maryvale High School
- Cartwright School District – 1998 - 1999
    Bilingual Computer Lab Instructor – Language Arts and Math
- Alliance Systems Aerospace Company – 1982 – 1999
  Various Support, Supervisory, Management and Staff Assignments involving International Business, Human Resources, Engineering, Lab Management and Quality Assurance.

REFERENCE COMMENTS
"...Always open to new ideas and different teaching styles...and she has a wealth of knowledge about the business world. Her teaching style is one of applied learning...resulting in few classroom management issues because the students are involved and interested". N. T. Chambers, Staff Development Director, Major Phoenix High School.

"...Sally is a very motivated, highly skilled individual... potential to become an outstanding Business Education teacher...works well with other department teachers...her Intel and Allied Signal experience help in the classroom... students appreciate the practical information". Bill Vance, Asst. Principal, Major Phoenix High School.

"...very (effective). professional with all levels of staff, teachers and students". A Rogers, Assistant Principal, Montrose High School

Rhonda Lucas

H: 314-219-8028 ▪ C: 314-897-3722 ▪ rlucas@hotmail.com
75 Sunset Avenue ▯ St. Louis, MO 63101

BUSINESS STRATEGY INNOVATOR   prepared by Barbara Safani

May 18, 2009

Fred Kaplan, EVP, Strategic Implementations
Kaine & Rowlings, Inc.
99 Smith Street, Suite 301
St. Louis, MO 63110

Dear Mr. Kaplan:

Developing the strategic roadmaps that help businesses define their market differentiators, optimize brand reach, and maximize customer acquisition and retention is my expertise and my passion. My strengths in e-business transformation, brand unification, new market penetration, and product innovation have been leveraged across multiple industries including consumer goods, technology, telecommunications, financial services, and advertising and span Fortune 50s, start-ups, and consulting practices. My accomplishments include:

E-Business Reengineering

- For MasterCard, accelerated online credit card applications by 60% in one year by repositioning the way the card product was marketed online, optimizing the user experience, and targeting an untapped segment of customers.

- For Kraft Foods, created the blueprint for an enterprise-wide initiative to align disparate lines of business within a more unified user experience to improve site usability and consistency of brand messaging.

Innovation

- For M&R Tech, a boutique software firm, redefined the value proposition and brand reach for the world's first proprietary software and 3D visualization technology used to create on-demand, made to measure apparel to target new and non-traditional markets.

Strategic Business Roadmapping

- For BPD Consulting, simplified complexities of sophisticated project processes for multi-tiered implementation plans to deliver on business goals, unify branding initiatives, and ensure a superlative customer experience.

Excited by the prospect of an opportunity with your company and impressed by the strength of your brand, I would welcome the chance to meet with you to discuss your company's business needs and my qualifications in more detail. I am confident that I can deliver results similar to those described above for your organization and look forward to a personal interview.

Sincerely,

Rhonda Lucas

Ronda Lucas

Attachment

> *"Rhonda is an exceptional strategist I truly admire. She drives strategic visions, influences team members, and achieves success with strong leadership and project management skills. She has in-depth knowledge of web analytic tools, their strengths and limitations, and gleans insights to improve customer experience out of complex web user behavior data. She constantly comes up with actionable solutions and brings them to completion."*
> **Colleague, MasterCard**

> *"Diligent, motivated, knowledgeable, and a great deal of pleasure to work with. We work well together and she seems to always be considering the needs of the project from various viewpoints, something I find rare in this industry."*
> **Colleague, MasterCard**

> *"Rhonda quickly assesses what is needed for the business, contributes new insights, and brings everyone to the table, eliciting the best from each team member. She develops effective plans to reduce costs and increase business results."*
> **Manager, Kraft Foods**

DAVID KENT

1623 St. Louis Way • Honolulu, Hawaii 96813
808-555-6256 • dkent@alohanet.com

January 14, 2003

John Jones, M.D.
Dean, School of Medicine
University of Hawaii
1234 East-West Circle
Honolulu, Hawaii 96822

Dear Dr. Jones:

Perhaps you remember our chance meeting at the Bio Asia-Pacific Conference at the Sheraton Waikiki on December 18 and 19, 2002. In our brief conversation, I shared with you the idea of utilizing Web Development as an administrative tool. You expressed interest in the possibility of implementing such a system within the School of Medicine.

May I suggest a formal meeting in order explore the idea?

I have some exciting and creative ideas, which may encourage you to take the next step towards realizing the positive impact a content management system would have in the School of Medicine. This would also be a great opportunity for us to discuss your goals and how an administrative intranet would help you reach them in a more timely and cost-effective manner.

In addition, there has recently been spirited discussion within the IT community on the topic of organizational continuity and its potential vulnerability due to advances in technology. I think you'll find the specific strategies I have to share with you worthy of consideration.

If you recall, my background is in Web Planning and Development, with specific skills in developing administrative intranets and public web sites, and designing web-based software to address the internal and external reporting needs of organizations.

Enclosed is my résumé attesting to my experience and specialties. I will contact you within the next few days to discuss the possibility of meeting with you.

Respectfully,

David Kent
Computer and Information Systems Manager

Enclosure: Résumé

MURRAY MAXFIELD

119 Montrose Road
Rocklin, CA 95677

■ ■ ■

Residence: (916) 6675 1123
Email: madmax@hotmail.com

2 March 2006

Mr. Fred Johnson
Human Resources Manager
ANX Insurance Inc.,
P.O. Box 123
Rocklin, CA 95677

Accounts Manager | Insurance Specialist

Dear Mr. Johnson

One of the most exciting things about the insurance industry is the many ways one can learn, specialize, and develop. Eleven years ago when I joined MSNB Insurance as a Tele-claims Officer, it would have never occurred to me that less than a decade later, I would be spearheading the establishment of an insurance recovery office in Malaysia, and acting as a "one man band" handling everything from marketing and business development, to operations, claims audits, recoveries, and more.

The last two years in Malaysia have been gratifying, frustrating, exhilarating, and challenging. Yet despite the rigors of establishing a new entity and promoting an unknown concept of third-party recovery services to a largely "closed" business environment, the new skills honed in managing accounts, servicing customers, and managing operations—all a departure from my prior career in insurance, have allowed me to offer a wide range of knowledge and talents with which to meet your needs.

With my contract in Malaysia now concluded, I have returned to Rocklin where I am keen to recommence my career offering so much more than was possible just two years ago. It is the sum of those talents that I present to ANX Insurance today—the ability to build and nurture important business relationships, expose opportunities, and look for alternative ways to get things done by moving forward to achieve business goals.

Possessing more than a decade of experience in the insurance sector, I know the structure and processes surrounding vehicle claims and claims recovery inside-and-out; I know the best people to call, the right way to achieve a result, and can do so expeditiously with a customer-focused mindset.

As such, I'm ready and able to provide the experience, credibility, and knowledge to your company in whatever way you feel I would best make a contribution.

Sometimes re-establishing roots in one's country of origin, means taking a step back to move forward. I'm prepared for that. With an arsenal of international and local expertise at my disposal, I'm confident that I can start making a quick and lasting contribution to ANX Insurance and I'm willing to take the necessary steps to do so.

Naturally I would be delighted to attend an interview to discuss your needs further and to prepare for our discussion, I have attached my résumé outlining my most significant achievements to date. I can be contacted at the numbers listed above, and look forward to speaking with you soon.

Sincerely,

Murray Maxfield

Project Synopsis

Murray had a unique situation which had to be summed up for his next employer and Murray and I had discussed his list of "pros and cons" that needed to be addressed in this letter.

On the list of "cons"

- Murray had spent the majority of his career developing and nurturing his skills in the specialist field of "recovery" work for insurance companies. As a result he had narrowed his employment prospects as there are very few third-party recovery companies and even fewer positions for these very job-specific skills. Someone seeking a person with expertise in the insurance sector would be expecting a set of generalist skills that Murray did not possess.

- In the past two years, Murray had accepted the job-of-a-lifetime to head up a new recovery company in Malaysia. It was a completely out-of-the-blue appointment, he had no idea why he was selected (other than his willingness to travel) and had never managed staff, started up a business, or been involved in sales previously. While this was a fabulous learning experience where he did extremely well, and in fact carved a new set of skills for himself in account management and business development, Murray was acutely aware that these new skills were only two years old at best. He felt pessimistic about his chances entering a business development role competing against candidates with many more years of expertise and felt it was important not to overstate his level of expertise.

- He had to re-establish himself back home and felt he had lost career momentum having devoted the past two years to a project in Malaysia—no matter how prestigious.

On the list of "pros"

- Murray had, through this incredible opportunity to head a project in Malaysia, added a vast bank of skills to his professional repertoire—making new opportunities available to him.

- Murray was open to anything and was happy to "lay his cards on the table" saying to the employer he was flexible and could fit in anywhere.

With that background in mind, I constructed the letter.

The opening paragraph set the scene where it tells the reader that he is experienced in the insurance industry, and has customer service experience. It then takes the reader on a journey mentioning the past two years heading up the Malaysian project and establishes his credentials in getting the business up and running.

The next paragraph reinforces the challenges he's faced, letting the next employer gain an insight on just how difficult it could be establishing a business in a country where even the concept of this type of business was foreign.

Paragraph three now brings up his return to Rocklin and reinforces that he now has so much more to offer by way of skills and experience thanks to the opportunities and challenges he has faced in the past two years. As he is interested in pursuing an account management or business development role I emphasized this aspect to elevate the employer's interest. The next paragraph continues with that theme showing that despite his new skills, he does have ten solid years of experience in the insurance industry and his background highlights his capacity to learn and get things done.

The penultimate paragraph sets the scene for what he hopes to achieve. Murray believes that by being frank about his expectations and realistic about his skills, he will be considered rather than being discounted for his lack of experience in some areas.

I concluded the cover letter by thanking the employer, and requesting a call to action—an interview to discuss their needs further.

Grace Maxfield

22 Queens Road
Rocklin, CA 95677

■ ■ ■

Cell: (916) 654-0900
email: gmaxfield@hotmail.com

22 July 2004

The Honorable Fred Fisher
Room 4 Rayburn Senate Office Building
United States Senate
Washington, DC 20510

Re: Industrial Relations Specialist

Dear Senator:

I hope you will allow me to be frank with you when I say that the health system in the State of California is failing to serve our community.

The combination of an industrial relations gridlock and an aging population has placed an unprecedented burden on resources, people, and infrastructure—and because of that—the best any government can achieve at present is to tinker around the edges. Despite our government's best intentions, a series of short-term "fixes" simply cannot be the answer over the long-term.

It is not my nature to criticize without offering a solution; a solution at least, to one of the significant issues in the health system as I see it—and that is the industrial relations arena.

As a specialist in industrial relations, I have a unique background in that I have ten years of experience as a union leader for some of our country's most militant unions. For years, I fought for worker's rights (winning many battles); observed and stood up to the inequities of "the system" and elevated the profile of members' issues in the media.

Now at this point you may be wondering if I have been part of the problem! On the contrary, I believe that this experience now makes me part of the solution.

For the past four years or so, I have been able to capitalize on my inside union knowledge as a senior advisor and consultant to executive teams and Boards of Directors within the health care sector, where I have turned around profits, contained industrial unrest, and led unparalleled change.

The health care system's industrial relations practices from my observation are ineffective. Plagued by political alliance issues, they ignore gross wastage from internal practices and top-heavy management structures that squander resources and divert attention from the government to provide top quality health care.

You have allowed me to frank with you, and if I may, I'd like to continue by telling you now what I am not. I am not a report-writer producing meaningless and costly reports designated straight for the filing cabinet. I am not motivated by glory and personal recognition as it is for you to take the credit for the successes I will deliver. I am ready to identify the bloat, take on the system, create the type of lean, responsive operations that deliver results, and win.

My clients—senior leaders in California's healthcare system, typically refer to me as "the iron fist in the velvet glove"—a description I believe is most apt, representing the dichotomy of my professional appearance and the relentless passion I bring to each and every battle.

Attached, you'll find my introductory biographical sketch, and naturally a full résumé is available. I will call your office in the next few days to see if either of us can clear our schedules for what I hope will be the beginnings of steering long-term definitive change that will revolutionize the state's healthcare system.

Sincerely

Grace Maxfield

DEVELOPMENT STRATEGY

If anyone could go against the union stereotype it was this client, Grace Maxfield. Grace is a character, who describes herself as the *iron fist in a velvet glove*.

From ten years in the union movement where she gained continuous press attention for chaining herself to railway tracks and whipping up a storm of emotion in street protests, Grace was fired from one of the country's most militant unions after management asserted she was "too radical" even for them!

In characteristic style, Grace turned a negative into a positive by opting to take that experience of playing "hardball" to benefit the "other side". Knowing how unions play the game, Grace was able to sell her insider knowledge to top executives of the health care industry and single-handedly turned around many ailing hospitals' operations through her "take no prisoners" style that focused solely on the bottom-line.

The hard-edged communications approach from her years in the union movement were disconcerting to negotiators who found themselves at a disadvantage when faced with a slightly-built, well-dressed woman of style, and exceptional courtesy, who had an answer for everything, the facts to back it, and the confidence to know she could call their bluff and win.

With renewed confidence and a healthy bank account from her consultancy work to match, Grace decided on an all-out assault on the state's healthcare system, seeing it as an industrial relations nightmare. This letter, cheeky and bold, is indicative of Grace's style and was designed to have either one of two results: to get thrown away, or to enlist the curiosity of the Senator!

Fortunately, it achieved the latter. Despite widespread opinion by "those in the know" who indicated to Grace that this letter would be viewed as arrogant and considered insulting, Grace received a telephone call from the Senator's representative a few days later with a request for a brief chat.

Since that time, Grace has continued to consult to the Senator and is poised to come on board as a government consultant.

Strategy

- Each paragraph is short and succinct; tight pack-a-punch phrasing that flows easily to the next paragraph.

- An opening "insult" over the state's failing health system is softened by a courteous "I hope you'll allow me to be frank with you". The answer is most politicians would say that they want constituents to be frank so they can learn more about their community. The opening line grabs attention.

- Instead of shying away from Grace's union background, I used it to best advantage—even humorously referring to her potentially having been "part of the problem" and then negating that by saying she was "part of the solution."

- Purposely used emotive words and phrasing such as "squandered" and "an unprecedented burden on resources" with a government that can only "tinker around the edges" indicates a problem that is huge, with little being done.

- Touched on what she sees is wrong (top-heavy management, political alliance issues, gross waste) so that the reader was aware that she knew what she was talking about, without giving away her solutions.

- Assured the reader that she was not out to make a name for herself, and that all her successes were his to raise his profile and take credit.

- A request for interview using an aggressive approach that she would call him, rather than a "please call me" ending.

VESA HALLERMAN
Ratsukatu 999 A 11, Espoo FIN-02611, Finland
Email: vesa.hallerman@iki.fi | Telephone: + (358) 40 555 7555

September 4, 2007

Mr. Joe Johnson, Chief Information Officer
Vision Incorporated
1134 Center Road
Rocklin, CA 95677

Re: Technology and IT Consultant

Dear Mr. Johnson:

"Sisu" is a Finnish term that can be roughly translated as strength of will, determination, perseverance and acting rationally in the face of adversity. "Sisu" is the overriding asset that I can offer you as a technology and IT consultant, software architect/engineer, or project manager with more than a decade of experience working with multinational companies and business leaders in Finland, Japan, and soon I hope, in the United States.

The enthusiasm, in-built customer-focus and the creative problem-solving streak that sets me apart from other senior software engineers and technical architects, are also the key attributes that have been instrumental in my employers' product successes and ever-increasing levels of customer loyalty.

Wherever I work, even when I don't aim to, I seem to have a knack for becoming the "go to" person that others refer to for help and assistance. Part of it is due to my determination where missing "impossible" deadlines or failing to surpass customer expectations is not an option. Whatever it takes, I find myself mastering the technology, or learning the ropes, or understanding customers' needs—sometimes even before customers can articulate what they want themselves!

Of course, having the vision and the determination are only half the requirements of my role. A solid knowledge of existing and emerging technologies, the ability to comply with best practice standards and agile software development for optimum product and version releases, and the willingness to return to the beginning if that means the best product will be delivered—all play a substantial part of my professional make-up.

The past two years as the Technology Consultant for Enterprise Java with ABC Technology Innovations in Finland has been exciting and tremendously gratifying. During this time I have been allowed the freedom to hone my strengths in the pre-sales consultancy phase to win new business, steer a team, manage the delivery of on-time projects, and turnaround a badly stalled project with potential to lose a major client's business. The efforts I devoted to sustaining the client relationship paid dividends with future projects commissioned.

But now, new challenges beckon. Keen to optimize products and deliver fresh solutions for your clients, following my relocation to Rocklin in October, I would be delighted to discuss your needs in more detail during an initial telephone conversation at a time convenient to you. I will call your Executive Assistant next week, say Tuesday before lunch to secure a brief time in your diary so that we may learn more about each other and the ideas I have for demonstrating "sisu" in driving your projects.

Thank you for reviewing my candidacy for this role.

Sincerely

Vesa Hallerman

Justification for this cover letter.

The key components of this cover letter are all there: Attention, Interest, Desire and Action.

Additionally, a further challenge existed and that was to persuade an employer to talk to Vesa—an individual who lives in Finland and who has not never worked in the US.

Consequently the letter needed to be more aggressive and show that Vesa was not a "run of the mill" IT person that an employer in the US could find any day of the week. This was achieved through the unusual opening that referred to the Finnish word "sisu", and continually reinforcing skills and strengths, right through to the closing paragraph where the client boldly states that she will be seeking to secure some time in the employer's diary—recognizing and bowing to the importance of CIO by knowing that he has an executive secretary.

The following spells out the strategy.

Attention: I composed an attention-grabbing opening that did two things. Established that the individual was not an American citizen, and reinforced the person as someone different by the way she approached her introduction with a description of a cultural term that applied to her.

Interest: In the next two paragraphs, I solidified facts so interest in Vesa could grow. I attack all the hot buttons of customer focus, creative problem solving and willingness to be a leader or a resource to others to build expectations further.

Desire: It is now time in the next paragraph to reinforce her hard skills. Her personality and character has been established in earlier paragraphs and now the employer should be able to visualize a person who possesses those attributes working as a valued asset in his or her team. But hard skills are very important and the CIO needs to know that Vesa has the necessary technology "cred". Here I bring up terms such as agile software development (a new and emerging trend) and her commitment to quality. Next I introduced where she is currently working and dangle a carrot for the employer by adding a few more skills, mentioning that she has been used in pre-sales work meeting with clients, that she has leadership strengths and that she can turn around troubled projects and maintain relationships sufficiently to drive new business.

Action: The final paragraph indicates that Vesa will be relocating to the US in October and suggests her enthusiasm to hit the ground running by requesting an initial getting-to-know-you session via the telephone. Instead of waiting for a call, Vesa suggests that she will call the employer's EA to secure a brief time in his diary (acknowledging his importance) to discuss mutual interests. I tie up loose ends by again using sisu to bring the beginning and the end of the letter to a tidy conclusion.

MATTHEW JOHNSON

6 Blackeye Drive
Rocklin C.A. 95677

Mobile: 0408 180 018
Email: mwane@bigpond.com

22 February 2007

Mr. John Johnson
Human Resources Manager
IBT Recruitment Inc.

Dear Mr. Johnson:

Re: Marketing Coordinator

Armed with a management degree majoring in marketing at the end of 2004, I did what many graduates do and took some time off to "see the world." Again, like many that have come before me, I made the trek to London and tried my hand at a few hospitality roles that would fund my travels. It never occurred to me that I would snare a role with a company like AtlanticVacations—a prestigious organization providing sales and marketing promotions for the top three cruise brands in the world.

That the initial role was an entry-level position supporting the Product and Pricing Supervisor held little concern for me. It was all about working in London, dealing with major brands, and gaining exposure to one of the most competitive sectors—challenging as it relied solely on the peaks and troughs of pricing to attract and sustain customers.

What was both gratifying and surprising however, was how swiftly my ascent at the company became. Soon after commencing I assumed many of the day-to-day tasks of the departing Product and Pricing Supervisor's role and from that time on, commenced doing the sort of things in marketing that I'd been trained to do.

Competitor analysis, statistical reporting, market research, trends analysis, pricing and package development—a rollercoaster ride of learning that allowed me to become a genuine contributor to a team effort. As my profile within the company increased as a person who could communicate, build relationships, and smooth the path towards improved productivity, my confidence also grew, providing me with the clarity to see how daily routines could be improved, how money could be made, and how strategies could be devised to attract customers.

I developed the company's first intranet, conceived an Excel spreadsheet that made producing competitive quotes a snap, contributed towards the content and layout of marketing price lists, attended trade shows, wooed tour operators, and raised the prospect of building revenues by changing the target demographics in times of passenger lulls.

Challenging yes! A wonderful learning experience in an almost chaotic environment where everyone had several jobs and needed to be an expert at all.

And now, I have returned home to Rocklin, equipped with a body of knowledge and experience that I would not have dreamed that I would possess just over two years ago. I know there is more to learn and that's exciting, yet the quality and the value of what I've achieved and experienced in the last two years I know will hold me in good stead and allow me to hit the ground running.

Could we meet? I'd be delighted to attend an interview at a mutually convenient time prior to resettling in Rocklin, and it would be a good opportunity to see if there is a mutual interest in moving forward. I can be contacted at the details listed above, and look forward to speaking with you soon.

Sincerely

Matthew Johnson

Exploration of Strategy

The Challenges
Matthew had less than two years employment following the completion of his degree, yet those two years had been jam packed with opportunities to learn new skills and excel in a "sink or swim" highly competitive environment. As such Matthew had become significantly more talented than would be expected of an individual with only two years postgraduate work experience.

Strategy
I decided to convey this information in a cover letter using a distinctive narrative style that would explain just how he came to be such a highly qualified person deserving of a position that would normally be out-of- reach for someone with just two years post degree.

The concept was to get the reader's attention by establishing two things immediately: the first that Matthew had a management degree in marketing, and that he possessed the confidence to travel to London to experience more of the world.

Next the strategy was to build excitement. "It never occurred to me…" sets the scene for the reader to continue as expectations are built. What awaited Matthew on his journey?

The next paragraph answers the question. He was placed in an entry-level role — but he was not concerned as it presented opportunities to grow and learn in such an incredibly exciting environment.

From here, the cover letter takes off as the excitement Matthew has for this experience builds. Clever placement of key words indicates that Matthew knows what he's talking about, and he has experienced challenges way beyond his contemporaries. Continuing on the journey, we then learn that Matthew has been so appreciated, that he has taken on the role of his supervisor, where he seeks to stamp his mark on the role through productivity improvements.

I opted to list his achievements in paragraph form rather than bullet points to maintain the narrative tone of the letter. Nevertheless it is clear that Matthew is a driven individual keen to excel.

The final two paragraphs bring the reader to the present time. We learn that Matthew has returned to his home from his travels and is now seeking employment. The final paragraph is a call to action to request an interview.

Matthew's entire career is encapsulated in this page that takes the reader on the journey of his life post graduation. It reflects his youthful enthusiasm, yet at the same time the reader is in no doubt that this is a young man with passion and talents worthy of consideration.

RECOMMENDED READING

RESUME BOOKS

There are hundreds of books about resumes. Too many to mention. One source I trust are the books written by Wendy Enelow and Louise Kursmark, probably the top expert resume writers in the United States, in my opinion. Here are a series of books they have written and you can find these at:

www.wendyenelow.com

EXPERT RESUME SERIES

Definitive guides for distinct fields and special circumstances

Expert Resumes for Baby Boomers
Expert Resumes for Career Changers
Expert Resumes for Computer & Web Jobs
Expert Resumes for Engineers
Expert Resumes for Health Care Careers
Expert Resumes for Managers & Executives
Expert Resumes for Military-to-Civilian Transitions
Expert Resumes for People Returning to Work
Expert Resumes for Teachers & Educators

$100,000+ RESOURCES

From the recognized experts in executive career management

Best Career Transition Resumes for $100K+ Jobs
Best Cover Letters for $100K+ Jobs
Best Resumes for $100K+ Jobs
Executive Job Search for $100K to $1 Million+ Jobs
Executive's Pocket Guide to ROI Resumes/Job Search
Sales & Marketing Resumes for $100K Careers
The Enelow-Kursmark Executive Resume Toolkit

COVER LETTER BOOKS

Practical advice and powerful examples

15-Minute Cover Letter
Best Cover Letters for $100K+ Jobs
Cover Letter Magic
No-Nonsense Cover Letters

KEYWORD RESOURCES

Tools to put the power of keywords in your job-search arsenal

Best Keywords for Resumes, Cover Letters & Interviews
Finding Needles in a Haystack: Keywords for Finding Top Talent
Keywords to Nail Your Job Interview

NEW GRAD RESUME BOOKS

Insider secrets and samples to help grads land top-level opportunities

Best Resumes for College Students & New Grads
College Grad Resumes to Land $75K+ Jo

Chapter 5
<<< Who Needs You?

"Who Needs You?"

There are millions of companies but only one that will employ you. Which one will it be? Why do you want to work for one company versus another? What makes one viable and others less so? In the 21st century, you also have to consider the technological revolution occurring around you. New technologies will drive some companies to greatness and bury others. Also these changes will, in greater degrees than we desire, drive our future. No one has a crystal ball and can predict what will happen to any given company. However, you can research trends, statistics and meaningful company data and then attempt to make the best choice you can. If you've done this, then you've done your best.

Technology is driving changing trends in the marketplace, thereby creating demands upon employers to compete in a global economy. These conditions are re-defining our concepts of work, job, workplace and profit-making decision models. U.S. companies are moving more and more jobs offshore.

Unless you understand what is required of you and are strategically planning on joining forward-thinking companies in making these 21st century transitions, you will be left behind, become a job-description dinosaur and find yourself out of work in the next 10 years.

History is the very best teacher, if we are smart enough to learn from it. Frank Jarlett, in an <u>outstanding</u> article published in the <u>Career Planning and Adult Development Journal</u>, Winter, 1998-99, stated that for 70 years the Swiss "owned" the watch-making market.

He stated that the Swiss watch industry had over 62,000 employees, 65% of the world's sales, and 90% of the world's profits. In 1967 they basically turned down the idea of the quartz watch movement and labeled it a useless invention. Electronic watches took over the market while the Swiss still maintained they made gears and springs. This backward thinking, old-workplace mentality resulted in a 90% watch industry unemployment rate. Now, move forward to today's marketplace and ask yourself what your company is doing to compete in the new world order economy.

You must ask yourself what are **<u>you</u>** doing insofar as education and retraining are concerned to keep up with lightning-speed changes in the workplace? What are the current and future trends? Which fields will keep you abreast of or ahead of super-fast marketplace changes?

Why don't you join the Gladiator? The website and newsletter contain articles by yours truly and other nationally known authors on topics ranging from resumes to transferable skills to interviewing and negotiating techniques. We also post a market watch to keep you abreast of changes affecting career direction and potential.

Which companies and industries will you choose and why? This is a tough question to answer in light of the above statements. If you stay where you are, will your industry survive long enough to allow you to retire?

If the answer is yes, great! If the answer is no, then you must re-evaluate what education and training you need to alter your profile and gain acceptance among the decision-makers in the new economy workplace.

Selecting Your Company

There are many issues to consider when

selecting a company that you hope will survive both your working career and your retirement years. To begin your understanding of these, start reading all you can in the *Wall Street Journal*, national business and news magazines, special journals, and any other reliable source of current, authoritative information.

Jarlett states, "the things you should look for are global, national and local changes occurring outside your current organization. These include technological, economic, political and demographic changes. No one company has the ability to control any of these but you do, insofar as your career goes." If you see changes taking place in the marketplace that your company isn't responding to, then think about a change, and soon. That advice is true no matter what the year.

In light of his statements about the future, Jarlett states you should also be concerned about your current or future company having patents, copyrights, unique employee skills, technology or other factors that will keep them ahead of the new "dot-coms" springing forth daily and failing by the thousands. What are the core values, vision, mission, short- and long-term goals of your company?

 Is your company, either current or future, keeping up with trends being projected by the national magazines and people in the know?

b-9

Is the company constantly looking to the future by examining their options and scheduling their future internal and external action strategies accordingly?

Is the leadership style of management one that constantly evaluates short- and long-term goals and adjusts corporate plans accordingly?

You will find answers to some of these questions by reading and studying your market segment. Others, you will not know until you interview and ask multiple persons throughout the interview process. Realize that some of the people with whom you interview won't know the answers either! Use your gut feelings.

> In my opinion, if the people with whom you interview look blank, or cannot at least frame an answer to many of these issues, then they work in an old-world work environment and the company will probably not be a growth candidate over the next 10-15 years.

Why, you ask? Because if management isn't communicating with every level of the company and lighting a fire under everyone with their "vision," why should customers buy their products or services and why should the people charged with producing their products or services care about P&L? Positive growth energy is vital to long-term survival. It begins and ends with people. Fire them up and you will conquer. Stifle them and the company will wither.

Under these circumstances, if you are under 45, you might consider looking elsewhere for employment, no matter how good the company looks today. If you are 45+, think carefully and do what is good for your economic well-being. Remember, if they have to downsize in 10-15 years it is probably because they are having financial difficulties competing in the global marketplace. If this is correct, then how solid is your retirement and pension anyway?

To summarize Frank Jarlett's thoughts, those companies with the greatest growth potential for the projected period from 2001 forward are ones that:

- provide better products or services

- encourage management to continuously improve on current practices using strategic alliances

- are virtual corporations or use outsourcing

- provide all employees with significant education and training in total quality management

- emphasize the self-managed team concept and support it with solid, well-constructed budgets managed by disciplined execution.

Finally, here's another sobering thought. People are changing jobs every 3-5 years now. Granted, this is influenced by the dot.com mentality and the IT industry, but it is still a developing trend.

 As more and more workers seek alternative solutions to the rigid workplace of the past, change is inevitable - both in their lives and in the workplace as a whole

b-10

Who Needs Me?

With that all said, let's focus on the next phase of "Who needs me?" by looking at what you want. When you completed earlier exercises (2.5 and 2.6), you focused on certain company characteristics, fellow-worker traits, geographical locations and other likes and dislikes.

As you search companies, don't lose sight of those desires. There are many ways to define the issue but only solid research will account for the majority of your search success.

There are two major market segments. These consist of the published, or "visible" jobs, and those that are "hidden." We will explore both in Chapter 6. The visible market consists of recruiters, associations, newspapers, television, journals, job fairs, magazines, Internet and other forms of printed media ads. The hidden job market consists of networking, direct mail and contact, and event opportunities.

What you must do is concentrate on companies closely matching criteria you developed from earlier exercises. Remember, just because a company is based in New York State doesn't mean that it doesn't have branches or representatives living elsewhere.

Researching Your Company

Good research is critical in making good company selections. Study each company and determine if they fit your criteria. If they do, then bookmark them with your Favorites button and hold them for further study later.

Exercise 5.1
10 Target-Specific Industries

Identify and establish criteria for your next job.
www.RAH2010.com

Any future research will be centered on industry sub-sectors you have already researched. Once you've identified these 10 industry sectors and sub-sectors, look carefully at the specific NAICS codes. Now, research companies falling within that broad NAICS code category.

One secret lies in determining a company's NAICS code. This stands for North American Industry Clissification System. Every industry and every company in the United States falls into one or more of these NAICS codes. The "world" of these codes may be found online at: (http://www.census.gov/cgi-bin/sssd/naics/naicsrch?chart=2007).

The initial list begins with the overall two-digit number listing in which all industries are divided. If you click on one of the two-number sections, you will see a further breakdown of the components of that section and, depending upon the clissification, it may break down into other sub-industry sections for even more classification refinement. Once you have identified the specific industry you wish to target, then use the logic strings online (found in Chapter 6) to investigate and discover the companies found that possess that specific NAICS code.

Market Investigation

As you do your research online or in the library, paying particular attention to individual company websites, review your personal likes and dislikes, family criteria, and the other factors you determined would make you happy from earlier units of this series. Keep these handy when reviewing information about each target company. Always see if that particular company falls within the "acceptable" range of personal options.

Don't forget to keep in mind all of your previous geographical and other selection criteria. As you print out company names and data, print copies of those of greatest interest because

this data will be used in the next phase of your search.

Also, don't forget the forms you filled out that contained information about you and your past work. Contained within these forms are the "keys" to your transitional skills. Just because you worked in one industry and managed projects doesn't mean you can't transfer these same skills to other industries.

Recruiters hate to hear this, but the fact is true, and doesn't alter your core skill sets. Your job, described in upcoming chapters, is to present these skills in such a way as to transcend the "he/she hasn't worked in this field" barriers and move on with your career!

Your first real assignment is to **identify a minimum of 100 companies** from each sector. With a minimum of 10 sectors or sub-sectors, by the time you will have finished this search, you will have developed many target companies that you can focus on with potential for your career future.

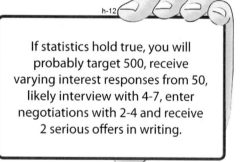

h-12

If statistics hold true, you will probably target 500, receive varying interest responses from 50, likely interview with 4-7, enter negotiations with 2-4 and receive 2 serious offers in writing.

If you look at these ratios, it means that you had better be doing a lot of things each and every day to generate this level of potential. These offers will come from **your** target list based upon **your** criteria for "ideal" regarding both company and location. For perhaps the first time in your career, you will no longer be without clear direction.

The data from the research described above will take you many search hours to develop and collect. It will also take you many hours to execute.

Exercise 5.2 150 Companies

Industry Criteria Exercise
Find 150 companies for each industry you identified. Write down and record those companies matching your criteria.
www.RAH2010.com

The research you will do should be done in the library and on the Web. There are hundreds of companies advertising on Monster or Career Builder or any of the other dozens of web sites so prolific today. Do your homework and match each company against your personal criteria for "acceptable." Then, use the methods described in other chapters to secure your interviews there. Use the more traditional SIC code method, or the web and the library or go to the site listed above when you want larger amounts of detailed information.

Exercise 5.3 NAICS Codes

www.RAH2010.com

If you decide to do the research yourself, know when enough is enough. I personally would rather spend my time interviewing and

negotiating than researching. The research mentioned above will take you considerable time and effort. Don't give up. Keep with it. Manage your time appropriately and select carefully. It is your future you are researching. Take Charge Now!

Don't fall prey to the lazyweb bug and just use the auto-responder services of some Internet job sites to drive your career choices. Don't relapse and go back to being a bobber in the lake, carried by whatever current drifts by. Target, target, and re-target until you have selected companies showing the most promise. Go after them. Pursue them until you land interviews with the decision-makers at each one.

Summary

You now have identified 10 industry sectors in which your skills are transferable. Within those industry sectors, you've identified hundreds of potential target companies that you would like to explore and where you could possibly become employed. Not all will fit your criteria. Keep paring them down and adding others as you can.

The next chapter on *Securing the Interview*, shows you how to do this quickly and effectively.

10 Target Specific Industries

How to find 100 target companies FAST

Industry

	Industry	SIC Code
1		-
2		-
3		-
4		-
5		-
6		-
7		-
8		-
9		-
10		-
11		-
12		-

Criteria

Geographic Location	(use Possible Geographic Locations sheet)				
Employees	Min	Max	Daily Commute	Min	Max
Annual Sales	Min	Max	Measured Units		

Identify as many industries as you can. Then start looking up companies within those industries that fall into the same SIC code group.

Make you Target List using Exercise 5.2

Use Exercise 5.3 as a broad guide to Industry codes.

Read the next Chapter on Internet Research to learn the "Killer Techniques" for finding almost anything.

150 Target Companies

Company	Location	Comment

Make 3 copies of this page, number 1-150, and add company information.

Chapter 6

<<<Internet Research

Simple Rules To Follow

This chapter is not for the faint of heart nor is it designed to be a book on internet research. It is designed to provide a range of assistance from simple to complex search rules and, depending upon your level of expertise, help guide you.

The following diagram has pictures to help you understand the beginnings of Boolean search. A Boolean search is simply a search that uses AND, OR, and NOT. Nothing fancy, really! The chart and the simple rules below come from an internet piece titled: "Where In The Heck Did I Find That?" In this chapter, I've extracted from several Internet sources. There are a few rules for searching. It seems that the biggest challenge you will face is to avoid your tendency to type anything into the browser, hoping that the results will yield something of value. There are a few rules you must follow. These rules and the Boolean Logic chart were developed by Cybèle Elaine Werts and you can find this at: http://www.supertechnogirl.com/articles/tech/internetsearch.html

- "Use a unique identifier when searching. For example, don't look for cake recipes. Look for mandarin orange crème bundt cake recipes.
- "Use the pearl-gathering technique. Pearl-gathering refers to the technique of studying a relevant citation and identifying additional terms to be used in your search query. Additional words, subject headings, or specific fields may be identified. A particular author may appear as an expert on your topic, suggesting a search by author."

∑ "Look for a relevant citation."

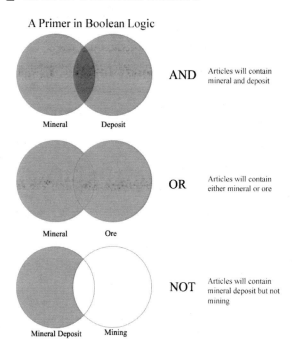

A Primer in Boolean Logic

Mineral — Deposit — AND — Articles will contain mineral and deposit

Mineral — Ore — OR — Articles will contain either mineral or ore

Mineral Deposit — Mining — NOT — Articles will contain mineral deposit but not mining

More Complex Rules - The following section of the book comes from Irina Shanaeva, an executive recruiter and expert sourcer. I simplified and edited her whole piece on this subject for inclusion here.

Googlean - Though other search engines are similar in many ways, each has its own syntax, somewhat different from Google's. Google syntax does, of course, implement Boolean logic, though in a limited fashion. I'd like to talk about the additional, "non-Boolean" part of Google. Google syntax (shall we call it Googlean?) contains much more than an implementation of Boolean logic. There are operators and special characters that instruct Google on how to use keywords in a search string. One doesn't need to learn about all of the operators to become successful in one's searches, but adding a few operators to your search will help quite a bit. Here I'll cover some operators that I think are a must for a serious web sourcer's toolbox.

The Minus - One very important special character is the minus "-", and in fact the minus works as part of the Boolean logic implementation. If you use it in front of a word, no spaces in-between, then it will mean "NOT": -jobs, (But if you write 7-3 in your string, Google will make a different guess and use its calculator instead.

The Question Mark - If you put a phrase in quotation marks, Google will look for the whole phrase. As an example, you could search for "Database Administrator." Google will recognize the operator OR within the quotes. You can search for "Database Administrator OR Developer" and you will find pages with either "Database Administrator" OR "Database Developer."

Finding The Employer - Pick a several-words-long phrase from a job description, put it in quotation marks, and search for it on Google. You will land on all web pages that advertise the job. Or, if you see a job description posted by a recruiter, and you are interested in who the client is, do the same as above, and you are likely to find the same job post made by the employer.

Looking for a person? If the person's name is rare enough, putting it in quotes and Googling it may help. I also use Google advanced image search (http://images.google.com/advanced_image_search?hl=en) with the "faces" option and often land on the person's blog or homepage.

Asterisk * - a very mysterious symbol in Google. Though it formally means "some words," in reality (or is it better to say in practice?) it stands for "one word or very few words." (The symbol * does not stand for a part of a word on Google as it does elsewhere.) Here's a quick example showing how it works. Search for "Oracle * Administrator" (plus keywords) and you will find Oracle Database Administrator, Oracle Discoverer Administrator, etc. The asterisk * is actually a very powerful tool. Here are some uses.

If you are looking for an email pattern for a company or are trying to collect email addresses, you can use "email * companyname.com" or "mailto * companyname.com. Since the symbol * typically stands for one word, you can add more asterisks to these strings and get different results. ("email * * companyname.com" etc.). Please note that since Google ignores special symbols, including the symbol @ in your strings is not necessary.

Phrases - Here are examples of Google searches for phrases. This would bring up pages written by people who work, or used to work for, or have something to do with Accenture. (Replace Accenture with your target company name.) Add your keywords to these strings to narrow down the searches. You can use phrases as a research tool: "I work * Accenture"; "I am * Accenture"; "when I * Accenture".

Tilde – Putting a tilde in front of a word means any word "like" this word. It needs to be used with care since you have no control over what Google may think is "like" your word. However, if the number of results is small or if you suspect you may not know of some synonyms for your keyword, using the tilde may help.

Plus Sign - The plus sign in front of a word tells Google to use exactly this word. This may be useful for two reasons. One, Google typically ignores what they call "stop" words, meaning very common short words like "the" or "in." If you put a plus + in front of "the," it will be included for sure. Two, Google "auto stems," which means that it will look for some variations of a word you include; if you search for manager, it will show results with management as well. Put a plus in front of manager, and the results will contain exactly this word.

More Research Tips

The following thoughts and ideas about internet search are provided by Shally Steckerl and Glen Gutmacher, and are extracted from a piece Shally prepared for me, and inclusions from the The Arbita Guru Guide at: www.Arbita.net.

Multiple Search Engine Sources

Don't depend on any single search engine for results. The overlap between Google, Live, BING, Yahoo, etc., even for the exact same search string is quite low and Thumbshots rankings prove it (http://www.thumbshots.com/Products/ThumbshotsImages/Ranking.aspx).

• Don't just look at firms in your industry (e.g., many accountants, attorneys, etc., work in places other than accounting and law firms)

• Consider targeting companies or organizations in growth industries or economically un(der)affected ones:

• Healthcare, Education, Energy, Defense, etc. They are updated monthly for large companies at Indeed.com in their section Indeed Industry Trends (http://www.indeed.com/jobtrends/industry)

• Or search by job at Wanted Analytics to see demand level by location (http://www.wantedanalytics.com/supplydemand/) or, again at Indeed.com create a custom hiring trend heat map by keyword (http://www.indeed.com/jobtrends?relative=1)

• Social Media and Alternative Technologies

• Hot niches within traditional industries (e.g., cybersecurity within IT)

• SMB companies that are innovating

• "Green-collar" jobs & technology (e.g., 100 green career resources (http://www.jobprofiles.org/library/guidance/100_tips_and_tools_for_better_greener_career.htm) or California green careers guide, Renewable Energy Jobs, green collar job board)

• Seek out companies that can benefit from larger firms' losses (niche firms, SMB)

If your search delivers good results, automatically receive new results that meet your criteria via email:

- click "News Alerts" in left-hand column (Google News)

- Google Alerts (for other Google queries)

- under "GET UPDATES" in right-hand column (Yahoo News)

- For Live.com searches, just click the orange/white RSS button (in MSIE v7+) or append &format=rss to any Live result URL

- Yahoo regular search results: append in this format http://api.search.yahoo.com/WebSearchService/rss/webSearch.xml?appid=yahoosearchwebrss&query=your+search+keywords+here

Focus on individual companies that are growing:

- Startups being funded by Incubators and VC's (www.masshightech.com) [type in key words to find specific section of site] e.g., these and VCs (e.g., these) which are more likely to be hiring (http://www.seattlepi.com/venture/374001_vc08.html) and other sites like: www.seattlepi.com

- Look at the annually-compiled lists of growing companies overall (www.inc.com) or by geography (e.g., Boston Globe's "Growth 50" within Globe 100. (www.boston.com)

- Target departments and areas that are necessary, and foster top-line growth: sales, product marketing, business development, R&D, specialized skills, etc.

- Look to competitors: not every company in the same industry is laying off.

- Analyze the media for trigger events that will cause hiring situations

- Look at news sites (e.g., Google, Yahoo, BING, Live) that will show you relevant stories during recent time ranges.

Sample Google News search queries:
– Company expansion: expands.operations|facilities|campus (http://news.google.com/news?ned=us&hl=en&q=expands.operations|facilities|campus)

– Add wildcard and variant word forms for even more results: grows|growing|expands|expanding.*.operations|facilities|campus

– Contract wins: receives|wins.*.deal|contract

– Or try searching against a laundry list of rela-tError! Bookmark not defined.

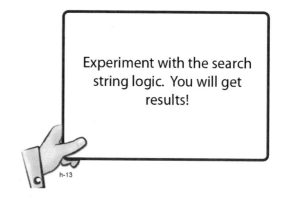

Experiment with the search string logic. You will get results!

h-13

– If you want to narrow geographically, the results count drops, so expand the date range a bit (e.g., 06/01/2008 - 02/25/2009) to compensate: receives|wins.*.deal|contract (boston OR massachusetts).

Incubators and VCs:
– Raises funds: raises|raised|funds|mezzanine venture.capital|incubator|vc

– Series A/B round: "series * round"

Recent financial statement is strong:
– Profit (has, that, margin) increased: "profit * increased"

Use job aggregator sites like Indeed.com or SimplyHired.com to find variant job titles as well as company names (note the left-hand column in all search results – e.g., if you want to be a concept artist, then find jobs reporting to an Art Director.

• To find reporting relationships, search for a job title plus ("report to" OR "reports to" OR "reporting to")

• Use site: command on search engines to look through an entire target website; combine with keywords, job titles, etc.:

> • Works on all major search engines (e.g., site:nike.com "design director")

• Can also run on blog-rich sites (e.g., site:livejournal.com)

• Or use a blog-dedicated search engine (e.g., Technorati)

• This often gets you early hints/rumors, inside

information, people are more likely to be named, etc.

• Also see industry sites which often have insider stories (e.g., CrispyGamer or Gamasutra for games industry; for Silicon Valley, ValleyWag or TechCrunch)

• You can find more sites (as well as interesting people) by typing search engine queries with an industry name plus rumor, like "industrial design" rumor 2009 or "fine art" industry (insider OR rumor) 2009

As I said at the beginning of this chapter, this is a ROUGH explanation of a very complex subject. There are hundreds of sites and literally thousands of experts who work with Boolean logic daily and perform internet search.

What I want you to gain from this chapter is an appreciation that it is OK to experiment with some of the guidelines provided by these experts in your job search. You **must** be able to research data on the internet or you will be left in the dust by those who can and will. Mastery of this subject is not required – experimenting with some of this in your job search process is!

Chapter 7
<<< Securing The Interview

"You Either Make Dust, Or Eat Dust"

his is an important chapter. It covers a lot of territory. Securing the interview is the most difficult aspect of your search effort. There are the gatekeepers, the nay-sayers (they can't say "yes," but they sure can say "no"), the "fearfulls" (they think you want their job and make it hard for your candidacy) and many other types of people, each with a different agenda than yours. Once you understand the competition, you must explore the visible and hidden job markets. Along the way you will encounter recruiters, human resource people, job fairs and many situational opportunities. Knowing how to work with each is important.

FEAR

Many years ago, I had the painful, but extremely beneficial experience of attending Dr. James Farr's institute in North Carolina. Why painful? My first exercise was to sit in a bathtub and play with a rubber duck and then report my feelings the next day to those attending the "stop being crazy" (my name for it) group. Dr. Farr forced me to look at perception and reality and understand the filters I was using to approach the world. These filters were being used to interpret the behavior of others towards me. Then, I reacted according to my emotional survival programming. Whew, heavy stuff!

Because I was wrongly filtering, and therefore misinterpreting most behaviors, I was reacting according to my "understandings" and approaching life in a way that was having a negative impact on myself and those close to me, both at work and at home. As I was going through the sessions, I was angry, frustrated and hated facing the reality of my fears. I worked through them and now assert that it was the most powerful and beneficial experience of my entire working career.

I now coach my clients to understand and incorporate a variation of FDR's famous saying, "We have nothing to fear but fear itself." The variation is: Fear *really* means - **F**alse **E**vidence **A**ppearing **R**eal. Go to EXERCISE 7.1, complete it, and identify your personal FEARs regarding the job search process.

Exercise 7.1 FEAR Quiz
Identify your personal FEARs **www.RAH2010.com**

The "Rambo's" among you can skip this exercise. However, for 99.99% of the American population, this exercise will be of value in helping you come to grips with barriers that might stand in your way as you attempt to manage and execute a meaningful job search.

You can see from the exercise there are multiple areas where FEAR can manifest itself and sidetrack your campaign. Let me take a moment and discuss these two concepts.

> The single most difficult part of your job search is, without question, securing an interview with the decision-maker. This is where even the strongest men and women falter and often fail. No interview, no job.

h-14

In my opinion, there are two main reasons for failure. The first is grounded in the concept of fear. The second is lack of determination and discipline. Think about this for a moment. Do you like rejection? Do you get up every morning saying to all who listen, "please reject me?" Of course you don't! No sane person seeks rejection. This, however, leads me to the main point of this portion of the chapter narrative.

Your job search is simply business. It isn't personal. When you don't get the interview, it isn't you. It might be timing, another candidate who actually might be more qualified than you and dozens of other reasons over which you have no control.

Jim Farr taught me an important behavior modification rule that I would like to share with you. When you were a child and put your hand on a hot stove, you soon discovered that if you repeated that behavior you would be hurt.

You didn't do it again, knowingly. These learned behaviors apply equally to the mechanisms we employ to protect both our physical and emotional health and survival.

During our lifetimes, all of us have been subjected to a multiplicity of experiences, some resulting in a feeling of rejection. At first, this created intense emotional pain. Each of us, of course, reacted differently. We either blocked the pain and avoided the causes, became callous and insensitive, or grew negative and hurtful. As we became adults, we eventually learned to minimize or avoid such encounters, as much as possible.

No matter what particular method you use to cope, you long ago developed behavior patterns, event-filtering mechanisms, and personalized retreat methods that you still employ today to survive emotionally.

Most people eventually employ these when going through a job transition. You will too, if enough "gatekeepers" won't let you get to the decision-makers, recruiters won't respond or are insensitive or rude, and hundreds of other rejection-reasons are experienced during your weekly search encounters.

Believe me, you **will** eventually lean towards familiar habits and possibly develop one or more patterns of behavior to avoid such encounters. Oh, do I hear you saying no? Poppycock! I am here to tell you that I have watched hundreds of job seekers go through this same avoidance syndrome.

The cure is not simple, but it is effective. The next time you have such an encounter, try to become aware of this vicious cycle of behavior and how you are reacting.

Every time you face rejection, stop and consider the <u>why</u> of the situation and then the <u>what</u> of your feelings. Figure out what the causes might have been and then take constructive action to change those things over which you have control, and do them differently. Remember: <u>you are either in control or out of control.</u>

Jim Farr used to call them "crazy tapes." He said the only way to modify behavior was to break the tape that is currently running and re-record, or substitute, a new set of behaviors and then practice them until they become the standard by which you operate.

> The key to your success is to keep on, no matter what! Break that negative cycle of "I'm not OK" by simply doing more, doing it better, evaluating your course of action, and attempting new strategies.

h-16

The second main reason for avoidance is lack of discipline. Poor discipline stems from poor habits. These range from being disorganized, procrastinating, having a lack of clarity as to your mission or purpose, poorly defining your objectives and goals, and a hundred other reasons. My personal shortcomings are disdain for detail and some procrastination. Evidence? The original version of this book was nearly two years in the making.

I promised you in Chapter 1, I wouldn't digress and philosophize in this book. I am not doing so now. Below, I have listed a few of my personal beliefs. If you practice these, and the 25 Rules you've already posted in your home, you will be extremely successful in your search. Who knows, you might also think about applying them to improve your personal life as well.

The rest of this chapter will focus on the published and hidden job markets and techniques to penetrate both.

REFERENCES AND NETWORKING

Fred's Rules h-17

"Good enough, never is!"
"You either make dust or eat dust!"
"Keep busy doing meaningful things!"
"Don't engage in 'Stinkin' Thinkin'!"
"All glasses are ½ full!"
"Worry about those things over which you have control, not those things you don't!"
"Stop, listen, evaluate, adapt, improvise, and move on!"

So far, we've developed the product (YOU) by defining who you are and describing why they should hire you through an attention-getting resume. We've also identified many companies as potential targets (Exercise 5.2) and are now ready to take the product (you) to market.

The first step is to let your references know of your availability and secure their help. Before approaching the Published Market, you must first explore your references. When you finish reading this section, I want you to put a list of references together.

Develop a 360 degree approach to references. There are two kinds of references - personal and business. I want you to list at least <u>three</u> personal and <u>six</u> business references. When you finish implementing the networking instructions, and you follow them exactly, you will have accrued over 1000 contacts in this search. Just as the longest journey begins with the first step, your list of 1000+ contacts begins with the development of your initial 9 names.

 You should begin networking after you have finished with recruiter follow-up.

b-19

Personal references are there to attest to your personal traits and character and should always be non-family members. Make sure that your selection of references includes people who are good on the phone and <u>ones that will return phone calls.</u> Most references are checked by phone.

Exercise 7.2

Actual Candidate Reference Check
www.RAH2010.com

As a recruiter, I always call all references, and I have a list of 12-15 questions I ask them. If you wish to see an actual reference check I did on a candidate, please refer to Exercise 7.2. Other recruiters and employers do the same.

Listing your last boss as a reference may not always be the best move. Your references are supposed to help you - not hurt you. So, if you and your last boss did not see eye-to-eye, or disagreed on a lot of issues, then don't use him or her as a reference. If you even suspect they won't be positive and upbeat, don't use them.

Under no circumstances are you to ask your references for a job! That is not their purpose. If you do, you might as well pack it in right here and now.

h-20

There are companies who, for a fee, will check reference and previous employer opinions about you. You may wish to avail yourself of these services. My recruiting staff performs this service

as a part of the search services we provide our clients. Other companies do as well and you can find them on the www.

However, because of lawsuits, both frivolous and valid, most companies, especially larger ones, only give out dates of employment. Consequently, should someone ask why you did not use your former boss as a reference, you can explain that the company only gives dates of employment.

Exercise 7.3

Example Reference Letters
www.RAH2010.com

Don't think for a minute that a letter of recommendation can be substituted as a reference. It can't. When you secure a letter of recommendation from a business associate or someone who knows you in a business context, it says to them that they have done a good thing, they then feel good about themselves and it signals them that they can now forget you.

Did you ever stop and consider the fact that sometimes the interviewer, after reading the letter, might want to ask a follow-up question?

You will need **five** reference letters from business peers or superiors in this search. Most of the time, references are busy. Here is a way to kill two birds with one stone. Ask your references if you can draft a short letter on their behalf that you will send to them for their approval, redraft and signature. 99% will say yes. What an opportunity! You can now take your SHARE stories, incorporate them into letters, create a different perspective in each one, make yourself appear more diversified and win, win, win. When this happens, you have constructed a nearly perfect scenario.

In the *Resume Worksheet* forms you have already completed, you were asked to describe five problems (SHARE stories), show how you solved them and what quantifiable results were achieved. This is one of the key places you will use this information. Be sure to incorporate at least one, preferably two, SHARE stories that reinforce your qualifications into a supporting letter from each of your references.

Basically, you wish to use a particular problem, state it in terms that are general and *include your quantifiable results*. The reference letter will begin with a statement of what your working relationship was with the author of the letter.

In your letters of recommendation, have the author insert a sentence opening the door to additional questions. For example, "Please feel free to call me at (put your reference's telephone number there) anytime, or email me at (be sure their email address is on the letter), to discuss (your name here of course)'s excellent qualifications."

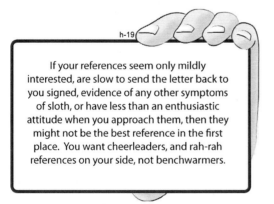

h-19

If your references seem only mildly interested, are slow to send the letter back to you signed, evidence of any other symptoms of sloth, or have less than an enthusiastic attitude when you approach them, then they might not be the best reference in the first place. You want cheerleaders, and rah-rah references on your side, not benchwarmers.

Be sure that they include their phone, fax number or email address. The email address is really important. No matter how well you think you know your references, make sure you have their permission to use their name and give out their phone, fax and email addresses before you do so. Have the reference sign the document and, bingo, you have a real reference letter.

No one likes surprises, no one! Your references are no different. Every reference has agreed to support you and push you as a great candidate. If they are caught off guard or it is inconvenient for them at the time, don't use them. You might get a surprise you will never know about.

It is a courtesy to give your references time to think about what they want to say if they initiated your reference letter. Be sure and tell them about the company and position for which you are applying. It will help them frame their responses when questioned.

> Whomever you contact in this search, no matter what they did for you, how small or large a favor or task it was, always follow up in writing with a thank you letter.

It doesn't hurt to also enclose your resume and your "business card" - the one you had made and are using during your search.

Be sure your business card contains the website address where your resume and work history can be found. You want as many people as possible thinking about you and your career move. Add your references to that group.

References are also handy in another way. When you go to an interview and the interviewer asks for your references, pull out your typed list and hand it to them. If they ask, you can assume your interview went well.

Use the Networking Chart we've developed

to manage your referrals and contacts. While awaiting responses from your inquiries and telephone calls to prospective references, spend your remaining time doing more web research for companies meeting your personal "ideal" criteria and standards.

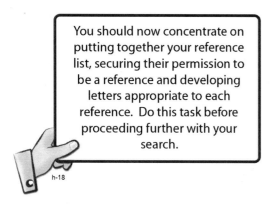

You should now concentrate on putting together your reference list, securing their permission to be a reference and developing letters appropriate to each reference. Do this task before proceeding further with your search.

h-18

RECRUITERS

There is much material written about how to deal with recruiters, so I'll be brief. My colleague, Darrell W. Gurney, a long-time executive recruiter, says that "recruiters **don't** work for you." They work for the company who is paying them to screen out all but the best candidates. They are paid when, and only when, they fill a job order.

So, here you come with your wonderful resume. To your great good fortune, they have a job order for which your skills are a match. Now, you are "gold," you are their best friend and they will be your advocate until either you are hired or until someone else is hired for the position. At that point, they go on to another bright and shining money-making star who fits the next job posting they must work on.

 When listing references, only list people who can freely discuss your work history and character.

b-11

On the flip side, if they don't have a job order for which your skills match, they generally won't give you the time of day. Oh, they may interview you, but when you finish your conversation with them, your name is put in their database and at some point in the future, generally 60-90 days, your resume is purged from their system. You feel good, but nothing has really transpired. Timing is everything with recruiters.

Don't think for a minute that submitting your resume to a few recruiters will do the job. It won't. It is best to circulate your resume to as many **appropriate** recruiters as possible. The best rule is to target recruiters specializing in your specific job-skills or targeted industries. Doing so ensures you of a higher probability of success. Sometimes you can get lucky with a recruiting broadcast service. There are many "blasting" services, but I don't recommend them. You will want to be very specific in your targeting of a recruiter type.

 There are basically two kinds of recruiters - retained and contingency.

b-12

When recruiters get job orders from companies, their own database is the first place they look for viable candidates. If they do not find a candidate in their database, recruiters go into a sourcing mode by first calling companies similar to the one that placed the job order to find people who might fit the job profile. They call you and try to convince you to switch companies.

If you choose to shotgun your resume to hundreds of recruiters, then go to the yellow pages or any of dozens of published directories of recruiting companies and mail your heart out.

No directory is completely comprehensive. Even the best ones contain mistakes and inaccuracies. That is not the fault of the directory. Recruiting is a tough business and turnover is very high. Change is the watchword in the recruiting field. You would do well to use my website as an up-to-date and accurate recruiter source. It is my personal belief that the paradigm of recruiting is changing and that at some point in the distant future, the internet will eliminate recruiters altogether.

Retained recruiters are contracted by companies to recruit people as positions become open. The retained recruiter is often called a "headhunter" and usually works with higher-salaried positions. Most people never hear from a retained recruiter. Most likely, you will hear from a contingency recruiter. The contingency recruiter is not on contract with any particular company. These recruiters usually work with lower-salaried or positioned employees. They are trying to pick as many qualified candidates as possible, to send them to their client company, and hope one fits. That is when, and only when, they get paid. The job or company may not be right for you but, many times, it appears this is not their main concern. Placing someone and getting paid is the name of the game. Beware.

You should seriously consider selecting both contingency and retained recruiters no matter how high your income level. Small emerging companies have neither the finances nor the status needed to utilize big name recruiters. They almost always start out using contingency recruiters.

Among these small emerging companies might just be the next Microsoft. If you are in the higher income bracket, select both kinds of recruiters but let the contingency ones know that you are looking for emerging companies.

Once you have a list of recruiters, you will need to send each of them a cover letter and a copy of your resume. Do not get carried away with fancy, heavy bonded paper. It is actually better, when dealing with recruiters, to submit your credentials on quality laser paper, keeping in mind that recruiters will want to forward your credentials to prospective clients. Don't fold your resume. Send it in a large envelope unfolded. They want your credentials on good contrast paper that can be easily copied, faxed or scanned. Also, utilize email if you have their addresses.

A mail-out to recruiters should be done as soon as your resume is finalized. Not only are recruiters an excellent source of job leads, but they can also provide valuable feedback on the market and how your skills might fit into that market.

- What is your employment status?
- Are you willing to relocate?
- What kind of money are you looking for?
- Are you willing to take a pay cut for a new opportunity?
- If you are currently unemployed, what is the lowest salary you will accept to secure a position?

One of three things will result from this mail-out to recruiters:

1) They will call you with questions about your credentials or with possible positions of employment. Long before now, you have already answered the following questions by completing the exercises found in Chapter 2 - Who Are You?

2) You will get a post card or a letter telling you that there is nothing currently available but that your resume will be kept on file.

3) You will hear nothing from some recruiters.

The recruiter's first question usually involves your current employment status. If you are working, say so. The next question will probably regard the reason you are looking. You should have an answer prepared. A good response might be that you are looking for more growth potential than your current company can offer.

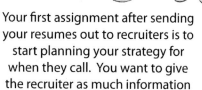

Your first assignment after sending your resumes out to recruiters is to start planning your strategy for when they call. You want to give the recruiter as much information and latitude as possible, while keeping them under control.

If you are unemployed, let the recruiter know. Present yourself as a victim of downsizing. And what if you have just been fired for some reason? Not too major of a problem when working with many recruiters! Remember that the recruiter is not the potential employer,

but merely a channel to that employer. It is the employer who will be making the decision regarding your hiring, not the recruiter. Save your explanations for the employer.

The recruiter's next question might regard relocation. Even though you might have no desire to move, keep the door open. Tell the recruiter that you would consider relocation for the right compensation package.

You want the recruiter to picture you as a highly flexible go-getter. If you give them too many restrictions, they will shift their focus towards more flexible candidates.

b-13

Another question will focus on your salary expectations. Bill Temple says: "Whenever possible, ask the recruiter what the position pays before they ask you your expectations. So long as their range is not ridiculously out of line, say, 'Thank you for sharing. That sounds like a good place to start.' If the range is too low for you, say so. Your honesty will be appreciated!" If you are employed, tell the recruiter what you are currently making and give him a brief description of your benefits package. Tell him that you anticipate increasing this package by more salary, responsibilities, benefits, equity or stock options.

A good rule of thumb is a total compensation increase of 15% or more. Don't forget to specify that this 15% _excludes_ any cost of living adjustments that may have to be made for relocation.

Here's a word to the wise. If you are offered an inexplicably high package by any company, look hard at their source of funding and their _BURN RATE_. It is not how much money they have, it is the speed with which they are spending it! If you ask and they won't tell you, then run away as fast as you can. Compensation is also determined by the econmic cimate of the time you choose to look. In 2010, salaries are somewhat flat to down, following the 2009 recession. But, my clients are still receiving signing bonuses and better packages. They followed the rules in the book and you can, too.

Let's take a moment to consider an interesting twist to desired salary increases. Suppose that the position under consideration is in another part of the country where the cost of living is substantially less and, consequently, the base salary may be less, simply because of the location.

Here you have a real dilemma. You will have to weigh the advantages of a less costly lifestyle against a career move that will cause a cut in salary. This type of move should not be taken lightly. If you decide to accept this kind of position, make sure that you can justify it as a true career advancement. On your next change, should you relocate to a higher cost of living area, you have just spent this amount of time participating in "marching in place" economics.

> Don't let yourself be wowed by money if your happiness depends upon the other criteria you've identified in the previous exercises.

b-14

Are you willing to take a substantial cut in pay for a new opportunity? This happens frequently, especially when someone is changing careers or moving from a large to a small corporation. Small companies, in most cases, cannot offer the salaries and slate of benefits that large

companies can offer.

But smaller companies usually offer more flexibility, stock options, growth potential and autonomy. Remain as open to new opportunities as your comfort level and credentials will allow.

h-22

The name of the game for the recruiter is volume. It is easier to place three candidates at $65,000 per year than one candidate at $180,000.

Additionally, you have to be very comfortable with your corporate skills and your family situation to take on something like this.

Recruiters often ask, "what is the minimum salary you will accept in a new position?" Be very careful here or you will find yourself being sent out for every low-paying job that happens to be on the recruiter's desk. Conversely, don't price yourself too high either.

Don't be fooled into thinking that the recruiter will naturally want to place you at as high a salary as possible because he/she will then make more in commission.

Employers make quicker hiring decisions for lower positions. Take a look at your budgetary needs and your cash reserves and give an <u>educated</u> answer to the "how low will you go" question.

Don't forget that while the recruiter is picking your brain, you should be doing likewise. Ask him/her what he/she found appealing about your credentials. Ask him/her about market conditions for someone with your skills and background.

Ask about his/her firm and his/her length of tenure in the industry. You can really waste time with green and inexperienced recruiters. If things look good, arrange to meet. Make a responsive recruiter a valuable ally.

Be realistic - not every recruiter will have a position that matches your credentials. The operative phrase here is "a position that matches your credentials." That, in a nutshell, is what the recruiting game involves. Matching! If there is a possible match, you'll get called. If not, you'll get a rejection card or letter, or silence. Do not take these rejections personally! Avoid attributing rejection to inadequate qualifications. It just means that, at this point in time, there is not a match.

> ### Here's another Fred's Rule:
>
> Keep calling until you get a court order telling you to cease and desist.

h-23

Some recruiters will not call or send a rejection letter. Don't let them get off that easily. Call them! This is your first opportunity to promote yourself. The purpose is to try and generate some interest in your skills. Pat yourself on the back if you can generate genuine interest, get

an interview with a potential employer or merely get an audience with the recruiter. Being able to generate interest in your skills, when none existed before, is a very valuable skill to learn.

To do this most effectively, you'll need to have an interest-generating opening statement prepared for the recruiter. The recruiter will probably respond that he has nothing that fits your credentials. That's perfectly OK!

You must then begin asking the recruiter questions about the general marketability of someone with your skills. Leave the conversation, if not with an actual job lead, at least with a referral to another recruiter who might be looking for someone with your skills.

Just remember, if you are dealing with an inexperienced recruiter, finding the position you desire is unlikely. However, it can serve as good practice in honing your skills. One or two practice sessions are all you need to arm yourself with excellent techniques. If you haven't learned to separate the "newlyweds" from the more tenured professionals, you will spin your wheels uselessly. The auto dealers have these guys all over their car lots. You know what I mean. You drive up and they descend upon you like flies, especially the newbies. Are you intimidated then? Good. Now I want you to view new recruiters in the same light as you do new-to-their-job car salespersons.

Exercise 7.4

Candidate Marketing Profile
www.RAH2010.com

If you are conducting a national job search and have mailed your resume to several hundred recruiters, following up with all of them may not be practical. To be effective, however, you must follow-up with all who are in the geographic locations that you deem most desirable.

 Start telephone follow-up about two weeks after mailing your resume to recruiters.

b-15

TRADE AND FRATERNAL ASSOCIATIONS:

A valuable, but under-utilized tool is the list of associations you will now compile. The *Encyclopedia of Associations* contains a wealth of information about current professional, fraternal, non-profit, educational and enthusiast associations, is regularly up-dated and is available at local libraries.

Step 1: As part of your action plan, you will select a group of associations appropriate for your professional and personal background. Prepare an opening statement that gives a brief description of your skills.

Step 2: Next, call the association, give your opening statement and simply ask if they have knowledge of any job openings with any of their members.

If the answer is "yes," you have hit pay dirt and can proceed with logistics on how to get your credentials in front of that member seeking additional staff.

Most of the time, the association will want you to fax, email or mail your resume so that it can be passed along to the hiring member. Do so, but make sure that you get the name of the person within the association who will be the one who conveys your credentials. <u>This person</u> <u>is your follow-up contact</u>.

Make sure that the association does indeed pass your credentials along and keep them posted on any contact or activity generated with the member.

Enter each contact in your ATS 2.0 sheets and be sure you document your contact activity.

Should the association not be willing to pass your credentials on to any of their members, don't worry about it or lose hope. Simply use the association to gather information on the market or common interests that they represent. Associations have been formed to act as information clearinghouses. In most cases, they are more than willing to pass general information on to the public. Try to secure a list of their membership.

h-24

The worst thing you can do is to appear too anxious. Also don't try to hustle them. They will know it, and not only be upset, but will probably put the word out about you and then you are dead! Don't let them see you sweat.

If you can get the name of even one member-company, you can find their industry code and start targeting all companies with similar classifications.

You should also ask if the association has a local chapter in your area. If so, plan on attending an open meeting or two. This is an excellent way of learning more about the group and also making *excellent* contacts.

The purpose of attending some local meetings is not to drop your resume on the members as soon as they walk in the door but to genuinely open conversations, form alliances and strategically let the members know of your employment availability.

Finally, don't forget about social and civic associations, your church, college alumni, or sorority or fraternity groups. These non-business associations can often offer excellent opportunities. Several of my clients come from the military and are West Point graduates. The armed service fraternal organizations are powerful and they communicate effectively. If you are able to participate in this group, by all means do so!

You should begin calling associations almost immediately after your resume is completed. The *Activity Tracking System* (ATS) (www.RAH2010.com) allows you to track your efforts throughout this search. Enter in all your data. There are, at least at this writing, two search management programs that I believe are perfect for helping you manage your job search. One is by Jason Alba, www.jibberjobber.com. The other is by Career Shift, www.careershift.com. There will be others, but such a tool is affordable and essential today.

Printed Media Ads

Of all the strategies available, answering newspaper ads exposes you to the most competition. As I said earlier in the book, they are mostly a waste of time. At senior levels within companies, they are virtually ineffective. However, some people still get jobs from ads so I've included a discussion about how to run an ad campaign.

Your source publications are your local newspaper, *The Wall Street Journal* and other trade publications. Don't forget your state and local employment agencies.

There are thousands of jobs online today found on various job boards. Jobs for senior management are rarely found in newspapers, these days.

If you are at the executive level ($100,000+), there are two sites I recommend: Exec-U-Net (www.execunet.com) and www.theladders.com. There are fees, but placements do occur and the advice they provide is solid and practical. They are listed on my website and you can contact them through the Resources page found in the "About Us" section of my website. The URL is www.stewartcoopercoon.com.

If you are lucky, your local paper will categorize their employment ads into specific categories such as high tech, health care, purchasing, etc. If this is the case, you should select as many pertinent categories and ads within those categories as possible.

> A good way of knowing if you are selecting appropriate ads is by looking at the requirements. If you match 50% or more, you are in the right category and should respond to the ad.

h-25

The simplest way of responding to an ad is to first make reference to where you saw the ad and what position is being advertised. Then simply match your skills to the requirements listed. Do not draw attention to areas where you do not match.

BLIND ADS

In a blind ad only a post office box, fax number or email address is given. There are some very sound reasons for a company to use blind ads:

1. Company confidentiality

2. Business strategy

3. Small company with no way to handle walk-in applicants

4. Front for multi-level marketing scheme

Many job seekers avoid responding to these ads. These ads normally generate about 40-60% fewer respondents than ads listing company names. Respond to these ads.

There is one additional risk to answering a blind ad. The company running the ad may be your current employer. Thus, we recommend that if there is even a remote possibility that the advertiser is your own company, don't answer the ad.

HOW TO ANSWER ADS

Most ads contain the company name. It's a very good idea to do a little research on the company before you answer the ad. Making a reference in the cover letter that shows that you know a little about the company may help set you apart from your competition.

The ad may mention a person to whom you may direct your cover letter and resume. If no

name is given, you can send it to the president or appropriate department head whose name you gleaned from your research. In almost all cases, I advise my clients to avoid Human Resources, if at all possible. Their job is to screen you out, not see that you get an audience. Some companies have internal recruiters and their sole purpose is to screen you out. Do your homework and find out the names of the persons in charge of your area and go after them.

In addition to looking at ads where you match 50% or more of the qualifications, you should also be looking for ads that are actually below your level of expertise. Below, you say?

A good rule of thumb for answering ads is to select as many as possible on the first pass. Then wait about 24 hours before you think about responding. Some of your first picks will not pass the test of time.

Look carefully at the Letterpack and Phone Scripts found at our web site www. RAH2010.com

Here's a secret. No one is suggesting that you consider moving down to entry-level status. But by stating in your cover letter that you are interested in a higher position within their company you might get your resume passed on to someone at the desired level.

Conversely, you should also be looking for positions that are higher than your actual level. Your cover letter should point out that you want to be considered by the successful candidate as he or she begins to put the team together.

Additionally, you should be looking through

the entire employment section and making a list of companies that are hiring in many different areas. These companies are growing. Growing companies are always looking for good employees.

 A better way is to wait four or five days after publication date before sending off your response to any ad.

b-16

This is fine, as long as you are not consistently rejecting all of your selections after this second reading. If this is occurring, you have lost your positive attitude and are being pulled into inertia. Break this cycle at once.

WHEN TO ANSWER ADS

Most job seekers are at the post office bright and early the day after an ad has run. They figure that they are getting a jump on the competition by firing off their response as quickly as possible.

If the truth were told, the person on the receiving end is inundated with hundreds of responses during the first three or four days. How much attention do you think each resume will receive?

Consequently, one of your most effective strategies as a job seeker is to send two resumes. Follow the instructions in the ad and send one resume to HR. Then, if you can ascertain the decision-maker's name, send a second resume to that person as well. Be sure to advise the decision maker that you also submitted to HR.

Your response will not arrive too late for consideration. Most companies generally allow a few weeks before the resumes are screened and

an interviewing schedule is set up. The risk you take by delaying your response is very small compared to the competitive edge that you gain.

ADDRESSING THE RESPONSE

Many ads will direct you to respond to the Human Resources (HR) Department. Their job is to review the hundreds - and occasionally thousands - of resumes and select a very small percentage for interviewing.

I don't want to repeat myself too much in this book, but this is an important point. To narrow the selection, HR compares the resumes coming in against a specific job description. HR people are not experts in manufacturing, engineering or marketing. As useful as their training and education may be in the field of Human Resources, they are often not qualified to evaluate candidates outside their area of expertise.

Needless to say, you are in much better shape if you can send your ad response to the functional hiring authority instead of HR. Unfortunately, it is often perceived as a breach of corporate protocol to bypass the HR Department and this tactic alone may screen you out of contention. My HR friends will not be happy with me when they read this section of the book. But the truth is the truth.

If the company only allows you to apply online, then that must be done; but this in no way relieves you of your responsibility to discover who your potential "boss" is in order to send him/her your resume.

Be quick to point out that you are not attempting an "end around run" and that you have responded in the manner stipulated in the ad. Then indicate that, because you see such an ideal match between your qualifications and the job described, you've made a special effort to bring your credentials to his or her attention.

With this technique, you will be penetrating the company at two different levels and increasing the odds for a response. Even if the hiring authority forwards your letter to HR, he or she may also request that you be put on the "short list" for interview scheduling.

One additional advantage to this approach is that it helps differentiate you from the competition. The vast majority of your fellow ad respondents will send their responses to Human Resources and just wait for a response.

Very few send their responses to the appropriate functional manager. Not only might you gain a strategic advantage, you might gain a numerical one as well. While the HR Manager is wading through 300 resumes, the functional manager may only have two or three to review.

HOW TO IDENTIFY THE HIRING MANAGER

The answer is simple. Make a phone call. Ask the receptionist who is in charge of the appropriate department. If in doubt, ask to be connected to a secretary in that department. Ask for help. Try to make a friend. If you are asked why you are calling, say that you have some information that you would like to send to the attention of the appropriate person. If you are told to send it to the "gatekeeper," tell them it is of a personal nature and would they mind giving you the information you need - name including the middle initial, proper title, correct address, *and the hiring authority's Email address!*

You can also use LinkedIn and other websites to "see" the e-mail structure of the company and then mail your future boss directly.

THE INTERNET

The Internet should play an essential role in your job search. Some of my clients are now finding their next position on the www. The Internet has become so significant to job searching that to not use it is a sin. The Internet is filled with opportunities and information just waiting to be conquered.

Companies provide links to job postings through their Websites. A growing number of companies expect you to seek job openings by looking through their specific Websites. Other Websites serve as clearinghouses for job postings from different companies. If you are not computer literate, you are <u>severely</u> limited in finding potential career possibilities and should consider computer training immediately.

 If your computer skills are lacking, you should strongly consider bringing them up to par.

b-17

ELECTRONIC RESUMES

More and more employers are requesting emailed resumes that can be popped right into their electronic tracking systems. Direct emailing is quick and efficient and cuts down on scanning errors. Here's what you, as the job seeker, need to know:

■ You must learn how to prepare your resume in three ways: a formatted paper resume, a scannable paper resume and a plain-text electronic resume.

■ You must learn how to email an electronic resume to an employment database, to an employer's Web site and to an individual's email address.

■ You must learn how to paste your resume into the body of your electronic cover letter.

■ According to employers, emailed plain-text resumes are their first preference.

■ Scannable resumes that are printed out on white paper and mailed via postal mail **(unfolded and unstapled)** are their second choice.

SEARCH ENGINES

Search engines are cyberspace's equivalent to the Dewey Decimal System. Here are some basic facts about search engines:

■ The best way to find out how to use a search engine is to <u>read the directions at the search engine site</u>.

■ A search engine is only as good as the database it's searching.

■ Read the directions!

■ Make sure that you have at least four key words on any given topic so that you can use the search engine most effectively.

■ Always try your keyword search in more than one search engine.

■ If you are having trouble using a search engine, use it to search a topic familiar to you. When you search for familiar items, you can quickly determine the value of the

search engine.

■ Look for search engine meta-lists that will give you immediate access to hundreds of search engines all gathered together into one place.

Your job is to get the name of their boss, boss's boss or the name of the hiring authority in the department where you want to work.

JOB FAIRS

If you've been to a job fair and didn't work it properly, you are probably tempted to skip this section. DON'T. You are probably saying to yourself right now, "I went and didn't find a thing there. What a waste of my time." If a job fair isn't properly worked, it can be a big waste of time.

Let's understand job fair rule number one: Your job *is not* to interview with the newest HR staff person who got stuck with the assignment for that day.

Your purpose in speaking with the staff at the job fair is to gain an understanding about the structure of that company and how you can get in to contact the real decision-makers.

Job fairs are places where both prospective employers and applicants go to size up each other. They provide an excellent forum for candidates and companies to meet. Attend as many as possible. At senior levels, you might think you are wasting your time. However, when you get there, grab the business cards from the target companies you wish to work for and then call into the company and figure out who is the decision-maker you want to speak with and then call her/him. The following are some strategies for working a job fair effectively:

PRE-REGISTER

Many times, employers attempt to pre-screen applicants. Your name in front of the career fair company representative will secure an audience, which works to your advantage.

ONE MINUTE "COMMERCIAL" OR "ELEVATOR SPEECH"

Should include the following:

1. WHAT I AM - This is your product identity; i.e., I am a senior operations specialist, or I am a C-level business manager, or I am executive director specializing in non-profit environments.

2. WHY I AM - This is the validation for what you are; it will include some statements about key skill areas or functional strengths you possess and some results you have achieved.

3. HOW I AM - This is more personal; it speaks to how you do what you do. For example, "The reason I have been successful is because I..." where you include some behavioral strengths that line up with the product definition above.

The length should not exceed 30-45 seconds. In fact, your whole introduction should not exceed 2 minutes tops. If you are doing all the talking the focus is on you and it should always be primarily on the other person.

NEVER GO TO A JOB FAIR WITHOUT A MISSION

Remember, offers are seldom made at the job fair. A job fair is a place where the whole process begins or where you gain more information about companies.

Write down exactly what you want out of attending each job fair. When you exit the job fair, compare your goal with what you actually accomplished. If you didn't accomplish at least 90% of your target objectives, then review your mistakes and don't repeat them at the next job fair. Set a high level of activity and be specific in listing your goals. It will help you FOCUS.

If you were a Stewart, Cooper & Coon client, at a minimum you would have the following job fair goals:

■ To meet four new target companies with openings in my field.

■ To find out salary ranges for people with my skill sets.

■ To practice face-to-face interviewing skills with 6 new companies.

> No matter what you're looking for, you can increase your chances for success by:
>
> Preparing well for the companies you want to meet.
>
> Having a system for working the floor - both inside and outside the main event site.
>
> To follow up with everyone you meet.

After you have set your goals, identify and research the companies with whom you want to connect. Analyze the list of attending companies, select your choices in advance and start researching. Don't just walk around from booth to booth.

JAMES K. LONG

999-999-9999   Jklong@comcast.org

CFO

www.webprofile.info/JLong

- Cross-Functional Leadership
- Performance / ROI   631 Charles Ct.
- Process Imp. / Project Mgmt.   Somewhere, IN 46999
- International Management   999-999-9999

- 20% reduction in compensation costs from productivity studies
- $6.0 million improvement from employee think-tank
- 89% improvement in manufacturing discrepancies
- $15 MM Cash Improvement From Inventory

Prepare a business card with 2 sides with the contact info visible and your webfolio or personal website prominent. Put three or four bullet points on the front showing your core competencies. No more than four accomplishments on the back of card. Give them out to everyone! But, collect more than you give. That way you can control the follow up.

Visit Websites. Read news releases. Try and get a copy of each company's job listings. Set up a grid to match your skills with companies that interest you. Be able to articulate why you are interested in a particular company. You WILL be asked this question.

Call the people whose names you found in your research and suggest meeting them at the job fair. If they aren't going to be there, ask for the name of the person(s) who will be representing their division. Having a contact's name helps focus your thinking.

Practice your 30-45 second career summary. This is the famous statement, "Tell me about yourself." Sometimes this is also known as your elevator speech. Write it down, commit it to memory and practice it OUT LOUD with your search partner. This is covered in the next unit, *Controlling Your Interviews.* Customize your career summary by focusing on the company, the product and the link to your specific skills.

Make a schedule and stick to it. Remember that job fairs tend to be crowded. Allow plenty of time to find a parking space. Prepare a 4-item tool kit consisting of business cards, resumes, notebook and manila folder. Put business cards in a jacket pocket and resumes in a folder.

Bring a notebook to make notes on EVERY conversation that you have. Be relentless in writing down the names of everyone you meet, highlights of your conversation and what you promised to send them. Attach a manila envelope to your notebook and put business cards from those you meet inside this envelope.

One never gets a second chance to make a first impression. First impressions are critical. Therefore, before you go, have someone evaluate how you look. People are prejudiced about the funniest things. This is a sure eliminator and your job search goal is to be the last one standing. Do your job and dress for success.

Working the job fair floor is an art. It involves critical time management and customized strategic planning for every company of interest. Plan on leaving a resume with every company where most of your skills match with the company's needs. Don't leave a booth without a business card and a follow-up commitment of some kind. Whatever you do, send a THANK YOU to everyone you met.

Create a positive "hook" so that people will have an easy time remembering you. Don't be another "me too" candidate. Remember that lots of jobs are obtained not because of technical qualifications but because of the right chemistry. Make yourself someone who interacts in a fun manner - someone with an upbeat attitude.

 The smart way to begin networking is simply by asking people for advice.

b-18

Go to all the social events no matter how tired you are. It's a lot easier to talk with a company executive while you are standing in a food line than it is to call the office and go through a gatekeeper.

THE HIDDEN JOB MARKET

The emphasis changes dramatically in the hidden job market. Here there are no defined or advertised job descriptions and, consequently, no competition. On the other hand, because nothing is clearly defined, finding a job in the unpublished job market can take longer than in the published job market. Here are three different avenues for creating your ideal job in the unpublished job market.

NETWORKING

Networking is a vital resource in your search. In fact, it may be the most important of all the methods you employ. The first rule you learn is that under no circumstance whatsoever should you approach networking by asking someone to help you find a job!

Here are some types of people who are probably in your network:

- Past and current peers, managers and subordinates
- Past and current customers and prospects
- Past and current vendors
- Consultants with whom you have worked
- Members of trade and professional associations of which you are a member
- Other business contacts and friends
- Alumni from high school, college or graduate school
- Past teachers or professors
- Neighbors
- Church, synagoque, temple or mosque contacts
- Sporting groups and fraternal organizations
- People who serve you - doctors, lawyers, accountants, etc.
- Military associations and groups

Start by saying that you are considering trying something new and, since they are already in the field, you would like to ask them a couple of questions about their industry. If approached in this way, most people are more than willing to give advice.

Step 1: The best way of getting launched into networking is to sit down with a pad of paper and list everyone that you know and where they work. Most people immediately begin thinking only of business associates.

While this may serve as a starting point, this approach is too narrow. Don't forget friends, neighbors, church members, merchants or vendors, old college roommates, fraternity brothers or sorority sisters. My barber once introduced me to another of his customers. This man has become an important contact in an industry I wanted to penetrate as a recruiter.

> ### Don't leave the office or get off the phone without having received the names and phone numbers of at least three other persons they know.
>
> h-27

Don't exclude people who are not at your professional level. I know of some very senior level clients who received leads from their barbers, gardeners or other unlikely sources

Step 2: Once your list is "complete," list all those people in the ATS system (www.RAH2010.com) or use one of the programs I mentioned previously.

The most likely approach will be to start with your list of business or trade associates. Plan on giving them a call or stopping by to see them. Graciously accept everything that they

tell you. Keep good notes on tidbits of information. But more importantly, find out whom they know or would recommend you contact to get more information.

> You should begin networking after you have finished with recruiter follow-up.
>
> b-19

If you are unemployed and have left your last position on less than stellar terms, you will want to carefully craft how you approach old business and trade associates. Under these circumstances, it is very easy to get sucked into airing dirty laundry about your former company or boss. **DON'T!**

Keep following any referral leads until you locate someone who can answer the burning question, "Does your company employ candidates with my qualifications?" "No? Then could you suggest three people or companies I can contact that are hiring candidates with similar credentials."

Networking can be fun but it can also be intimidating. Start out with people you know and let them lead you to people they know. As you move farther away from your circle of reference, realize that you will have to sharpen your information-gathering techniques. Hanging over the back fence is acceptable with a neighbor but not when you are meeting with your neighbor's boss.

Networking is unique in another way. It is a rich field that you can continue to cultivate for information and leads. Keep members of your network informed on your progress. Keep asking them for advice. Send personal thank you notes or buy them an occasional lunch. This is most appropriate for very good leads. This represents a process that can evolve into a continuing source of good leads.

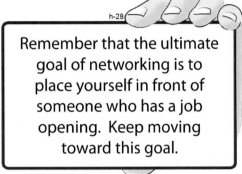

Remember that the ultimate goal of networking is to place yourself in front of someone who has a job opening. Keep moving toward this goal.

There is a very good reason for this short delay. Recruiters should be able to tell you how marketable your skills are in any given area. This information will allow you to tweak your career summary, resume and other documents and hone your presentation to fit market conditions.

It is very easy to get locked into a networking group that is fun, but is offering no new information. Make friends out of the members of this networking group, but move to more goal-oriented networking.

EVENT OPPORTUNITIES

Another way of penetrating the unpublished job market is by reading business articles in newspapers, trade magazines and business journals. These articles usually revolve around four topics: growth, executive change, new product launches, or corporate problems. Many of these might offer an opportunity for someone with your skills.

If a company is growing or launching a new product, they might be hiring. An executive change indicates that someone might be putting a new team together. Problems within a company also offer opportunities, especially if you have the management or marketing skills to solve that problem.

The approach to use is to write a "fan" letter. Reference the article that you have read and offer your congratulations on positive events. Briefly present your skills and ask if they would be willing to talk with you regarding possible employment.

If you are responding to an article regarding company problems, do not reinforce the negative. Point out that you have lived through a similar situation and have the skills to help the company through their current challenge.

If you are incredibly lucky, someone on your networking list may help open the door into the very company about which you have just read. Use your LinkedIn Network to reach out and "touch" the person you wish to contact. Also, plan on following up by telephone with all people to whom you have written.

 You should begin looking for career opportunities immediately.

b-20

DIRECT MAIL CAMPAIGNS

This is the job seekers equivalent of junk mail. Here you select a list of companies that fit certain research criteria. Your approach is to prepare a snappy direct-marketing letter about yourself and your skills and mail it out.

As I said before, there are companies advertising on the web that, for a small fortune, will send out 3000-12,000+ letters, claiming that this will get you a job. Well, that's great, but a 7,000-item mailing could turn out to cost $10,000, or more, when all is said and done. Too expensive for me. How about you?

The purpose of this initial mail-out is to inform companies of your existence. Many will find your background attractive. However, only a few (typically 1 to 3%) will have a current need. It is from this smaller percentage that your interview invitations will come, if at all.

YOUR MARKETING LETTER

Your marketing letter should be straightforward and short (1 page), expressing interest in employment with the company and highlighting those qualifications most likely to be relevant to their company's needs.

The letter should make a strong benefits statement and outline relevant skills. It should be addressed to an appropriate member of the management team, either by name or position title (i.e., Director of Operations or Manager of Systems Analysis).

If in doubt about who is the proper addressee, aim high. Stuff rolls downhill, not uphill.

Your cover letter should NOT contain data already stated in your resume. Include two accomplishments to support your proposed "fit" with that company. The cover letter **should** identify your specific strengths that address specific issues.

FOLLOW-UP STRATEGIES THAT WORK

1. References - Let them know if a prospective employer might call them. Provide them with information about both the company and the position. Keep them informed regarding your progress.

2. Recruiters - Depending on the number involved, you should follow-up with all recruiters who do not contact you. Your objective is to generate interest in you and your skills, to gain some valuable information about the market and how it applies to your particular background, or to gain a referral to another recruiter.

3. Associations - Follow up with any association or association member who expresses an interest in you or your skills.

4. Ads - You should plan on beginning your follow-up about two weeks after you send in your resume. If nothing more, you want to learn where the company stands in its hiring process.

   Try and locate the person booking the interviews. Ask if you are on the list to be interviewed or when that list will be chosen.

5. Networking - Follow up on all leads and keep your networking contacts informed of your progress.

6. Event opportunities - Begin your follow-up about two weeks after you mailed your "fan" letter.

7. Direct mail - You should anticipate following up with about 10 to 15% of those companies who do not contact you.

8. Social Networking - Keep building your network!

Important Note

Create a separate section in your three-ring binder and track all 50-250 weekly activities.

SUMMARY

STINKIN' THINKIN' OR ACTION PLAN BLUES: The secret is staying consistently active and following-up. You should be doing about **50 - 250 job search activities** (ads, trade associations, job fairs, networking, direct mail or business articles) **every week,** depending upon whether or not you are employed, until you find your next position. Enter all activity into the ATS and chart your progress, or use one of the programs I've already recommended.

False Evidence Appearing Real:

If perception is reality, and it is to most people, we also need to recognize that we follow input.

Sample 1-Minute Commercials

Manufacturing Executive:

I am an Executive Manager with proven international experience in Products Manufacturing businesses. The industries I worked include both consumer and industrial electro-mechanical products like semi-conductor switches, heavy duty truck components, flow meters and instrumentation.

My core competencies include Leadership & Management, Start-Up Initiation and Management, Technical & Operations Management, Sales & Marketing and Total Quality. I have successfully managed operations in the USA, Ireland, UK and Germany, and have established manufacturing Joint Ventures in India and China. I have co-founded technology based Start-Ups, created their organizational structure, and grew sales exponentially. In one situation I increased operating income 413% (from $0.75 million to $3.1 million) by increasing sales from $18.3 to $21.1 million and reducing product cost by $0.5 million.

I am an effective leader who can apply my strategic, operational and technical know-how to solve business problems, introduce new products, penetrate new markets, reduce cost, and grow the enterprise in a profitable manner.

Strategic Business Development:

I am a strategic business leader specializing in enterprise technology planning, implementation and business development. My strategic planning and business development efforts have led to over $40 million in new business with total forecasted revenues of over $100M. I have supported the planning, evaluation and development of enterprise technology architectures including a $2B transformational mission operations system for the US Air Force and led engineering and integration of the largest data network in the history of warfare in support of Operation Iraqi Freedom and Operation Enduring Freedom.

I have supported the turnaround of countless projects through process improvement and team building, contributing to saving a $200M telecommunications management agreement and growing the account by $35M. My strategic business recommendations have led to multi-million dollar corporate investments and sustainable revenue and profit growth.

I have been successful because I listen carefully and take practical approaches to solutions. My ability to develop lasting customer and stakeholders relationships is critical to my success. The relationships I develop allow for open and candid communication on critical issues leading to a more effective assessment of needs and resulting solution approach.

Sales and Marketing:

I am a senior level executive specializing in Sales and Marketing.

I possess high level skill sets in Leadership, Sales Management and Business development. I established and grew a start up Footwear Company by producing $700,000 in the first year of sales and reached $2.3M in revenue during the second year of operation. I launched an Italian shoe brand in the US that had struggled for 3 years prior to me arriving to produce annual revenue of $1M. In just short of two years, I drove sales to $12.5M and established a brand in the US. I grew a non-existent (major shoe company name) business at (major retailer) from virtually nothing to $6M in 18 months and then took that $6M to $19M over the next three years.

I have succeeded in every role or venture I have been a part of because of my leadership and relationship management skills, strategic thinking and planning abilities and my knowledge and understanding of retail and how to build and grow a brand.

Marketing and Sales:

I am a marketing and sales professional for with over 20 years of experience primarily in cable and telecommunications. I have substantial expertise in areas including New Product Launches; Strategic Planning; Customer Acquisition and Retention; Project Management; Budget Development & Control; Team & Employee Development and Product Branding/Bundling. In fact, a recent bundling and customer contract program has generated over $6 million in incremental revenue and is being embraced nationally by the company.

I've been successful due to a focus on driving results with special attention to ROI and Cash Flow and the ability to fill my teams with strong executives.

IT Director:

I am a senior level IT manager with a broad IT background, and experience in programming, business analysis, plant operations, environment architecture and Data Center operations management.

I posses strong people management skills and have a track record of building successful technical teams. I've successfully designed, built and implemented a worldwide Data Center operation from the ground up. The facility was 5500 square feet and provided offices for 20 people. It was the network-operating center and access point for all worldwide systems implemented including the company ERP. The facility and all its contents were implemented on time with a budget of 5 million dollars. I've led a technical team through a successful recovery of a Data Center that was destroyed by a natural disaster. I also have strong budget management skills, having created a 10 million dollar expense budget. I've also provided architecture leadership for the creation of two Data Centers.

I've been successful because I believe in providing an environment for team members to participate and not fear failure. I believe management must allow for risk taking and individual involvement. I'm a very approachable, passionate person that believes hard work produces satisfaction and success. Eliminating obstacles from team members so they can have success is a key component of my management style.

Chief Marketing Officer:

I'm a senior executive with more than 20 years of management experience in the healthcare industry. I've worked for large multi-million dollar supplier organizations, the largest healthcare system cooperative in the US and a technology start-up company. I have consistently excelled at integrating existing businesses resulting in the development of effective internal processes and the introduction of cohesive brand image and product lines to the market.

The foundation of my success has always been my ability to learn new areas of healthcare and the businesses that support them. Throughout my career, I have built effective strategies based upon the critical business objectives and the current market conditions. While at VHA, I had marketing responsibility for six very different businesses ranging from clinical to IT to administrative business services and outsourcing with a wide range of target audiences including administrative executives, clinical leaders, department heads and individual physicians. I also led the pharmacy business unit for (major drug company) and started the Non-Acute Care business unit for XXXX. At YYYY, I quickly learned the claims processing business and the healthcare insurance market.

What sets me apart is my ability to get results through a high-performance team made up of cross-functional team members. I care about their success and can define the purpose of a company objective, paint the vision as well as their role in that vision. I introduce the high level plan and lead them through the planning process for their respective areas. As a team, we execute the plan and celebrate the successes.

Chief Information Officer:

I am a senior executive, team leader and accomplished individual contributor. My expertise ranges from re-engineering business processes to developing information systems. I am a leader in the organization first and a technology resource second. Within the technology framework I have managed project portfolios in excess of $40 million in size and staffs in excess of 100.

As someone with excellent communication skills and broad management experience, I have distinct competency in understanding all sides of complex issues and brokering the conversations between business and technology organizations. I have the ability to integrate technology, human capital, financial, and business objectives as to increase the bottom-line performance across all business operational sectors. I am successful in these endeavors as I can communicate effectively to, with, and between engineers and end users to achieve productivity between these often diverse elements.

The foundation of my success has always been my flexibility to quickly learn new industries, implement innovative strategies or tactics, and adapt to dynamic companies and industries. I thrive with a challenge and excel in situations that seem impossible or unattainable.

Engineering Executive:

I am a business executive, team leader and accomplished technologist, having worked in both small business start-ups and billion-dollar corporations. My expertise ranges from re-engineering business processes to developing information control systems. As someone with excellent communication skills and broad management experience, I have distinct competency in understanding al sides of complex issues and brokering the conversation of problem resolution and change management.

I have consistently excelled in realizing business enhancements at increasing levels of responsibility, whether in operations initiatives such as cost reductions, cycle time improvements and process automation, or management programs such as outsourcing partnerships, personnel growth and new ventures.

My overall success in 25 years of product development, international business management and cross-functional team leadership comes as a direct result of skillfully leveraging my key professional assets - proven innovation skills in several technology disciplines, and proven management skills in both product- and service-based business.

VP Marketing:

I am a proven leader with 18 years of marketing experience in business-to-business, service companies, complimented by a background in sales, sales training and customer care. Throughout my career, I have built or overhauled departments; infused teams with energy and motivation, and established cohesive cultures that produced results.

At every company I served, I have increased target market awareness, while doubling or tripling the size of the account base and annual revenues; regardless of whether they were in new and emerging categories, struggling to navigate identity changes or in the middle of acquisitions. For example, my present company contracted with the number one companies in the categories of retail printers, office superstores, newspapers and direct mail based on the marketing messaging and materials I created, which ranged from design templates for end customers to training tools for their associates.

The foundation of my success has always been my flexibility to quickly learn new industries, implement innovative strategies or tactics, and adapt to dynamic companies and industries. A case in point is that, in just a few weeks at no cost, I developed customized materials for various vertical markets that both (major office store chain and (major office store chain), with all their marketing resources, used to promote design services and drive store traffic.

What sets me apart is my ability to exceed expectations despite minimal budgets, resources and time. Whether it's re-branding a company in 45 days with a very minimal budget or creating a unique, week-long sales training program in 30 days with no budget, I thrive in situations that seem impossible or unattainable.

Director of Operations – Manufacturing:

I am a senior operations/manufacturing leader specializing in food and beverage products and processes.

I have successfully transformed multiple facilities and achieved a 300% production capacity increase, cut employee turnover by 80% and raised the quality performance by 27% using Lean Manufacturing and 6-Sigma tools and techniques. I have doubled a business unit's profit in a turn-around situation as well as led an already successful plant to even higher levels of profitability and achievement.

I am successful because I am skilled in cross-functional management, and have the ability to focus on people and their professional needs while taking a big picture/holistic view of the entire process to maximize results for the customer and the company.

Management Executive – Operations:

I am a veteran with 24 years experience in management, operations, and resource management through the U.S. Army.

I am a team player and a team builder with a "hands-on" style. I have molded several staff elements into highly successful teams, proactively addressing the many needs of 205,000 soldiers. I am a strategic planner, who looks at not only the big picture, but can analyze the details to mitigate risk. I have made significant contributions to congressionally mandated programs involving the annual justification of 15,000 manpower requirements and the $527 million dollars needed to support the Army and its soldiers. The Army has recognized me for these skills through promotion to Lieutenant Colonel and several awards for meritorious service.

I am currently looking for a position where my leadership experience, my management style, and operational and resource management skills are used to the benefit of a progressive company and its employees.

FEAR Quiz	Exercise 7.1

False Evidence Appearing Real:
If perception is reality, and it is to most people, we also need to recognize that we follow input to create these perceptions. One filter is our own fears. In most cases, we don't use the right evidence to draw proper conclusions.

In the list below are words or tasks you may be uncomfortable with. Indicate your feelings as follows:

Identify F.E.A.R.'s

1.	
2.	
3.	
4.	
5.	
6.	

Now you must write down why you feel uncomfortable and at least two things you are going to do to attack the problem areas indicated by all 1 & 2 responses.

Problem:		
FEAR

1 | What two things are you going to do to attack this problem?

1.

2. | |

Problem:		
FEAR

2 | What two things are you going to do to attack this problem?

1.

2. | |

Problem:		
FEAR

3 | What two things are you going to do to attack this problem?

1.

2. | |

Exercise 7.1

Problem:		
FEAR 4	What two things are you going to do to attack this problem?	

1.

2.

Problem:		
FEAR 5	What two things are you going to do to attack this problem?	

1.

2.

Problem:		
FEAR 6	What two things are you going to do to attack this problem?	

1.

2.

Example: ACTUAL CANDIDATE REFERENCE CHECK

REFERENCE # 1 -
        Mr. John W. Smith, President
        Stewart, Cooper & Coon
        1234 West M St.
        Phoenix, AZ 85037   602-777-8888

1. Relationship with Candidate at last position   : Worked under Candidate in Alabama working for Allcrest Pipeline Construction Company. Worked not only for him, but also with him, as a peer. Both were in a consulting capacity.

2. Strengths : Candidate has a very broad knowledge base of construction, engineering, field procedures and all the requisite skills needed to identify and solve problems. Candidate was involved with a lot of technical and environmental issues. Candidate was the overall program manager charged with responsibility to get the company out of hot water with the Department of Energy and the US Congress. He pulled people together and saw that they stayed focused.

   He had a lot of inexperienced people working for him and it required him to take technical staff with very little knowledge or direction and bring them up to speed quickly. He did an excellent job and when he left it was a self-running program. Candidate spent about half his time in the field in the trenches and half in the office.

3. Weaknesses : Very goal- and task-oriented and drives himself a little too hard.

4. Accomplishments   (example) At Allcrest, he took a company under litigation and staggering revenue losses with high pressure to stop the bleeding and when he finished they had credibility, trust of the government, state regulatory agencies and the field personnel of Allcrest Pipeline Co. At the Nordstrom Nuclear facility, he worked with a diverse number of groups, each with its own agenda, to get them to pull together on difficult tasks. Candidate was totally responsible for entire program.

5. Ethical/Honest : Absolutely

6. Left employment because: Contract expired

7. I would hire (not hire) him again because   : The way he is able to work with both employees and management to build a team that produces.

8. Overall Opinion : Candidate would be an asset to any company.

9. Ability to Perform: Intelligent person with excellent performance

10. Work ethic : Exceptional

11. Meet deadlines : Never know him to miss one.

12. Ability to work under pressure and example: The Nordstrom Nuclear Facility was facing sanctions and fines by the NRC. Candidate developed a program the NRC recognized went above and beyond the issues and charges and caused the facility to receive a clean bill of health.

FINAL COMMENTS: Any company that would end up with the candidate will have a tremendous team player and a person able to get performance from all levels of personnel without adversarial nature of doing so.

Exercise 7.3
Example Reference Letter

June 5, 2010

To Whom It May Concern:

I've been asked to provide a reference for John Archer. I believe John is a very accomplished marketing professional with a wide array of experience, particularly in the areas of database and direct marketing. Perhaps the best way to describe his ability is to cite a specific example of results he and his company, Database Marketing Associates, achieved for me.

When I met John, I was (title) for FEC Enterprises, Inc., a start-up dot.com company. We had recently hired a sales force to handle inquiries, but our media advertising wasn't working. We needed to quickly generate inquiries. John developed a highly targeted direct mail program using both postal and email, delivering messages containing a specific offer to incent response and providing several convenient ways to respond. We literally began to get responses the same day the campaign dropped. The combination of postal and email provided both immediate and ongoing sources of inquiries. The program resulted in 1,120 postal inquiries at a cost of $84 each, and 1,764 email inquiries at $64 per inquiry, compared to a cost of over $1,200 each for the few inquiries generated through media advertising.

This is just one example of many inventive and successful direct marketing programs John developed and implemented on our behalf. I'd encourage you to give him the opportunity to achieve the same kind of results for your organization. Please contact me if you would like to speak personally.

Yours truly,

Reference #1
Title

Exercise 7.3
Example Reference Letter #2

June 4, 2002

Re: John Archer

To Whom It May concern:

John Archer has asked me to serve as a professional reference for him as he pursues career opportunities. At the time of our association, I was Senior Vice President of Sales for Digit Corporation of Chicago, the county's leading printer. In June of 1996, Digit purchased John's firm, Apex Industries. Digit purchased the company in part because we wanted to leverage our sales organization by giving them an entirely new line of products to sell our existing clients. Since Apex's sales force was calling on the same customers as Digit, there seemed to be a lot of synergy. However, it soon became obvious that expecting check sales people to sell direct response products wasn't realistic. We needed to quickly develop a workable sales model.

Because of his experience in the industry and his role as National Sales Manager at Apex, I asked John to head up the creation of a Field Sales Specialists group made up of people from the direct response industry with a lot of technical expertise and some sales background. These people would work as a team with our check sales reps, our folks getting the appointment, and the FSS demonstrating the product and answering technical questions. This allowed us to capitalize on long-established relationships without embarrassing our check reps in front of their customers by asking them to sell something that they didn't understand.

John accepted the challenge and agreed to serve as Director of Business Development for Digit's newly created Direct Response Division. In this capacity he reported directly to me. Not only did he do a superior job of recruiting and training our nineteen-member FSS group, but he demonstrated a unique ability to manage and motivate his team in a very difficult situation. Although John's FSS group's only charge was to introduce the new direct response product line to Digit customers, he and his team members had to depend on our check reps to get appointments and close sales. Since direct response products were not the check reps' only responsibility, John's job also involved promoting teamwork between the two groups, a task he was unusually well suited for.

Although John and I ultimately both left Digit through a series of divestures, we have remained in contact. Because of my respect for John's abilities, I have retained him as a consultant on a number of occasions in my current capacity as Senior Vice President of Sale and Marketing for Home Land Purchase Systems. I can heartily attest to John's qualifications as an outstanding sales, marketing and business development leader. Should you wish to discuss John's qualifications further you may feel free to contact me at (phone) or via email at (email).

Truly yours,
Mitch Honner
Title

CANDIDATE MARKETING PROFILE

Name:	
Address:	
Contact Info: Home # Cell # Office # Pager # Email Note best time to call & where	
Job Titles/Positions Held:	
Compensation Expectations Current Rate/Salary	

Top Skills	Yrs. Of Experience	Rate 1-5 (5=Guru)

Current/Last Assignment/Project: Scope of Work Where Duration Who do you report to Team	

You should copy this form, fill out each section, and have it ready to send to a recruiter who expresses interest in you.

Exercise 7.4

Why change? For each position on the resume, tell us why you were no longer employed there. Example: Most Current: Next to Most Recent: Next Back: Next Back: Next Back: Were you ever fired or asked to resign, and for what reason(s).	Promoted
Do you anticipate counter offer or more projects at this current company?	
Availability: If contract work, when is the start date for next Assignment: Best time to interview	
Ideal Assignment 1st Choice 2nd Choice 3rd Choice	
Ideal Work Environment	

Date: _____

Signature: _____

Exercise 7.4

Ideal Companies to Work For	
Career Goals	
3 Primary Motivations or Hot Buttons	
Recent Achievements/- Accomplishments What Where When How With whom	

List Past Supervisors/References	Titles	Contact #

Date: _____

Signature: _____

Exercise 7.4

Pending Opportunity Position (Where have you been submitted in last 5 mos.)	Company	Rate	Interest Level Rate 1-5 (5=Highest)	Consulting Company
Interviews in the Last 5 Mos.				

Who would you consider Gurus in your fields of interest? Locally Nationally	
Best resources of employment opportunities?	
What are your expectations of our company?	

Chapter 8
<<< Controlling Your Interviews

"Always Half-Full"

If you are not in control, you're out of control...
(Fred E. Coon)

K. You now have an interview scheduled. Now, you must *really* do important homework - both written and verbal - to survive the next phase of this process. I mean, why would you have worked so hard to get this far and then blow it because you thought you could wing it.

In this chapter, I've avoided the really heavy in-depth discussions of cognitive dissonance. However, I've described them in terms of how to use this technique to control the interview. This is a critical issue in your achieving more money and a better position with the company with which you are interviewing. This chapter also addresses do's and don'ts of interviewing dress, styles, language and other eliminator issues.

PRELIMINARY ISSUES

In this chapter, I would like to share with you the exact interview control techniques I teach my clients.

Before we get to these, however, I want you to think back to when you interviewed for your last position. Were any of the following questions being asked, "What did your W-4 show for last year?" "What are you currently making or what did you make last year?" or, "What are you looking to make?" All of these mean trouble. Answer them up-front and YOU LOSE, BIG TIME.

Most of my clients have told me that not only were these questions asked in some form or another, but that they found themselves capitulating to company probing and information gathering pressure tactics far too early in the interview process. If you, like them, give in easily, then you are giving away not only precious position advantage, but also your power to control your monetary package.

No matter what form these questions take, most candidates feel compelled to quickly provide the interviewer an answer. I mean, if you don't, won't you be considered dishonest or evasive? Absolutely not. Don't be foolish and give your power away. If you do, you lose! It's that simple.

> You are there to learn as much or more about them than they will learn about you so that you may make an intelligent decision about working there.

h-29

An Italian advisor to the great houses of Italy, Prince Machiavelli, said that knowledge is power and any person who has it has the potential to control the events surrounding her/his destiny. You are asking right now, "OK, how do I take control and not lose my power?"

Before you ask this question, I want to explain my concept of power and control. I believe that to have control, you must gain power (knowledge) and in order to use this power to your advantage, you must build a *two-way* communication street.

Communication must flow in two directions. Your power begins with a minor amount of interview "housekeeping" or, what we call a thorough understanding of the protocols involved in scheduling and managing the interview process.

Knowledge begins with the gathering of information. Before you are hired, you will engage in several rounds of interview activities. Each activity will involve different methodologies. Each methodology requires a different approach and has a different set of rules. Ignore any of these, and you will eliminate yourself from competition. Follow these strategies, and you will remain viable in the interview game.

To this point, you have submitted your resume and, by doing so, have provided them with sufficient background information to justify the interview. The interview process is the ultimate gladiatorial event. As you already know from reading other chapters in this book, you either win or lose - there is no second place or chance.

The purpose of the traditional interview process is to allow the interviewer to justify why they should hire or eliminate you when they compare you with the half-dozen other finalists in front of them, any one of which would be qualified to fill the position for which you are applying. The other equally important purpose is for you to be able to size them up and make a good decision about working there.

Whenever you send correspondence, speak with secretaries, interact with other support personnel, conduct a telephone screening, or someone has told them about you, they will have begun to form an impression of you. They also provide a great source of potential knowledge.

Any material you send to them must be thoroughly checked and rechecked for grammar, spelling, punctuation, syntax, correctness of sentence structure and factual content.

 You never get a second chance to make a first impression.

b-21

Of equal importance is being nice to everyone you encounter. Remember, in small companies, the secretary who you just brushed off may very well be the owner's wife, daughter, or girlfriend.

Stop and think about everything you say before you say it and always show a positive attitude. Any conversations must be professional and friendly in nature.

However, save any jokes until you report to work. What do you want to be said about you before you report your first day at work? This impression follows you always and can open doors or create barriers.

PRE-INTERVIEW ISSUES

Interviewing is a deadly serious business. Blow it and you have eliminated yourself.

h-30

When they call you and tell you they would like to speak with you, or you call and arrange your meeting date and time, there are two questions to be answered. What is the time period for making a hiring decision? How long do you think the interview might last? These questions are important because:

■ They allow you time to prepare your interview answers and research the company.

■ They allow the company the opportunity to adjust the focus of the job description and duties. Nearly all job criteria change during the interview process. Therefore, be on the later time slot because you will want to interview against their latest criteria, not the earliest.

■ The latter question alerts you as to how well you're doing in the interview process. Knowing that you have been scheduled for an hour interview but it ends after 20 minutes is not a good sign. Being at the company for two hours when the original interview was only scheduled for one is a good sign.

Exercise 8.1

The Pre-Interview Questionnaire, Workbook, Unit 4, is a very useful tool. The information required to plan a "great" interview begins with these items and will help you be seen as better than the competition.

www.RAH2010.com

Print this out and put into your 3-ring search binder. Make copies for each of your interviews. Secure the following information as early as possible. You will need to incorporate the answers into your contact strategy long before a telephone, or face-to-face, interview.

Job Description

The job description provides invaluable information for planning an interviewing strategy. It also might help you determine a salary range and a benefits package.

Company Brochure

The company brochure will tell you what products or services they produce and what their overall corporate direction might be, thereby affording you an insight into the corporate philosophy and thinking so you can determine if you are a right fit.

Key Contacts

You should attempt to secure the names of the President and VP of whatever you are applying for and in whose division you will be employed. More importantly, you should attempt to secure the name of the person you will be reporting to and the name of the person they report to, as well.

Company's Products

Can you imagine anyone going to an interview and not knowing what products or services are produced, much less how they are made or delivered? How many divisions do they have? Are they a multi-location or multi-plant company?

Are these products or services obsolete? Do your homework!

WWW Address

Check the World Wide Web. It is almost overwhelming the amount of information available with the stroke of a finger. Use Linked-In or Zoom.info to develop a background on the person who is interviewing you.

Any information about your interviewer

This is critical intelligence you must have to be well-prepared. When calling a secretary or someone else in the company to ask another type of question, always inquire about the person who is to interview you and see if you can glean enough information about their background to help you form a strategy. Use light questions, not interrogation techniques. The web is the most powerful information source available to you.

If you are to interview with a human resources staff person, your approach will be entirely different than if it is the hiring manager or the person reporting to them.

Three Competitors

Not only are you to be concerned with internal interviewing, but you must also focus on the external issues as well.

You will recall in Chapter 5, how the Swiss missed an entire technological revolution and nearly buried the watch industry there.

10-K, other SEC filings or annual reports

If it is a public company, these tools become your best friend. It is like having a spy on the inside to tell you what you want to know - good and bad. These are the most valuable resources you can get your hands on to develop your response questions in the interview process. This information can be secured from the public

library, on the www and from your stockbroker. Do yourself a great favor and read the auditor's footnotes.

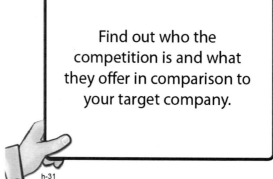

Find out who the competition is and what they offer in comparison to your target company.

h-31

Directions to the interview location

Prior to the actual interview you should plan on doing a drive-by or check out the directions on a map.

People often do not give good directions and nothing is more embarrassing than looking the hiring authority in the face and saying… "sorry, you're hard to find" or "sorry I'm late." He/she will most certainly think in the back of their mind, "You're hard to hire because we don't hire careless or unprepared people." A client of ours had four telephone interviews and was finally flown in for a face-2-face interview. When he left the hotel to go to the interview he asked the desk clerk for directions. You guessed it. They were wrong and he showed up over 30 minutes late, missed his panel interview, and, of course, did not get the job. Enough said.

Of course, you will have already identified the company and will have done your strategic homework. But in case you don't remember, here is a brief recap.

You should explore economic trends of the industry sector to which the company belongs.

Are the trends moving up or down? Is the targeted company moving with or counter to these trends?

 You must begin to prepare for the interview immediately after the date has been set.

b-22

Why or why not? Remember the Swiss watch industry example from earlier in the book.

The *Pre-Interview Questionnaire* should be completed as soon as possible after the interview is scheduled. Obtaining this information will set you head and shoulders above your competition.

Now that you know more about the company, take the job description and other information you learned in your preparatory investigation, put yourself in the interviewer's position and make a list of all the skills, technical proficiencies and character traits that you would want an employee to have.

Here is where you pull out your *Resume Worksheets, Exercise 3.5,* and use your "SHARE" stories to address the specifics of the job description. For example, if they want someone with supervisory experience, then develop a SHARE story to fit their need. You will use this in some form or another in your interviews. If you don't have a SHARE story already prepared that addresses these specific needs, develop one immediately.

The next move is to take the job description and list the items required down the left side of the paper and then a quick summary of your qualifications down the right side of the paper. This could take several pages of paper.

Use only cryptic notes on the right-hand side. No sentences! They take up too much paper. Now that you have completed this exercise, how do you look? During the interview process, each interviewer is taking mental or written notes. They are comparing you to the identified and hidden criteria for the listed position.

Exercise 8.2

Commonly Asked Interview Questions

If you look like you qualify for the position, use this exercise. Bear in mind that the main issues on the interviewer's mind are:

1. What can you do for me?

2. How will you fit in?

3. Can I justify the cost of hiring you?

www.RAH2010.com

You will do the same thing, only you will do it in advance of the interview. Take the job description and use this information in two ways. First, to write a letter to secure your interview and then, following the interview, as a beginning point for your follow-up letter.

Exercise 8.2.1

Interview Stress Questions
www.RAH2010.com

These will help you understand the do's and don'ts of constructing a proper answer. You can also revise your SHARE stories to fit the company where you are interviewing. You should now be ready to customize and develop answers specific to your situation. GO PREPARE YOUR INTERVIEW ANSWERS NOW.

From previous exercises, you have already prepared, in one form or another, all of the information you need to complete this exercise. Type the answers to each question.

Your answers should be succinct and never exceed 45-60 seconds in length when spoken. Whatever you do, don't "over share." Too much information could possibly eliminate you as well. Stick to the question and make your point, then SHUT UP!

The last bit of your pre-interview presentation is preparing your interview outfit. This should be completed well in advance. Don't wait until you are getting dressed to discover that your suit needs pressing and that you are out of shoe polish. Don't eat food that drips or splashes just before your interview nor during a second interview lunch with the hiring authority. If you are interviewing out of town, be sure to check the local weather forecasts before heading out.

INTERVIEWING PROTOCOLS: THE DO'S AND DON'TS

I almost didn't include this section in the book, but as a recruiter having to listen to some of my client companies complain about simple things that I take for granted about dress and simple protocol, I've included a few basic rules.

THE DO'S

1. **Dress Appropriately.** Business attire, business attire, and more business attire! Remember you are the CEO of your career and you are planning a major merger. Look the part.

If they tell you it is a casual office and everyone is wearing jeans and t-shirts, then dress casually but not sloppy. On the other hand, when in doubt-overdress.

2. **Come Prepared.** Have additional resumes and reference sheets. Carry these in a leatherette folder. Why not a brief case? Simple. Have you ever looked into someone's brief case and wondered about their organizational skills as they rummaged through it looking for something? With a folder it's hard to get too messy. Don't forget a professional looking pen and make sure that it works. Don't take one from the motel or your favorite insurance salesperson, with their logos displayed, to the interview.

3. **Arrive Strategically.** Not too early and not too late. About five minutes before the appointed interview time is about right.

This does not mean, however, pulling into the parking lot with two minutes to spare and bolting for the interviewer's office. Arrive with about 10 to 15 minutes to spare, casually collect your stuff, and confidently walk into the interviewer's lobby about 6-10 minutes ahead of schedule. Who knows, they might take you early and you will then have more time for your interview session.

I'm sure you don't want to be running to get there, worried about whether or not you have all of the requisite materials you need and sweating profusely over this. Like one great sports coach said, "Never let them see you sweat."

THE DON'TS
HOW TO BLOW ANY CHANCES WHATSOEVER...

1. **Those D---- Phones and Beepers.** There is nothing more irritating than sitting with a candidate and having their phone or beeper split the silence or an intense dialogue with rrrrriiiiinnnnnggggg or bbbbbuuuuuzzzzzzzzzz (representing some obnoxious or loud song).

2. **The Limp Noodle.** Shaking the interviewer's hand like you are a limp noodle causes most interviewers to feel very uncomfortable. Most likely, they think that you are insincere or weak or indecisive or not really interested in being there. Whatever they think, if they feel uncomfortable, then you failed the number two selection criteria - "will they fit in here?"

3. **The Bone-Breaker.** Breaking their hand while shaking it makes the interviewer feel uncomfortable. It also hurts.

4. **Perfumes and Colognes.** Some men and women insist on smelling like they are an advertisement for a perfume company. I don't know who told them to wear enough to knock over the office. Also, some perfumes and colognes don't mix with your body chemistry, no matter how expensive or trendy they may be. I worked with an HR person once who bought expensive perfume. Unfortunately, her body chemistry didn't work with that chemical oil base and it smelled like bug spray.

   I can't tell you how many times I've had to gasp and try to go with the interview, all the time thinking about how long it will take me to clear my office of the stench. When I am thinking about that, I am not focusing on you. It is the same for any person who interviews you. Think before you douse yourself.

   Worse yet, some interviewees put hand cream on their hands and then want to shake mine. The first thing I want to do is wipe it off. If I can't, all during the interview I sit there thinking about wiping my hands and not touching my tie or items on my desk instead of listening to what the candidate is saying. Ask yourself who loses in these encounters.

5. **Know-It-All.** Overbearing, over-aggressive, or "know-it all" attitude - Remember, "you attract more flies with honey than vinegar."

   In this context it means that you must do more listening than talking and quit trying to impress them with your ability to pontificate. If you are really good, your SHARE stories will speak volumes for themselves.

6. **Inaudible or Poor Voice Tone.** No one wants to have to strain to hear you. On the other hand, no one wants to run out for earplugs either. I remember a fellow I once knew who literally shouted everything he said and was a real embarrassment in public situations. It also goes without saying that if you have a uniquely unpleasant voice tone, and it calls attention to your "non-blendable" qualities, you should seek the help of a voice coach.

7. **Poor Grammar and Slang.** Almost without exception, if your grammar is poor, you might as well forget a long-term career ladder. Oh, you might get a job and decent

pay but at the point you decide you want to advance and fill a senior manager role, you are dead in the water.

Stop and ask yourself how many senior corporate managers from reputable, well-known corporations have you personally met who have poor grammar and language usage.

Do you think you will be paraded in front of an investor group to do a presentation to raise capital or communicate the growth potential of their company?

I've had clients who graduated from really well-known schools that verbally murdered sentence structure. Upon hearing it, to those of us who are in hiring roles or screening roles, it is like a grenade going off and can have extremely unpleasant after-effects for you.

This is one of the silent prejudicial barriers that will never be legislated against in this society. Many persons I interview today, especially young people, don't seem to be as well-spoken or prepared these days, but that is the subject for another book.

8. **Lack of Planning.** Almost always, you will be asked to tell them what your long- or short-range goals are or why you want to work at this company. If you can't provide them with a well thought out answer, you look unconcerned, unprepared and unprofessional. Any one of these will eliminate you from further consideration.

9. **Acting Passive.** The words passive and passion are very close in spelling and worlds apart in meaning and potential outcomes.

The difference between them is often the difference between winners and losers and those who will be hired and those who are not.

10. **Lack of confidence.** If you seem too nervous or ill at ease, you could not only make the interviewer feel nervous too, but also have them begin to suspect you might have something to hide.

The way you make sure to control this is to practice what you have prepared - over and over and over and over and over and keep repeating it until it is good enough. When you think it is good enough, remember my rule stating, "good enough, never is."

11. **Talking about your past failures.** The only time, and I mean the **only** time, you ever talk about "the" past failure (notice singular case) is when they ask you the interview question, "tell us about a past failure you've had and how you handled it." What a great opportunity to take one of your SHARE stores *that you have prepared ahead of time,* and share to your heart's content.

Why? Because you have the chance to turn a negative into a positive with the "E" portion of the SHARE story. This will demonstrate you are smart enough to learn from mistakes and to correct or modify your decision-making procedures to be a better manager or whatever you are. Please don't tell the worst thing that ever happened. Be smart enough to pick a not-so-bad story then build on that. Demonstrate what you learned.

12. **Bad-mouthing a past employer.** This one

is self-explanatory.

13. **Making excuses or being evasive.** Being evasive is a really bad interview technique. If you don't know the answer to something, tell them you don't and immediately follow up with, "I will provide you the answer in an email or follow-up interview." You may not come off looking quite as professional, but they know you are honest and not a BS artist, and will also realize you know how to deal with uncertainty and pressure. Then, follow up. Not to do so will eliminate your future with that company. Putting it in a more positive light, you get another shot at the interviewer.

14. **Poor eye contact.** I have a current client who is superior on paper, has a great personality, is verbally correct and otherwise presents a polished and professional image. He is also a really nice guy. Unfortunately, if you were interviewing him, and were to try to look where his eyes are moving, you would go dizzy and then crazy. I don't know who he is constantly looking at on my office ceiling, but they must be having a great conversation.

It is a real shame that some people don't understand this vital aspect of body language. The old expression, "the eyes are the window to the soul," is true. How many times do you pass judgment on someone by the expression on their face as seen through their eyes? Look straight at the interviewer and don't take your eyes off them for a moment during any question they ask you or during your responses. No exceptions.

15. **Industry Knowledge.** If you won't extend

the courtesy of gathering information and understanding their company, why should they take a further interest in your career?

16. **Being Late For The Interview.** We've covered this previously in its positive form.

17. **Seemingly Focused on Money and Benefits.** You are there for the money, of course, and in due time the entire discussion will focus on this critical issue. BUT NOT NOW!!

Letting them back you into the corner with statements like, "what did you make last year," or talking about money at all early in the interview process guarantees that you will give away your personal power and lose any chance at successful negotiation sessions. This will be explained further in a later section of this chapter.

18. **Bad Manners.** This area really needs no explanation other than to emphasize that your manners and your courtesy toward others are critical in establishing your image, and ensuring your position within your future workplace.

19. **Being Cynical.** It is rude, uncaring, unprofessional and unacceptable behavior. You are masking those "crazy tapes" Jim Farr said are being played because of past experiences.

Change this lifestyle and behavior, or suffer the consequences throughout your personal and professional life.

20. **Condescending Attitude.** I have interviewed with many people in my life. In some cases I was older, more experienced, more technically competent and just plain knew more about life than they did. Not one of them ever felt this from me. I really try to

take a genuine interest in people and feel I can learn from everyone I meet.

On the other hand, people who viewed themselves as the person who had invented sliced bread have interviewed me. When you meet them, and you will, grit your teeth, smile and then determine if you have to work with or for them, or if they might have an influence on your work or success, once you've been employed. If the answer is yes, then drop that company like a hot potato. It only gets worse, never better, when dealing with those people. Believe me, life is too short for that nonsense.

21. **Bad Handwriting.** There is nothing worse than getting something you can't read. Sloppy handwriting on any submitted material is inexcusable from you as an applicant, much less when you are working there.

My handwriting is really, really bad. I make it a special point to slow down and attempt to be legible whenever I fill out a form.

22. **Over Sharing**. When interviewing, don't over share. It's rude and, worse yet, wastes valuable time that could be spent on your SHARE stories or information gathering (power building).

The fact that you have a cat and two dogs and came from somewhere, USA, isn't that germane to your being hired. I interviewed one client and after 20 minutes, I just wanted to see how long he would actually ramble, he looked at me and finally said, "I guess I blew that, huh?" Point made.

23. **Indecisive**. As you should know by now,

people hire you because you can solve problems. Solving problems means that you can construct a plan of action, make a decision, and then properly execute it, regardless of the problem being managed. Go back to the SHARE exercises and practice your answers before your interview sessions. Know what you want from the company and the job before you walk into the interview.

24. **Being Intolerant.** I don't know of any organization worth its salt that actually likes hiring bigots, critical or generally intolerant people, do you? If you have an opinion about a particular ethnic group or belief system, keep your mouth shut, and hold your opinions to yourself.

Your personal opinions are just that, personal; don't take them to the office with you. Working as a professional is about focus on business. If you feel strongly that your opinions and personal beliefs are in conflict with company policies or workforce makeup, then look elsewhere.

25. **Smoking or chewing gum.** Don't ever smoke or chew gum in an interview, even if the interviewer offers you the opportunity. Don't ever go outside for a smoke between multiple interview sessions. It makes your breath smell, your clothes stink, and, if you put a mint in your mouth to cover it up, you violate rule number one - nothing in your mouth. More and more companies are now implementing a no-smoke or limited smoke zone at their companies. Every day, more are adopting a "no-hiring smokers" policy. Be smart, be kind to others and yourself and just plain don't smoke. In fact, just quit and

you will be better off.

26. **Whining.** Like I said earlier in the book, "nobody likes a whiner, but everybody loves a winner."

27. **Lack of a Sincere, "Thank You."** When you leave the interview, please remember to say a simple "thank you." Don't do this, and you will probably be remembered for it.

Thank them for their time, consideration, and informative session and BE GENUINE about it.

28. **Slouching and Posture.** Just like your dad or mom told you when you were younger, sit up straight, don't cross your legs, put your hands in your lap when not gesturing or making a point. Don't clasp your hands behind your head, don't look at the ceiling, don't swing or jiggle your crossed legs (if you must cross them) and for sure, don't pull or scratch at any of your body parts.

29. **Lack of Verbal Expression.** Only full sentences with understandable answers should come from your mouth. No techno-jargon unless you are interviewing with a techno person who asks you to explain a complex, technical issue and you are absolutely certain they will understand your answer.

Think about this a moment. You are being asked a question and they expect an answer. If you give them a simple "yes" or "no," you will have completely given up another wonderful opportunity to communicate why they should hire you. It's like going to the battlefield without any ammunition in your gun.

The good thing about this list is that everything on it can be cured. The difficult part is admitting that you have any of these problems.

TYPES OF INTERVIEWS

There are two or three types of interviews. The **info/referral interview** is just as the name implies - it's to get information. IT IS NOT TO BE USED TO ASK FOR A JOB! The **info/referral interview** usually comes about through a networking contact and works something like this.

1. Call up the referral, and tell him/her you have been referred by so and so and that you are considering a career move. Tell him/her that you have always been interested in either the products or services their company produces or delivers and that your networking contact suggested that you meet with him/her to get a better feel for his/her (industry, products, company type, etc.).

2. Go prepared with a list of specific information that you need to obtain. Since this is an **info/referral interview** only, you cannot immediately start asking questions regarding possible job opportunities at his/her firm. You initially want to ask some of the following:

   ■ How did you get started in this line of work?

   ■ Where do you see this industry going over the next 5 to 10 years?

   ■ What do you like best about this industry and company?

   ■ Where did you get your training? If

you were looking for a new position in this industry, what companies would you approach?

■ Does this industry generally promote from within?

■ What is a typical career path like? Having looked at my background, are there any other options or industries you think I should consider?

■ I am interested in the ABC Company. Do you know anyone over there with whom I might speak regarding opportunities?

3. At the end of the interview, ask the most important question, which is "Are there competitors or other companies in related fields where you would point me or where you might know anyone personally who I might contact."

4. If your interaction continues to be positive, you should close the interview by asking if the interviewer would like to be kept appraised of your success.

5. When you get home, the first thing to do is sit down and write a thank you note, and recap your experience, and attach an executive summary for their information. You never know when your Friday interview will be discussed at Saturday's golf game with your new boss.

The second type of interview is a **traditional, one-on-one interview.** Here, the objective is simply to sell your skills. Three types of **traditional interviews** are frequently utilized. They are telephone, panel, and face-to-face. There are also SKYPE interviews, which can be

either panel or single person interviews. These are becoming more widespread as of this writing. You should familiarize yourself with all forms of interviewing.

The telephone interview is usually a screening interview, and is often done in place of a face-to-face initial interview, if there is geographic distance involved between the interviewer and the interviewee. The HR Department usually handles this interview. Preparation for such an interview is the same as for a face-to-face interview.

Most telephone interviews are scheduled in advance.

 Don't accept a call without preparation time.

b-23

When the HR person or recruiter calls, do the following:

1. Thank them for the call.

2. Indicate you cannot talk then and set up a time to reconnect.

3. Request a copy of the job description (it may have changed).

4. While confirming your email address, ask the caller what the position pays. They Know! That eliminates pressure over salary questions later.

The panel interview is usually set well in advance so you'll have plenty of time to prepare. The strategy here is to try and find out the titles of all the panel members.

Then, try and address specific concerns of

each of the panel members or common concerns of several panel members. Have a sheet available to you so you may write down the names of the panel members.

Call each of them by name and be sure before the panel is over that you secure each person's correct name spelling, their title and specific function within the company. You WILL be sending each of them a thank you letter when you get home that day.

Panel interviews can be confusing and difficult. You might receive the same question from more than one member. Usually, they are not trying to trap you. It is more likely that one member didn't hear the other's question previously.

The traditional face-to-face interview is going to be either with a Human Resources Department employee or with the hiring authority or other key decision-makers within the company. As I've already said, you are better off interviewing with the hiring authority because the hiring authority is better able to match your skills to the needs of the position.

Often, you must start out with an initial interview with Human Resources. Take my word for it and, if at all possible, avoid HR at all costs. Try to get in front of the actual decision-maker as early in the process as possible.

Also, try to understand the function of HR in the interviewing phase. Out of all the resumes submitted, HR has the duty of selecting a small number for an initial interview. From this number an even smaller number of candidates are selected for an interview with the hiring authority.

There are certain points to keep in mind when interviewing with HR:

1. HR people generally know a lot about the company but really don't have a comprehensive understanding of the desires of the hiring authority nor the true daily duties as envisioned by that person.

2. The interview with HR is basically a chemistry test to see if you fit into the organization.

3. You almost certainly will be asked the question "tell me about yourself." In response, you will have prepared your opening statement that briefly describes your past positions and accomplishments. Pick accomplishments that match the position requirements and would be impressive to the interviewer. Don't forget you are trying to show them why you meet the three criteria better than anyone else they will interview.

4. Do your homework and be prepared. The type of questions you ask will form, in some small part, their overall opinion of you and indicate your level of interest in the company, position and future there. Here are some questions you should feel free to ask HR.

■ What is the company trying to accomplish that is new or different from what was done in the past?

■ How does the position that we're discussing fit into present and future goals?

■ What are the principal skills required to perform effectively in this position?

■ What about my resume, background or experience caught your attention?

■ What are some of the things you are looking for in how the person in this position works with you/your department?

VIDEO AND INTERNET(VC) INTERVIEWS

More and more, these days, companies are turning to video-conferencing (VC), or SKYPE-type interviews, which are very cost-, space-, and time-effective methods of interviewing. One of my former clients recently experienced several VC interviews and I asked him to share his thoughts for incorporation into this book. Here they are.

1. Video-Conferencing(VC) is an extremely cost-effective alternative to a face-to-face interview in a distant city. Consider the cost of air travel, hotels, ground transportation and meals compared to the cost of a one-hour VC session, which runs about $250.00 on the high side to $0.00 on SKYPE.

2. VC is also extremely time-effective. Consider the time it takes to go through security, wait for a flight, board a flight, travel to your destination, get your bags, get a car or cab, travel to the interview site, get ready for the interview (you didn't wear your suit on the plane, did you?) and then traveling back home again. Compare that to your own laptop. You'll have accomplished in a couple of hours what might have taken a day or more to accomplish. Moreover, those doing the interviewing get their shot all at once so they are not wasting time waiting for you.

As an aside, I recently had another client who interviewed with two decision-makers who happened to be in Australia on business from the U.S. He wound up among three finalists from a starting field of 16 contestants in line for the Presidency of a Washington DC corporation. Anyway, not to digress.

3. Before your VC session begins, review how you appear in the near (local) window of the monitor. Adjust the camera to shoot you from the chest up. Think of yourself as a newscaster.

4. Don't make sudden moves with your head, body or arms. VC transmission speeds (now familiar to anyone who has recently watched a video-phone newscast on CNN from Afghanistan) will blur quick movement, making you look to the viewer as if you're underwater. Keep still and if you have to move, do so smoothly. Periodically check your appearance in the "near" window to make sure you're head isn't tilting to one side and that you're still centered in the screen.

5. Aim the camera so that the viewer can't see the table in front of you. This allows you to spread out notes that you can refer to without the viewer seeing them. HOW ABOUT YOUR SHARE STORIES? RING A BELL? Feel free to glance at notes, your resume, the job description, printouts about the company, write notes, or whatever makes you feel more comfortable during the interview. But, always keep your eyes on, or returning to, the camera. No way do you have this level of freedom in a face-to-face interview!

6. Make sure that if you're having trouble

hearing or seeing, let the other person know so that it can be addressed and fixed, or even rescheduled. Don't risk blowing an interview because you can't hear the questions clearly.

7. Keep an eye on the time. Some VC sessions give you a warning 5-10 minutes before the session ends, some don't. It can be pretty jarring to have a VC interview end mid-sentence, so be aware of the time. It's better to have a clock on top of the monitor or on the wall in front of you, but if those aren't available to you, take off your wristwatch and put it on the table in front of you to avoid any potentially embarrassing movements checking your wrist for the time.

8. Suggesting to the employer that you start with a VC interview will win you points: You're on top of new technology, you're innovative, you're practical and you're interested in saving your potential employer money. The fact that you're saving yourself even more time and gaining advantages as well only increases the appeal of VC interviewing.

9. VC interviewing has advantages over phone interviewing, since the visual component adds comfort and intimacy missing from the phone. It's a great compromise between the hassle and expense of travel and the importance of a face-to-face- interview. However, it never replaces the power of a face-2-face interview.

10. If you know that the VC interview is only going to last an hour, prioritize a list of issues you'd like to address during the interview. Most VC sessions are billed in full one-hour increments, so make sure you make the most of the limited amount of time available to you. Scheduling a follow-up VC session is more of a hassle than simply continuing a successful face-to-face interview, so make sure you've covered your key points in the current VC session.

Overall, VC interviews offer the interviewee some real advantages over other types of interviews, though you should expect a face-to-face interview to follow if the employer is interested in you. But since you'll have already broken down many interpersonal barriers, expect a much warmer and more comfortable face-to-face interviewing experience when it comes.

No matter what else happens, your first priority, at all costs, short of losing the opportunity to interview, is to delay any discussions of salary or compensation.

CONTROLLING THE INTERVIEW

Let's start with the big question some of my clients ask. Most don't ask because they don't even know that the interview can be controlled. Confused? Let's start over. The interviewer asks you: *What did you make last year? Or, what did your W-2 show last year? Or, how much money are you looking for?*

What do you say?

If you answer too much you are eliminated. If you answer too little, you are eliminated or abused. Then you really get angry when you report to the job and find that you are being paid less than someone with equal skills, or less.

SUCCESSFULLY AVOIDING THE MONEY QUESTIONS

Let's get one thing clear from the beginning. You need to take control of this situation. To take control, here are a few retorts you may use to answer the question about money. Use the one you feel most comfortable with and best fits the nature of the position. Jack Chapman is an acknowledged expert in the negotiation area. Once again, I highly recommend his quick to read and high-impact book, Negotiating Your Salary: How to Make $1000 a Minute. All of us in career coaching have our own methods of delaying this question. I've condensed some of Jack's excellent recommendations and included a few of my own as well. These are in order of my preference, but feel free to select which ones work for you. Also remember, some interviewers are smart, have been there many times, and may press you for an answer. Try to fend them off two times. I tell my clients to use #7 the first time and #10 the second time. If those fail, give a range acceptable to you. If you've done your homework beforehand, you already know what that position pays in that geographical area so you will be pretty safe stating a range.

1. Are you making an offer?

2. Well, I'm sure we can come to an equitable agreement in that area since I'm sure you offer a competitive plan. What is the range for this position?

3. If you don't mind, let's hold off on salary discussions until we explore the nature of the position, the responsibilities and whether or not I'm the right person for the job.

4. You also might say, "I always feel uncomfortable discussing salary, so if you don't mind…, or, I'm happy to discuss my prior salary and packages in a few minutes but if you don't mind, for right now…"

5. I'm glad you asked that. I have researched positions with comparable titles within this geographical area and I'm sure you are within this range. What is your range for this position? OR, If you don't mind, let's hold off, etc.

6. In the past, I've been paid fairly for my efforts and skills and I'm sure you will do the same. Before we talk about money, why don't we determine if I'm right for this position and if the company if right for me?

7. I'm sure you and I can agree on a fair and equitable salary when the time comes, but right now, I would like to fully understand the responsibilities of the position and what the criteria are for meeting or exceeding company performance expectations.

8. Don't worry about salary because you and I can easily work that out. Quite frankly, the amount you pay me is not the highest criteria for whether or not I accept any offer you might make. I am more concerned whether I can exceed my own performance expectations and be happy working here. Could you tell me more about…?

9. Look. You and I are going to agree on salary. If I tell you what I want, you might

eliminate me before you even begin to know my capabilities. On the other hand, if you tell me what you want to offer, I might not like it and then for a few dollars, we both lose. Why don't we postpone this area of discussion until we have a clear understanding of expectations and capabilities? Could you tell me about…?

10. Salary? Well, I expect to receive what others of comparable responsibility in this company are being paid. By the way, what is the range for this position? I'll be happy to tell you if it fits. When they respond with a range simply reply, "Well, that's what I thought and we should have no problem reaching an accord in this area.

Now, could you tell me about…?"

Be aware. If, after two other solid uses of Number 1-10 they <u>still</u> ask you about salary, give it to them if you sense they are upset or will be so by not getting the information.

Immediately, upon acceptance of your range comeback, you must use one or more of the questions I provided earlier in the Controlling My Interviews Unit to engage them in a discussion of the responsibilities they see for this position. REMEMBER that you are trying to tell a SHARE story at every turn. This is the perfect chance to do so.

Well, enough about that. Let me put on my recruiter hat and share my views, as well as those generally practiced by my fellow recruiters, on this subject.

If the question of money comes from a recruiter, go ahead and discuss your past history with them. Remember, recruiters are in the business of placing you and, if you fit the criteria for the open job order, they will help sell you anyway. Also, we try to get the highest amount for you because recruiters are paid a percentage of your first year's salary. The higher your agreed-upon salary, the more money recruiters make. On the other hand, please keep in mind that we have multiple candidates to provide to the company, so don't be greedy about your negotiating position.

Your job description, especially during the interviewing and negotiation modes in your campaign, is closely akin to that of a salesperson, whether you like it or not. You are selling a product (YOU) to a corporate buyer (YOUR NEW BOSS). The universal rule any salesperson worth their salt will tell you is that he/she who speaks first loses!!!

Therefore, if you mention money first, you lose. Remember, they are not going to get mad at you for delaying the discussion. In fact, just the opposite often happens. Respect is earned.

Another important concept to remember is that the interviewing strategy shifts when speaking with the hiring authority. This person knows the job specifics and wants you to tell him that you have the skills needed.

You will be working for this person and they must feel comfortable you are the right fit, have the right skills and that they are getting their money's worth by employing you.

Now, I would like to introduce you to the term called *cognitive dissonance*. Basically, the theory is that if you create enough positive agreements between yourself and the interviewer and something goes wrong in the interview, using this technique effectively can salvage the interview.

Sometimes, you may not have all the qualifications they require; however, given your experience base, you are the best qualified. Your role is to help them see that. If, for any number of reasons, things go awry, and believe me they will, using the following techniques will put you light years ahead of your competition.

Let me give you an example. The "questions" shown below are general in nature, but will set the framework for using your SHARE stories to confirm "fit."

There are <u>five</u> major question areas you must address in exactly the following order to gain control of the interview and the negotiation sessions. They are: 1. Personal, 2. Job Description, 3. Performance Measurements, 4. Support, 5. Career Path, and 6. Personal and Growth Issues. There is a sixth question to be asked when all of this is done. It is, 7. "Where do we go from here?"

Each major question area builds toward a logical conclusion - that you are the right peson! None should be left out.

You would do well to follow this sequence in order to have a truly great interview and negotiation session. This sequence will help you determine if you really want this position, decide if you are capable, examine the work environment, predict your chances of job and economic success or failure, and whether you have a future with the company. Another advantage of using this method is that you have a really strong method to use when negotiating your package.

In presenting a discussion of the major issue areas, I used a summary from a coaching session with one of my recent clients, a regional sales representative with a Fortune 100 company. **After reading the following questions, take time and write out your own questions in each of the major categories. This is critical to a successful interview so don't get lazy now!**

> **At the beginning of each interview session you must ask permission to ask questions. The following statement works well. "Do you mind if I ask questions as we go along?" In most cases they will say yes. Always say, "THANK YOU" when they say "yes." Saying "Thank You" puts <u>you</u> in control of the interview.**

PERSONAL: GENERAL QUESTIONS FOR ALL JOB TYPES

1. Who occupied this position before?

2. What was their background?

3. How long were they in the position?

4. What successes did the person have in that position?

5. If successful, what caused them to be successful?

6. If not successful, what prevented their success?

7. What kind of personal qualities are you looking for in a person who takes this position?

   For example, self-directed, motivated, understand relationships, good with people, etc.

When they reply with what they are looking for, ask them to expand on a particular issue for which you have pre-prepared a SHARE story.

You then say to them: "It sounds like you are looking for a person with XYZ personal traits. Do you mind if I share an example of how I ....?" At this point, provide a SHARE story for the qualities or things they are looking for. An Example: "What is your definition of motivation? Could you be more specific?" Then, when they are specific, hit them with your "employee motivation" story.

JOB DESCRIPTION

In the questions below, insert relevant phrases from your particular field into the parentheses. If no parentheses exist, then it is a general enough question that you may use it regardless of the position you are seeking.

1. Please tell me about the job, what this position does and how it fits into the department, product line group, regional structure and company.

2. What will my specific duties be?

3. What is the extent of my authority?

4. What about my resume, background, or experience caught your attention?

5. Do I (acquire new accounts)?

6 Where do (they come from)?

7. Do I (take over existing accounts and grow that market segment of the business) or, do I primarily (look for new business)?

8. Tell me about the (type and number of existing accounts).

9. What problems seem to be developing or are on the near horizon?

10. How do you feel the (product or service) stacks up against the competition?

11. What do you feel your pricing and product advantage is over your nearest competitor?

12. How did your area do compared to (budget last year)?

13. How did this compare with other similar sized regions in the company?

14. How does the team I work with fit into (accounts management)?

15. Is an account team already assembled?

16. Do I assemble my own account team?

17. Do I solely call on the account or is there a team approach?

18. What is your role (in the acquisition) or (management) of my (accounts)?

PERFORMANCE MEASUREMENTS

These are critical to understanding how your performance will be measured. Develop your own questions as they apply to your field.

1. What is your expectation for (new account growth) in the next year, two years and five years?

2. What (dollar amount or percentage growth) are you looking for?

3. What is the (current budget)?

4. What factors do you see influencing (expected growth)?

5. How do you measure my success with (my

accounts)?

6. How many (contracts are coming up for renewal?)

7. How will I be measured? ($), (relationship), (levels), (account growth)? Put your specific area here. They are taken from the job description gathered during your research.

8. What is the timing for (learning the accounts), (processes), and (core business)?

SUPPORT

1. What comprises the current team?

2. How long have they been there?

3. Tell me about them.

4. How do they interact with the rest of the (company, division, accounts, etc.)?

5. What resources are available?

6. What type of people or manpower?

7. How much money?

8. What technical resources support this position?

CAREER PATH

1. Is there a comparable position in this area?

2. How long have they been with the company?

3. How is their career path structured?

4. How do you see this position in the company and where do you see it heading?

5. Are there other divisions in the company and

how are inter-division transfers handled?

6. What professional development path do you see for me?

PERSONAL AND GROWTH ISSUES

1. What is the company's continuing education policy?

2. Is successful completion rewarded by an increase in the package?

3. Is there a tiered perks structure?

4. Stock Option Plan?

5. 401-K plan?

6. Other Financial Plans?

Question 1 + Your SHARE story + Your closing question for this particular SHARE story area is: "does this seem to be what you were describing that you wanted?" + their confirmation that it is = A reason to hire you

Question 2 + Your SHARE story + Your question "it seems that my experience here is what you were describing, yes?" + their confirmation that it is = A reason to hire you

Question 3 + Your SHARE story + Your question "does this seem to be what you were looking for?" + their confirmation that it is = A reason to hire you.

Question 4 + Your SHARE story + Your question "this experience appears to match what you were describing, don't you agree?" + their confirmation that it is = A reason to hire you

Question 5 + Your SHARE story + Your question "it seems to me that this story really reinforces what you were looking for, agreed?" + their confirmation that it is = A reason to hire you

Question 6 + Your SHARE story + Your question "does this seem to be what you were describing?" + their confirmation that it is = A reason to hire you.

Later, when you sum up your interview session, you have at least six "agreements" about why they should hire you. If you are told that you are not qualified or there is something wrong with your candidacy, you have a concrete foundation to refer back to and to build upon in your attempt to salvage the interview.

By reminding them of all their agreements as to why you should be hired, you reinforce their positive thinking and possibly force them to rethink their objections and to be more open to exploring your candidacy further. As I said in the beginning of this chapter, communication is a two way street, but you must guide the flow.

Moreover, if you sail through without a hitch, then you now have a basis upon which to build for your package negotiations. Either way, you win.

HOW TO USE THE SHARE STORIES

Remember, they want someone who can make profitable decisions, will fit in, and from whose sweat they can make money. Let me take a minute and show you how to use your SHARE stories effectively.

You should have at least 5-6 SHARE stories for each position you've held during the last 15 years. For most people, this averages 18-24 SHARE stories, assuming 6 per position and each position held approximately 3-4 years.

At a minimum, you should develop 15

SHARE stories addressing the following areas: P & L management, people management, working with a group to succeed, working under pressure and succeeding, building working relationships with other (people, groups, accounts, vendors or whatever is specific to your job), a difficult technical problem or challenge and how you managed it, a personal SHARE about a failure and how you would do things differently now, among others. You may not ever have to tell your "failure" story, but trying to wing this one in an interview is guaranteed employment suicide.

Now, let's discuss the actual physical techniques of the interview process that incorporate your SHARE stories.

In CHAPTER 1, we mentioned your need to secure a portfolio that could contain a writing pad, your resumes and references and business cards for your search. Our focus is on the writing pad, your pen and how to use them to support your question/answer technique to control the interview.

After you tell your SHARE story, secure acknowledgement that you are the right fit for that criteria by putting a + sign on the left side of the same line, put your SHARE story name (two or three words). Write nothing else on the page at this point.

h-33

When you open the pad, all the interviewer should see is a blank writing pad. However, below the top (BLANK) page are two important pages. The second page down will contain two columns. The left column will have a list of your questions so you won't forget. The right column will be the place for you to take notes. The third page down will be a list of your SHARE stories, numbered and listed down the left side of the page.

When sitting across from the interviewer, all they will see is a blank page each time you lift it to look at your notes. It won't be blank for long, however.

As you progress through the questions we just discussed, you will have a SHARE story for each one. Mark off each SHARE story with a checkmark so you don't repeat yourself.

As you continue to tell your SHARE stories and receive acknowledgment that you are a "fit" against that criteria, add a + for each one down the page. These must be no less than ½ to ¾ inches in height and made to be bold. PRINT, DON'T WRITE, THE NAME OF YOUR SHARE STORIES. Take a ruler and see how big this is so you can make it the right size during the interview. The reason? You want the interviewer to be able to see your SHARE story name even upside down at a distance of at least 3-7 feet.

For example + **FAST LEARNING CURVE.**

What the interviewer sees psychologically is a plus sign, you are positive, and a statement addressing one of their concerns with a positive associated with it. With enough of these on the page, it becomes clear in his/her subconscious mind that you are a strong choice for the position. However, you're not finished yet.

When you have concluded with your

SHARE stories and have a feeling that the interview might be coming to a close, **draw a line under the + all the way across the paper just as if you were getting ready to add the column of plus signs.**

Now comes one of the critical questions you must ask them. *"Is there anything we haven't covered today that we might have or is there anything you see that might stand in the way of my consideration as a candidate?"* The purpose of this question is to dig out any objections that might be hidden or in the back of the interviewer's mind. These must be addressed right here, right now! You can be absolutely sure that the interviewer will address them with others after you've left. By the same token, if your SHARE stories have hit the mark, they will be shared as well.

The second reason to ask this question is to find out how strong your chances are. Another way of putting this question is: *"How many candidates have you interviewed and how many do you have left to interview? My reason for asking is that I would like to know your opinion of their strengths."* If they tell you, it is good because you now know what they are looking for and if it doesn't jive with what they have told you so far, you are afforded one final chance to tell another SHARE story to overcome any perceived weaknesses. When you share the final story, put another + and print the name of the positive point, just as you have done up till now.

If there is a negative comment or a deficiency identified, then draw a negative sign - under the column of plus signs. Here it gets a little tricky. Let's hope you have done your homework and have a pre-prepared SHARE story for each of your identified weaknesses. Use the one that most closely approximates the objection. When you've finished, ask your usual question - "Does this seem to fit" or "Is this what you are looking for?" If they say yes, turn the - into a +.

Now, you are ready to close the interview. You state the following:

"Mr./ Ms. Interviewer, we have covered a lot here today and I wanted to review just to make sure we haven't missed anything. Do you mind if I take a second and review my notes?" Nine times out of ten they will say yes. When they do, recap your SHARE stories one by one taking no more than 6-12 seconds to do so. For example:

"When we started, you said you were looking for **(FAST LEARNING CURVE)** *and you recall our discussion about the short timeframe I was given at XYZX company and the fact that I brought the project in both ahead of schedule and under budget."*

"Then you said you were looking for..." Repeat the above strategy, keeping it under 12 seconds and exactly to the point. Even if you think of something else that is critical to the point you are reviewing, **don't** bring it up now.

They have heard one version and telling another at this point will throw things out of kilter and maybe cost you a second interview.

After you have covered your points, you look them in the eye and say: *"It seems to me that, based upon the points we've covered, we have a match."*

The reason for this is one of the first things any salesperson worth their salt learns. After the "close," say nothing, because he or she who speaks first loses. No exceptions to this rule. I once sat in a gentleman's office and we

stared at each other for nearly two minutes. He finally spoke first and said he knew what I was doing and wanted to see if I would capitulate. Everyone else before me had done so. We signed a $500,000 deal that day which grew to over a million dollars within two years. Believe me, it works.

When you have said this, shut up and don't say a word. Make them be the next to speak.

Hopefully, the next thing out of their mouth will be *"Yes, it would appear that way."* When they say that, write in big letters the word QUALIFIED to the right of your plus sign at the bottom of the page.

Another thing they can say is they want to look at other candidates before making a decision. This is where you can ask them about other candidates as described above. If they have already interviewed some candidates, simply ask them the following question: *"How do their credentials and experience stack up against mine?"* Now, you can really find out what your competition is and how you compare in their mind. If they indicate you are lacking in a particular area, or you identify an area you feel needs beefing up, you have the final opportunity to jerk a SHARE story out of your bag of tricks and give it to them. The very last words spoken are.......

WHERE DO WE GO FROM HERE?

Never leave any interview without asking this question. Otherwise, what have you accomplished? Don't waste their time, or yours, by not asking this question.

GENERAL INTERVIEW DIALOGUE TECHNIQUES

Remember, you are trying to demonstrate your ability to solve problems. How can you do this if you don't know what they are? You must take a consultative role in the probe during your interview. Expect to again be asked, "tell me a little about yourself." Have your opening statement prepared <u>but close with the feedback question,</u> "What about my background caught your eye?" or "Why are you interested in me?"

---

1. More than likely the interviewer will focus on a position, skill or accomplishment from your resume. Have your SHARE stories ready, as well as your "does that seem like what you are looking for?" question at the ready.

2. Deliver your SHARE story and close by asking if the interviewer needs someone with that particular skill for the position.

In most cases, the interviewer does need someone with this skill and will proceed to give you valuable information about the problem that he is trying to solve. Keep responding with positive information about your ability to handle the job.

You have now turned the interview into a consultative sale. You are telling the respective buyer, the hiring authority, how this particular product, YOU, can solve their problem.

When you have exhausted discussing the current problem, ask, "what's the next problem that you want to solve?" and so on.

DEALING WITH OBJECTIONS

Objections are multi-faceted in nature. An objection is really another way of identifying a "real" concern that underlies the question being asked. The "real" issue is their concern about how fast you can overcome the deficiency, learn what you are supposed to and ultimately make a profitable contribution to the company.

Whether or not the objection is simple or complex, the objection has two parts. First, they are concerned that you don't know something about the subject being addressed and second, how long will it take you to become proficient?

Whenever an objection is identified, the strategy proposed by most experts is to acknowledge the concern, rephrase it to focus on an offsetting strength and then demonstrate that you have that offsetting strength. What follows is a step-by-step method for overcoming objections. In this case, let's say the objection is lack of experience in the employer's industry.

Step #1: Acknowledge the Interviewer's Objection.

You want to *acknowledge* the objection, not *validate* it. To accomplish this you might say to the interviewer:

Actually, I'm not surprised you brought that up.

Note that you have not indicated agreement with the point being made by the interviewer. You have only acknowledged that his observation merits discussion.

Step #2: Surface the Real Concern and Restate it in Favorable Terms.

Shift the focus to the real, underlying concern. In this case, since lack of industry-specific experience is evident from your resume, the interviewer's actual concern is how long it will take you to become productive. Restate the objection in those terms. Your response might go something like this:

I'm sure that whomever you hire must become productive quickly. Am I right? It is important to ask a question at the end and get agreement before you proceed.

Step #3: Provide an Example SHARE Story Aimed at Neutralizing the Concern.

Once agreement has been reached, provide a SHARE story highlighting your ability to meet the challenge and overcome the objection parameters. The whole transaction might go like this....

Interviewer: *"It appears that you don't seem to have experience in (some aspect) of our industry."*

Candidate: *"I'm not surprised you brought that up. You want to be sure that the person you hire can become productive quickly. Is that right?"*

Interviewer: *"Yes, it is."*

Candidate: *"In the past, I've proven multiple*

times that I can not only get in front of a learning curve quickly, but afterwards, can produce as well. In fact, let me SHARE an example with you."

> Interviewing, from the interviewer's position, is much easier. They are only concerned about the following:
>
> 1. Can they justify paying you the amount you want?
> 2. Will you create harmony or disrupt the organization?
> 3. Can they make money from your efforts?

The SHARE story you offer should illustrate your ability to adapt quickly to an unfamiliar setting and to make tangible contributions. Don't forget to conclude with the feedback question "is that the type of quick response you are looking for?"

Do not expect an employer to be so impressed with your response that he offers you a job on the spot. The objective here is to dissuade the employer from making a *no hire* decision based on an objection that was raised.

Exercise 8.3

Post-Interview Worksheet
www.RAH2010.com

POST INTERVIEW FOLLOW-UP STRATEGY

Step 1: Immediately after each interview you should find a quiet place and begin taking notes on:

1. What questions were asked?

2. What questions did you answer well?

3. What questions did you not answer so well?

4. What is the next step in the hiring cycle?

Enter these notes into the forms provided in the Workbook, Unit 4, Exercise 8.3.

Step 2: Next, you'll need to write a short thank you note to each person with whom you interviewed. This note should thank them for considering you, express your continued interest in the position and, most importantly, reinforce any areas that you thought were weak during the interview.

SUBSEQUENT INTERVIEWS

Here's a news flash. The higher the position, the more pay involved or the greater the influence your potential position has on others within a corporation, will determine the number of interviews it will take to land the job. Each interview, from the first to the last, requires the same amount of intense preparation. But the subsequent preparation involves learning more about the internal workings and politics of the corporation.

 Remember to analyze and write thank-you notes for subsequent interviews also!

b-24

This isn't as difficult as it sounds. If you did your job during the first interview session, you will have surfaced information useful in developing your next round of questions and in directing your company research.

Exercise 8.4

Interview Thank-You Letter
www.RAH2010.com

Information obtained from answers to these questions is vital to your analysis of the job, should a job offer be forthcoming.

SUMMARY

You now know how to avoid the issues of money and not shoot yourself in the foot. You have learned the proper protocols for pre and post-interview activities. Hopefully, you have been offered a second or third interview or, maybe even have been made an offer.

What you do at this juncture is really important and will set the tone and direction for your future. The next chapter, *Behavioral Interviewing*, will show you how to explain your behavior and how well you play with others.

Pre-Interview Questionnaire   Exercise 8.1

Company

Company Name	Web Address
Home Office Address	Local Branch Office Address
Name of CEO	Name of President

Gathering Information
    Do you have a brochure?
    Do you have a 10-K?
    Do you have a www address?
    Business Articles

Key Contacts
    Who are your key contacts at this company? Include anyone with whom you have already spoken.

Products and Services
    What are this company's main products and services?

    What are the products and services at the locations/divisions that you are contacting?

Competitors
    List at least 3 of this company's main competitors.

Pre-Interview Questionnaire   Exercise 8.1

Who's Who

Network

Who in your network might have done business with or have contacts with this company?

[ ]

Summary

Summarize the nature of the company, its position in the market relative to its competitors, long and short term economic factors influencing its lines of business and its management reputation.

[ ]

Job Description

What the Job Needs	What You Have

The Interview Preparation Sheet

Company

Date   Time   Length

Location

Interviewer(s)

Phone   Email

Mailing Address

Map

The Week Before

Do the pre-interview exercise
Have business cards ready
Do questions exercise
Answer top 20 interview questions
Find out about your interviews
Get suit cleaned
Should already be don   e
SHARE exercises
Resume

The Night Before

What to do:

Review job description
Review SHARE stories with somebody else
Memorize interviewer's name
Prepare clothing for the morning
Shine shoes
Check weather forecast
What you will need for tomorrow

SHARE exercises
3 Resumes
Your interview questions for them

Do

Dress appropriately
Come prepared
Be on time
Have confidence
Make good eye contact
Speak clearly
Be positive
Have good posture
Learn about the industry
Leave with a sincere thank you

Don't

Shake hands too hard or too soft
Wear too much smell
Be a know-it-all
Act passive
Lack confidence
Talk about past failures
Bad mouth past employer
Make excuses or be evasive
Focus on money or benefits
Be cynical
Have a condescending attitude

Exercise 8.1.1

business cards
appropriate interview dress
folder and notetaking material
umbrella
breath mints or chewing gum
overcoat

Over share
Be indecisive
Smoke or chew gum
Whine
Lack verbal expression

Last Minute Pointers

Turn off phone and pager
Arrive 5 to 10 minutes early
Be nice to receptionist
Ask as many questions as they ask you
Tell at least 3 SHARE stories
Secure a business card from everyone you meet
Confirm another meeting or follow-up time
Thank the interviewers
Thank the receptionist on the way out

After the Interview is Over

Complete the Post Interview Worksheet
Write a follow-up thank-you letter to everyone you met.
Write a thank you note to the person who referred you.
Follow up with a phone call if you committed to do it.
Did you compare your notes to your company criteria list?
Did you write down a list of items to improve on in your next interview?

Exercise 8.2

Commonly Asked Interview Questions

Here are some of the most commonly asked stress or interview questions and suggested approaches for answering them. Bear in mind that the two main issues on the interviewer's mind are...

♦ What can you do for me?

♦ Do you fit in?

Consequently, if you can use your answers to score points on either of these issues, you'll gain an edge on your competition. The answers also keep you from getting yourself in "hot water" with extreme answers.

---

1. Tell me about yourself.
   This is not an invitation to ramble on. Take some time in advance to think about yourself and those aspects of your personality and/or background that you'd like to promote or feature for your interviewer. Write this in about a 90-second to 2-minute format and practice it until delivery is smooth.

2. What do you look for in a job?
   State what you want in terms of what you can give to your employer. The key word in the following example is "contribution."

   "My experience at the XYZ Corporation has shown me that I have a talent for motivating people. That is demonstrated by my team's absenteeism dropping 20 percent, turnover steadying at 10 percent, and production increasing 12 percent. I am looking for an opportunity to continue that kind of contribution in a company and with a supervisor who will help me develop in a professional manner."

3. Why are you leaving?
   You should have an acceptable reason for leaving every job you have held. If you don't, pick one of these six acceptable reasons. The acronym for it is CLAMPS:

   - Challenge: You weren't able to grow professionally in that position
   - Location: The commute was unreasonably long.
   - Advancement: There was nowhere for you to go. You had the talent, but there were too many people ahead of you.
   - Money: You were underpaid for your skills and contribution.
   - Pride or prestige: you wanted to be with a better company.
   - Security: The company was not stable.

   For example: "My last company was a family-owned affair. I had gone as far as I was able. It just seemed time for me to join a more prestigious company and accept greater challenges."

Exercise 8.2

4. <u>What can you do for us that someone else cannot do?</u>
This question will come only after a full explanation of the job has been given. If not, qualify the question with "what voids are you trying to eradicate when you fill this position?" Recap the interviewer's job description as you highlight your skills.

    Finish with a question that asks for feedback or a powerful answer. If you haven't covered the interviewer's hot buttons, he or she will cover them now, and you can respond accordingly.

5. <u>Why should we hire you?</u>
Your answer should be short and to the point. It should highlight areas from your background that relate to current needs and problems. Recap the interviewer's description of the job, meeting it point by point with your skills. Finish your answer by remarking: "I have the qualifications you need [itemize them], I'm a team player, I take direction and I have the desire to make a thorough success."

6. <u>Can you work under pressure, deadlines?</u>
You might be tempted to give a simple "yes" or "no" answer, but don't. It reveals nothing and you lose the opportunity to sell your skills and value profiles. Whenever you are asked a closed-ended question, answer the question and add a skill-selling example story.

7. <u>What are your most significant accomplishments in your present or last job?</u>
Keep your answer job-related. You might begin your reply with a statement such as: "Although I feel my most significant achievements are still ahead of me, I am proud of my involvement with...I made my contribution as part of that team and learned a lot in the process. We did it with hard work, concentration and an eye for the bottom line."

8. <u>What is your primary strength?</u>
Isolate high points from your background and add key values. You might want to demonstrate pride, reliability and the ability to stick with a difficult task yet change course rapidly when required.

9. <u>What is your primary weakness?</u>
This is a direct invitation to put your head in a noose. Decline the invitation.

    Design the answer so that your weakness is ultimately a positive characteristic. For example; "I enjoy my work and always give each project my best shot. When I don't feel that others are pulling their weight, I find it a little frustrating. I am aware of that weakness and I try to overcome it with a positive attitude that I hope will catch on."

    Also consider the technique of putting a problem in the past. Here, you take a weakness from way back when and show how you overcame it. It answers the question but ends on a positive note. An illustration: "When I first got into this field, I always had problems with my paperwork – you know, leaving an adequate paper train. To be honest, I let it slip once or twice. My manager sat me down and explained the potential troubles such behavior could cause. I really took it to heart and I think you will find my paper trails some of the best around today. You only have to tell me something once." With that kind of answer you also get the added bonus of showing that you accept and act on criticism.

Exercise 8.2

10. <u>How long would it take you to make a contribution to our firm?</u>
    You are best advised to answer this with a question: "That is an excellent question. To help me answer, what are your greatest areas of need right now?" When your time comes to answer, start with "Let's say I started on Monday the seventeenth. It will take me a few weeks to settle down and learn the ropes. Do you have a special project in mind in which you will want me to get involved?" That response could lead directly to a job offer but, if not, you already have the interviewer thinking of you as an employee.

11. <u>What do you think of your boss?</u>
    People who complain about their employers are recognized as the same people who cause th most disruption in a department.

12. <u>What features of your previous jobs have you disliked?</u>
    Criticizing a prior employer is a warning flag that you could be a problem employee. No one intentionally hires trouble. Keep your answer short and positive.

13. <u>Would you describe a few situations in which your work was criticized?</u>
    This is a doubly dangerous question. You are being asked to say how you handle criticism and to detail your faults. If you are asked this question, describe a poor idea that was criticized, not poor work.

14. <u>How would you evaluate your present firm?</u>
    Always answer positively and keep your real feelings to yourself, whatever they might be. Your answer should be, "Very good" or "Excellent." Then smile and wait for the next question.

15. <u>What would you like to be doing five years from now?</u>
    The safest answer contains a desire to be regarded as a true professional and team player. As far as promotion, that depends on finding a manager with whom you can grow.

16. <u>How do you organize and plan for major projects?</u>
    Effective planning requires both forward thinking ("Who and what am I going to need to get this job done?") and backward thinking ("If this job must be completed by the twentieth, what steps must be made, and what time to achieve it?")

17. <u>Describe a difficult problem you've had to deal with.</u>
    This is a favorite tough question. It is not so much the difficult problem that's important – it's the approach you take to solving problems in general. It is designed to probe your professional profile, especially your analytical skills.

18. <u>What would your references say?</u>
    You have nothing to lose by being positive. If the company checks your references, it must by law have your permission. That permission is usually included in the application form you sign. Despite these points, never offer references or written recommendations unless they are requested.

19. <u>Can we check your references?</u>
    This question is frequently asked as a stress question to catch the too-smooth candidate off-guard. It is also one that occasionally is asked in the general course of events. The higher up the corporate ladder you go, the more likely it is that your references will be checked.

Exercise 8.2

Your answer may include: "Yes, of course you can check my references. However, at present, I would like to keep matters confidential until we have established a serious mutual interest [i.e., an offer]. At that time, I will be pleased to furnish you with whatever references you need from prior employers. I would expect you to wait to check my current employer's references until you have extended me an offer in writing, I have accepted, we have agreed on a start date and I have had the opportunity to resign in a professional manner." You are under no obligation to give references of a current employer until you have a written offer in hand. You are also well within your rights to request reference checks of current employers wait until you have started your new job.

20. What type of decisions did you make on your last job?
The interviewer may be searching to define your responsibilities or he/she may want to know that you don't overstep yourself. It is also an opportunity to show your achievement profile.

21. How do you handle tension?
This question is different from "Can you handle pressure?" It asks how you handle it. You could reply, "Tension is caused when you let things pile up. I find that, if you break those overwhelming tasks into little pieces, they aren't so overwhelming any more. So, I suppose I don't so much handle tension as handle the causes of it."

22. How long have you been looking for another position?
If you are employed, your answer isn't that important. If, on the other hand you are unemployed, how you answer becomes more important. So, if you must talk of months or more, be careful to add something like, "Well I've been looking for about a year now. I've had a number of offers in that time but I have determined that the job I take and the people with whom I work need to be people with values with which I can identify."

23. Have you ever been fired?
Say "no" if you can. If not, act on the advice given to the next question.

24. If so, why were you fired?
If you were laid off as part of general work force reduction, be straightforward and move on to the next topic as quickly as possible.

Having been fired creates instant doubt in the mind of the interviewer and greatly increases the chances of your references being checked. Consequently, if you have been fired, the first thing to do is bite the bullet and call the person who fired you, find out why it happened and learn what he or she would say about you today.

Your aim is to clear the air. So, whatever you do, don't be antagonistic. Reintroduce yourself, explain that you are looking (or, if you have been unemployed for a while, say you are "still looking") for a new job. Say that you appreciate that the manager had to do what was done and that you learned from the experience Then ask, "If you were asked as part of a pre- or post-employment reference check, how would you describe my leaving the company? Would say that I was fired or that I simply resigned? You see, every time I tell someone about my termination, Whoosh, there goes another chance of getting another paycheck!"

Whatever you do, don't advertise the fact you were fired. If you are asked, be honest, but make sure you have packaged the reason in the best light possible.

Exercise 8.2

If you can find out the employee turnover figures, voluntary or otherwise, you might add, "Fifteen other people have left so far this year." A combination answer of this nature minimizes the stigma. You have even managed to demonstrate that you take responsibility for your actions, which shows your analytical and listening skills. If one of your past managers will speak well of you, there is nothing to lose and everything to gain by finishing with, "Jill Johnson, at the company, would be a good person to check for a reference on what I have told you."

25. <u>Have you ever been asked to resign?</u>
When someone is asked to resign, it is a gesture on the part of the employer: "You can quit, or we will terminate you, so which do you want it to be?" Because you were given the option though, that employer cannot later say, "I had to ask him to resign."

26. <u>Were you ever dismissed from your job for a reason that seemed unjustified?</u>
The sympathetic phrasing is geared to getting you to reveal all the sordid details. The cold hard facts are that hardly anyone is fired without cause and you're kidding yourself if you think otherwise. With that in mind, you can quite honestly say "No" and move on to the next topic.

27. <u>In your last job, what were some of the things you spent most of your time on, and why?</u>
Employees come in two categories: goal-oriented (those who want to get the job done) and task-oriented (those who believe in "busy" work). You must demonstrate good time-management and a goal-oriented attitude, which is what this question probes.

28. <u>Do you have any questions?</u>
A good question. Almost always, this is a sign that the interview is drawing to a close and that you have one more chance to make an impression. Create questions from any of the following:
- Find out why the job is open, who had it last, and what happened to him or her. Did he or she get promoted or fired. How many people have held this position in the last couple of years? What happened to them subsequently?
- Why did the interviewer join the company? How long has he or she been there? What is it about the company that keeps him or her there?
- To whom would you report? Will you get the opportunity to meet that person?
- Where is the job located? What are the travel requirements, if any?
- What type of training is required and how long is it? What type of training is available?
- What would your first assignment be?
- What are the realistic chances for growth in the job? Where are the opportunities for greatest growth within the company?
- What are the skills and attributes most needed to get ahead in the company?
- Who will be the company's major competitor over the next few years? How does the interviewer feel the company stacks up against them?
- What has been the growth pattern of the company over the last five years? Is it profitable? How profitable? Is the company privately or publicly held?
- If there is a written job description, may you see it?
- How regularly do performance evaluations occur? What model do they follow?

Exercise 8.2

29. <u>Rate yourself on a scale from one to ten.</u>
Bear in mind that this is meant to plumb the depths of your self-esteem. If you answer ten, you run the risk of portraying yourself as insufferable. On the other hand, if you say less than seven, you might as well get up and leave. You are probably best claiming to be an eight or nine.

30. <u>What is the most difficult situation you have faced?</u>
The question looks for information on two fronts: How do you define difficult? And what was your handling of the situation? You must have a story ready for this one in which the situation both was tough and allowed you to show yourself in a good light.

31. <u>What have you done that shows initiative?</u>
The question probes whether you are a doer. Be sure, however, that your example of initiative does not show a disregard for company policies and procedures.

32. <u>What are some of the things about which you and your supervisor disagreed?</u>
It is safest to state that you did not disagree.

33. <u>In what areas do you feel your supervisor could have done a better job?</u>
You could reply, "I have always had the highest respect for my supervisor. I have always been so busy learning from Mr. Jones that I don't think he could have done a better job. He has really brought me to the point where I am ready for greater challenges. That's why I'm here."

34. <u>What are some of the things your supervisor did that you disliked?</u>
If you and the interviewer are both nonsmokers and your boss isn't, use it. Apart from that answer, "You know, I've never thought of our relationship in terms of like or dislike. I've always thought our role was to get along together and get the job done."

35. <u>How did your boss get the best out of you?</u>
This is a manageability question, geared to probing whether you are going to be a pain in the neck or not. Whatever you say, it is important for your ongoing happiness that you make it clear you don't appreciate being treated like a dishrag. You can give a short, general answer:

"My last boss got superior effort and performance by treating me like a human being and giving me the same personal respect with which she liked to be treated herself."

36. <u>What personal characteristics are necessary for success in your field?</u>
You might say, "To be successful in my field? Drive, motivation, energy, confidence, determination, good communication, and analytical skills. Combined, of course, with the ability to work with others."

37. <u>Do you prefer working with others or alone?</u>
This question is usually used to determine whether you are a team player. Before answering, however, be sure you know whether the job requires you to work alone. Then answer appropriately. Perhaps, you could reply, "I'm quite happy working alone when necessary. I don't need much constant reassurance. But I prefer to work in a group—so much more gets achieved when people pull together."

Exercise 8.2

38. <u>Explain your role as a group/team member.</u>
You are being asked to describe yourself as either a team player or a loner. Most department depend on harmonious teamwork for their success, so describe yourself as a team player.

39. <u>Do you make your opinions known when you disagree with the views of your supervisor?</u>
If you can, state that you come from an environment where input is encouraged when it help the team's ability to get the job done efficiently. "If opinions are sought in a meeting, I will give mine, although I am careful to be aware of others' feelings. I will never criticize a coworker or a superior in open forum. Besides, it is quite possible to disagree without being disagreeable.

However, my past manager made it clear that she valued my opinion by asking for it. So, after a while, if there was something I felt strongly about, I would make an appointment to sit down and discuss it one-on-one."

40. <u>How would you handle an unfair or difficult supervisor?</u>
If you need to elaborate, try, "I would make an appointment to see the supervisor and diplomatically explain that I felt uncomfortable in our relationship. I felt he or she was not treating me as a professional colleague, and, therefore, that I might not be performing up t standard in some way. I would ask for his or her input as to what I must do to create a professional relationship. I would enter into the discussion in the frame of mind that we were equally responsible for whatever communication problems existed and that this wasn't jus the manager's problem."

41. <u>Do you consider yourself a natural leader or a born follower?</u>
If you are a recent graduate, you're expected to have high aspirations so go for it. If you are already on the corporate ladder with some practical experience in the school of hard knocks you might want to be a little cagier. Assuming you are up for (and want) a leadership position, you might try something like this, "I would be reluctant to regard anyone as a natural leader. Hiring, motivation and disciplining other adults, while at the same time molding them into a cohesive team, involves a number of skills that no honest person can sa they possessed from birth. Leadership is a lifetime learning process. Anyone who reckons they have it all under control and have nothing more to learn isn't doing the employer an favors."

42. <u>When do you expect a promotion?</u>
Tread warily, show that you believe in yourself and have both feet firmly planted on the ground. "That depends on a few criteria. Of course, I cannot expect promotions without the performance that marks me as deserving of promotion. I also need to join a company that ha the growth necessary to provide the opportunity. I hope that my manager believes in promoting from within and will help me grow so that I will have the skills necessary to be considered for promotion when the opportunity comes along."

Exercise 8.2

43.   <u>You have been given a project that requires you to interact with different levels within the company. How do you do this? With what levels are you most comfortable?</u>
This is a two-part question that probes communication and self-confidence skills. The first part asks how you interact with superiors and motivate those working with and for you on the project. The second part of the question is saying, "Tell me whom you regard as your peer group?"

To cover both bases, you will want to include the essence of this: "There are basically two types of people I would interact with on a project of this nature. First, there are those I report to, who bear the ultimate responsibility for its success. With them, I determine deadlines and how they will evaluate the success of the project I would outline my approach, breaking the project down into component parts, getting approval on both the approach and the costs. I would keep my supervisors up-to-date on a regular basis, and seek input whenever needed. My supervisors would expect three things from me - the facts, an analysis of potential problems, and that I not be intimidated, as that would jeopardize the project's success. I would comfortably satisfy those expectations."

"The other people are those who work with and for me. With those people, I would outline the project and explain how a successful outcome will benefit the company. I would assign the component parts to those best suited to each and arrange follow-up times to assure completion by deadline. My role here would be to facilitate, motivate and bring the different personalities together to form a team. As for comfort level, I find this type of approach enables me to interact comfortably with all levels and types of people."

44.   <u>Tell me about an event that really challenged you. How did you meet the challenge? In what way was your approach different from others?</u>
This is a straightforward two-part question. The first probes your problem-solving abilities. The second asks you to set yourself apart from the herd. First of all, outline the problem. The blacker you make the situation, the better. Having done that, go ahead and explain your solution, its value to your employer and how it was different from other approaches.

45.   <u>How would you go about making a decision when no procedure exists?</u>
This question probes your analytical skills, integrity and dedication. Most of all, the interviewer is testing your manageability and adherence to procedures. You need to cover that with, "I would act without my manager's direction only if the situation were urgent and my manager were not available. Then, I would take command of the situation, make a decision based upon the facts and implement it. I would update my boss at the earliest opportunity."

46.   <u>That is an excellent answer. Now give me a balanced view, can you give me an example that didn't work out so well?</u>
Here, you are required to give an example of an inadequacy. The trick is to pull something from the past and to finish with what you learned from the experience.

Exercise 8.2

47. <u>What kinds of decisions are most difficult for you?</u>
You are human. Admit it, but be careful what you admit. If you have ever had to fire someone, you are in luck because no one likes todo that. Emphasize that, having reached a logical conclusion, you act.

48. <u>What area of your skills/professional development do you want to improve at this time?</u>
Another "tell-me-all-your-weaknesses" question. You should try to avoid damaging your candidacy by tossing around careless admissions.

49. <u>Your application shows you have been with one company a long time without any appreciable increase in rank or salary. Tell me about this.</u>
To begin, you should analyze why this state of affairs does exist. Then, when you have determined the cause, practice saying it out loud to yourself as you would say it during an actual interview. It may take a few tries.

Try to avoid putting your salary history on application forms. No one is going to deny you an interview for lack of a salary history if your skills match what the job requires.

50. <u>See this pen I'm holding? Sell it to me.</u>
In today's business world, everyone is required to sell—sometimes products, but more often ideas, approaches and concepts. As such, you are being tested to see whether you understan the basic concepts of features-and-benefits selling, how quickly you think on your feet and how effective your verbal communication is.

You say calmly, "Let me tell you about the special features of this product. First of all, it's a highlighter that will emphasize important points in reports or articles and that will save you time in teaching the important features. The casing is wide enough to enable you to use it comfortably at your desk or on a flip chart. It has a flat base to help it stand on its own. At one dollar, it is disposable and affordable enough for you to have a handful for your desk, briefcase, car and home. And the bright yellow color means you'll never lose it."

Then close with a smile and a question of your own that will bring a smile to the interviewer's face, like, "How many gross shall we deliver?"

51. <u>Why should I hire an outsider when I could fill the job with someone inside the company?</u>
The question isn't as stupid as it sounds. Obviously, the interviewer has examined existing employees with an eye toward their promotion or reassignment. Just as obviously, the job cannot be filled from within the company. Ifit could be, it would be and for two very good reasons: It is cheaper for the company to promote from within and it is good for employee morale. Your answer should include two steps.The first is a simple recitation of your skills and personality profile strengths tailored to the specific requirements of the job.

For the second step, realize first that whenever a manager is filling a position, he or she is looking not only for someone who can do the job, but also for someone who can benefit the department in a larger sense. No department is as good as it could be. Each has weaknesses that need strengthening. Therefore, in the second part of your answer, include a question o your own, such as, "Those are my general attributes. However, if no one is promotable from inside the company, that means you are looking to add strength to your team in a special way In what ways do you hope the final candidate will be able to benefit your department?" The answer to this is your cue to sell your applicable qualities

Exercise 8.2

52.   <u>Why were you out of work for so long?</u>
       You must have a sound explanation for any and all gaps in your employment history. If not, you are unlikely to receive a job offer. Emphasize that you were not just looking for another paycheck. You were looking for a company with which to settle and to which to make a long-term contribution.

53.   <u>Why have you changed jobs so frequently?</u>
       If you have jumped around, blame it on youth (even the interviewer was young once). Now you realize what a mistake your job-hopping was and, with your added domestic responsibilities, you are now much more settled. Or you may wish to impress on the interviewer that your job-hopping was never as a result of poor performance and that you grew professionally as a result of each job change.

54.   <u>What was there about your last company that you didn't particularly like or agree with?</u>
       You are being checked out as a potential "fly in the ointment." If you have to answer, it might be about how some employees disregarded the bottom line by consciously misunderstanding directives.

       Or: "I didn't like the way some people gave lip service to 'the customer comes first' but really didn't go out of their way to keep the customer satisfied. I don't think it was a fault of management, just a general malaise that seemed to affect a lot of people."

55.   <u>What are some things you find difficult to do? Why do you feel that way?</u>
       This is a variation on a couple of earlier questions. Remember, anything that goes against the best interests of your employer is difficult to do. If you are pressed for a job function you find difficult, answer in the past tense. That way, you show that you recognize difficulty but that you obviously handle it well.

56.   <u>What were some of the minuses on your last job?</u>
       A variation on the question, "What interests you least about this job?" which was handled earlier. Use the same type of answer. For example, "Like any salesperson I enjoy selling, not doing the paperwork. I grin and bear it."

       If you are not in sales, use the sales force as a scapegoat. "In accounts receivable, it's my job to get the money in to make payroll. Half the time, the goods get shipped before I get the paperwork because sales says, 'It's a rush order.' That's a real minus to me. It was so bad at my last company, we tried a new approach. We met with sales and explained our problem. The result was that incremental commissions were based on cash in, not on bill date. They saw the connection and things are much better now."

Interview Stress Questions

Now that you have read the questions and answers in Exercise 7.2, answer the following using your ov words. <u>DO NOT SKIP THIS EXERCISE!</u>

1.   Tell me about yourself.

2.   Why are you leaving?

3.   What are you most significant accomp   lishments in your present or last job?

4.   What is your primary strength?

5.   What is your primary weakness?

6.   How would you evaluate your present firm?

7.   Describe a difficult problem you've had to deal with.

8.   Have you ever been fired? If so, why?

9.   What kinds of decisions are most difficult for you?

10.   What are you short-range objectives?

11.   What are your long-range objectives?

Post-Interview Worksheet   Exercise 8.3

Company Name	Interview Date

Part A and B of this worksheet should be completed immediately following the interview. Find a quiet place where you will not be disturbed.

A. What questions were asked? What were your answers? Were they good?

	Question	Summary of Your Answer	Good or Bad?
1.			
2.			
3.			
4.			
5.			
6.			
7.			
8.			
9.			
10.			
11.			
12.			
13.			
14.			
15.			
16.			
17.			
18.			

Post-Interview Worksheet   Exercise 8.3

B.   If you were the interviewer, how would you have ra   ted the interview? The form below is a typical interview evaluation form. Fill this form out from the interviewer's point of view.

1. Interest in the position					
2. Knowledge of company					
3. Education or training					
4. Experience					
5. Maturity					
6. Adaptability					
7. Assertiveness					
8. Ability to communicate					
9. Appearance					

10. What are the applicant's major strengths?

11. What are the applicant's major weaknesses?

12. How does this applicant compare to other applicants for this position?

13. Overall Rating (circle one)   Excellent   Good   Fair   Poor

The following   should be completed   within 24 hours of the interview.

C.   Write a s hort thank you note to each person with whom you interviewed.
   ❑   Thank Them
   ❑   Express continued interest in the position
   ❑   Reinforce any areas that you thought were weak during the interview.

Exercise 8.4
Interview Thank-You Letter

Dwight H. Gesson
14451 South 8 th St.
Phoenix, AZ 85048-4440
480-283-6234

Dear Ms. Klausen:

Thank you for including me in your interview schedule while you were in the Phoenix area. I feel like I gained further knowledge of Oscarmove Solutions and the regional sales manager position currently available.

It came as somewhat of a surprise that your western territory is generating such low sales volume. Based upon my research of your company, the competitors operating in this arena and the great products you offer, I believe the southwest territory has tremendous growth and, as of yet, untapped market potential.

At the conclusion of our interview we agreed that my candidacy is under strong consideration because of my requisite skills and past experiences in moving sales numbers quickly and profitably. I also feel that not only can I acquire new clients, but I can also deepen your market penetration in this territory and develop numerous profitable long-term relationships.

Your company needs, and my skills and proven track history in moving numbers, makes our future working relationship a good match. I would be proud to work for Oscarmove Solutions.

Again thank you very much for the opportunity to interview with Oscarmove. I look forward to hearing from you soon.

Sincerely,

Dwight Gesson

Controlling the Interview and Eliminating Your Competition

Generally, the interviewer will review your resume with you. This process will also result in a few questions asked. This is the point at which you MUST ask the following question:

"During this interview, do you mind if I ask a few questions?" Of course, the interviewer will say no, not at all and you MUST respond immediately with a question that will allow you to bring up your first share story.

As you can see, the interviewer is trying to see what is being written and is looking at the job description lying next to my pad. Write the requirements and qualification in single words on the left side of page two of the pad and the names of your SHARE stories on the right side of the pad page that match the requirements for the position.

The objective of this exercise is to make very subtle changes in the interviewer's perceptions of you and your candidacy. Most of this portion of the technique involves non-verbal techniques using your pen and your pad of paper.

As you can see, the interviewer is now looking at the first page of the pad which is held vertically. The interviewer is reading what you have written from both an upside down and backwards point of view. This fact causes the person to remember more about you than anything you can say verbally.

Each SHARE story has a name that consists of one or two and no more than three words. Each time you tell a SHARE story, you write down the name of that SHARE story on the first page of your pad. As you begin to tell the stories, each one is shown on the first page of your pad.

Controlling the Interview and Eliminating Your Competition

Exercise 8.5

You will keep referring to your notes on the second and third page of your pad. When you do, the raised page cannot help but be seen by the interviewer. Why don't you try this with a friend and watch their eyes go to the pad, whether or not they want them to. This physical response cannot be helped by anyone sitting across from you.

Don't forget to watch the interviewer's eyes when you close with the phrase: "*That is what you are looking for, isn't it?*". The answer, will usually be positive or call for clarification.

DO NOT write anything down until the answer is YES! When you get this response, write the SHARE story title down and "review your notes" so that the interviewer will once again look at the page and take in the list of reasons why you should be hired.

When you close the presentation say to the interviewer: Well, it looks like we have a match." At this point SHUT UP AND LISTEN. If the answer is yes , or yes in some variation, write the word, **MATCH**, at the bottom of the list of SHARE story words. Make sure you also put the + sign in very large print next to the word match.

I would remind you not to forget to ask "*Where do we go from here?*" before you leave the room. This will tell you exactly where you stand and also allow for further dialogue if there are obstacles standing in your way of receiving an offer.

By following the entire SHARE story technique demonstrated above, you will have accomplished three very important things simultaneously.

1. You have created value for yourself as a prime candidate.

2. You have eliminated the competition. Can you imagine anyone else doing this to establish value?

3. You have created **EXCESS VALUE**. Excess value is the difference that you see when you ask for more money, larger package and a signing bonus. Excess value is established by your control of the situation and your clear demonstration of your value beyond the expectations the company has for an "average "candidate.

This area, called "above and beyond" is where you justify why the company should pay you more than advertised. Why? Because you have established a far greater worth.

Good luck with your interviews!

Chapter 9
<<< Behavioral Interviewing

enry Ford had it right many years ago when he said, "I hire the man, not the history." He was likely dealing with how the person acted towards and with others, and that method was the forerunner of Behavioral competency Interviewing/Hiring - 60 years before the concept showed up again in the work place. Let's focus on the following revision: "I hire the person, not the history."

Think about it and ask yourself, what is the right person? What does right mean, or what does the whole person mean? Another question to ask yourself is what is going to make money - the history of the person or the person? You guessed it. The answer is the right person. Why? Because the right person is going to be a match for their business, the position, the team, and their needs, and this will be wrapped up in the person with the right qualities, technically and behaviorally. That's probably you.

Also, ask yourself why you are the best? If you do not come up with terms like persistent, conveys credibility, motivation, interpersonal savvy, able to identify the needs of others, action oriented, innovative, and approachable, then you do not know why you are effective and, more importantly, who you are. Behavioral interviewing deals with your individual character. A properly conducted behavioral interview investigates the character of the person being interviewed, and when the right questions are given, you will either succeed in beating your competition or you will fail, and they will receive the job offer.

In the 21st Century interview, if you do not prepare well, and cannot demonstrate how you have used your job knowledge and experience and behavioral competencies to solve a problem when you are asked, you will see some strange facial expressions. It takes a lot of self knowledge and confidence to explain how experience and your personality (behavioral competencies) helped to solve something or contribute to a company.

Faking behavioral actions and competencies is virtually impossible.

h-35

You, the applicant, must be able to demonstrate a behavior being used. To do this task effectively, you will have to know yourself and what you are selling, tie that knowledge to the needs of a company, and then show the skills you use to do that. One would have to be a great actor to just pick something, and show it working in an actual event during their career.

WHAT ARE BEHAVIORAL COMPETENCIES?

In matching people with work, we intuitively try to do the best we can to assess those underlying factors or competencies that will affect people's success in the job. Often the company wants to know HOW you go about getting things done as well as WHAT you know how to do. For instance, they might want to know...

■ HOW does this person take initiative and ensure results in work assignments?
■ HOW does this person communicate and

work with other people?

■ HOW does this person deal with conflict or obstacles?

Behavioral competencies target those HOW factors. Behavioral competencies are abilities and characteristics that help people make the most of their technical competencies on the job. The thoughts offered here act as a catalyst for critical thinking about what you bring to your work and to the interview table (demonstrating value to the new company) with regard to your personal competencies.

Consider the question, "How will I demonstrate my level of executive intelligence?" I am sure that you can recognize that being able to effectively discuss your corporate intelligence level could have a significant impact on the outcome of an interview.

It is said that *executive intelligence is comprised of the ability to use conceptual thinking.* There is nothing more difficult than thinking about thinking – conceptual thinking. Keep in mind that there are the four sides of you that you have to sell: job knowledge or skills; behaviors; conceptual, innovative, analytical thinking; and executive intelligence, or using your knowledge or executive smarts, as some refer to it. Your task is to be prepared to sell all of them as the opportunity is presented. Even if an opportunity does not come up during an interview, it is your job to figure out how to get those messages delivered to the interviewing company.

A study by Ohio State University concluded that during the interview situation and maybe even in life, you have up to 30 seconds to make or break a first impression. Other studies have revealed that most opinions about candidates are formed

within the first few minutes of an interaction between people and the rest of the interaction or interview is spent validating those opinions. This material is a tool to help you think about how best to make that positive first impression and keep it positive during the interview.

There are a few different types of interviews, but basically they break down into the following structures:

General/Traditional Interviews, which may appear to have a lack of focus and are usually directly related to the resume information and the job description.

Behavioral Interviews, which are focused on your personal behavioral makeup and its use.

Case Interviews, which are focused on your ability to THINK and REASON quickly, with the emphasis on quickly.

Know your personal competencies – the real you – and know how to talk about them. Fit has little to do with job knowledge or job skills. The reality is that it does not matter what kind of interview structure you are in. As aforementioned, it is a conversation, and it is about answering questions; it is about delivering a message about your value and what you are like to work with.

Some companies have been using competency-based or behavioral-based interviewing for years, and more companies are moving towards a behavioral approach to their interview programs. When a job description is written, not only are the job skills and job knowledge identified, but also the behaviors, competencies, and traits desired in an employee.

By the way, an important question to ask the company as an interview session is being scheduled is what type of interview system they use. If by some chance you get into an interview, and do not know the system or type, and are being asked questions that begin with, "Tell me about…" "Describe a time…" "Give me an example of…" or any question that sets up a situation, you are in a behavioral / competency-based interview. Situation interview inquiries are very similar to case interviews; however, case interview inquiries are most always dealing with a hypothetical business problem and are mostly focused on examining your ability to think and reason. You must prepare for both.

This is a good place to comment further on case interviews. What is a case interview? Simply, it is structured by asking for an analysis of some kind of business situation, and it can also include questions, which may seem ridiculous. On one end, you could be presented with a question about a firm that is losing market share and is experiencing profitability problems and the questions becomes, "Give me a picture of how you would go about examining this problem and what actions would you take to turn it around?"

On the other end, the ridiculous end, you could get questions like, "How many fire hydrants are there in a square mile of a city or in a city of 5 million people?" Another is, "If you were a tree, what kind would you be and why?"

Keep in mind that brainteasers often give you the opportunity to talk about yourself. Consider the tree question: a tree that grows with a wide spread could be interpreted to mean that you are interested in having a large span of influence.

So what is at stake in these interviewing strategies? What is at stake is your ability to demonstrate executive intelligence, which has been defined as "Conceptual thinking ability; the ability to demonstrate the use of your job knowledge." Intelligence is the skill of using knowledge to solve a problem. If you are presented with a case, you need to go down a path that includes the following:

1. **diagnostics** - you discuss possible issues showing a logical outline;
2. **analysis** – showing understanding of the impact;
3. **communication** of solution or process to achieve an outcome.

In other words, what you are demonstrating are the abilities of qualitative and quantitative analysis, problem-solving, synthesizing thoughts, and communication with a professional demeanor.

A thought about thinking: THINKING INVOLVES THE MANIPULATION OF INFORMATION AND IS NEEDED TO ALLOW YOU TO MODEL AND DEAL WITH YOUR GOALS. THE USE OF IMAGINATION IS IMPORTANT.

Competencies are defined as behavioral skills, and when combined with technical knowledge, serve as indicators of success in a position. The premise behind behavioral interviewing is that the most accurate predictor of future performance is past performance, which includes what you have used behaviorally to get something done in similar situations. Habits and behaviors are repetitive.

Competencies are also used because they give the corporation a tool to evaluate the qualities and character of individuals, and evaluate their ability to make effective contributions to the organization. Competency or behavioral-based interviewing places the emphasis on the applicant's character, and the individual's ability to relate learning from past experience to the position in question.

Competency interviews tend to obtain in-depth information on an applicant, how they perform, and what they use to get work done. During a competency interview, the applicant can expect to be quizzed in depth, because the company is trying to learn if you have specific behaviors needed for the position. They want to hear the actual behavior in words, so you will need to factor those thoughts into an interview answer.

The word "hear" is used for a specific reason. During the interview, the interviewer expects to hear the specific behavior in the answer given to a question. For example if you were demonstrating the use of your "command skills," then that term, command skill, should be used in your answer. Unfortunately, many times the interviewee thinks his or her message is getting out, and that is not a safe assumption. Tell your audience what you want them to hear.

Remember that some behavioral questions are aimed at getting the applicant to respond to negative situations; therefore, you will need to have examples of negative experiences. Identify such negative experiences, turn them into a S.H.A.R.E. in such a way that indicates in the results that you were able to make the best of the situation, or better yet, how you were able to bring about a positive outcome. Keep in mind that <u>all</u> negative experiences are learning situations; be prepared to talk about what you learned.

In a "traditional" interview, you can get away with telling the interviewer what he or she wants to hear. There is not much accountability. However, in behavioral interviewing, the interviewer is actually dealing with your character. So it is somewhat difficult to not pay attention to the real you. That is why in this process you should spend some quality time really looking at yourself in terms of what you use in terms of behavior, traits, and habits to get work done. These attributes carry an important message.

Examples of competencies / behaviors / traits / habits are: • persuasiveness • customer service • drive for results • stress tolerance • planning • strategic thinking • flexibility • initiative to problem solve • team work • business acumen • tolerance and dealing with ambiguity • strategic leadership • energizing • interpersonal savvy • political savvy • intellectual makeup • approachability • conceptual thinking • decision making • innovative and analytical thinking • problem solving • customer service • managing and measuring • integrity and trust • compassion • and perseverance.

Sometimes these types of skills are referred to as soft skills, but the business world is calling them behavioral competencies, behaviors, and/or traits. In addition, as you look at core competencies, please consider that each are made up of several items. Take the idea of Strategic Agility. As the words imply, this is someone who can see ahead, can anticipate consequences accurately, has broad knowledge and perspective, is future oriented, and is a visionary who can create breakthrough strategies.

Please notice that you do not see technical job skills or job know-how used in this definition, but you do see personal competencies along with action and results. Look again at what makes up strategic agility, and it is those thoughts. If that is a skill for you, you must get it across during an interview. Breaking down a competency this way gives you the information you need to demonstrate why the competency is a skill of yours.

As one explores his/her background, one is likely to discover that there about 15 to 20 behaviors, habits, and traits, which are used often to get work done. These represent your key, saleable, personal behavioral strengths; strengths that you want your listeners to know about so that when they finish talking with you, they know the real you.

Keep in mind that there are three sides of you, which you need to be able to discuss during an interview. One involves your job skills. The second is job knowledge. These are the easiest to talk about, because you do them every day. The third major area is behavioral competencies; they are difficult to talk about because we do not think about them each day. As was mentioned earlier, ask yourself how often do you sit back and think about thinking, analytical, conceptual and innovative thinking , how often do you consciously think about how you have used your executive intelligence. Take a moment and think about something you accomplished and identify the behavioral competencies which contributed to its success. As has been said, these are used to get work done, and directly impact your "likeability factor." This personal area is the most difficult to talk about, because folks tend not to think constructively while communicating about who they are from a personality viewpoint, and what they use to get work done.

Ask yourself, how often at night do you take time to sit and "think" about what it really took to get a job done that day? Many individuals may have the same job skills as you do, but we are all different when it comes to knowing who we are, and knowing how to present our personal behaviors, habits, and traits. Therefore, communicating these characteristics is a way for you to make yourself stand out in someone's mind.

During the interview, pay close attention to how a person speaks, what he or she is doing while you are talking, and their clothing. These can give you clues to their behavior. Also, the way their office is decorated can offer clues, as well as the types of things that are on the desk. So too can clues be found in how the security people respond to strangers, and even how the reception room is decorated, so observing and interpreting your surroundings is important.

A recent survey of more than 800 managers and hiring professionals concluded that 67% said they would hire an applicant with strong, "demonstrated" personal skills, competencies, habits, or traits, where technical skills were lacking.

Only 9% said they would hire someone who had strong technical skills but weak interpersonal skills. It is interesting that the survey concluded that 93% said technical skills were the easiest to talk about because they are used every day.

Behaviors, thinking, and intelligence are the most difficult to discuss because people do not think about the role of such characteristics in each of their achievements. Remember that your "likeability factor" is based on your knowledge of, and ability to, present/demonstrate behaviors, traits, and habits as attachments to your technical interview answers using your S.H.A.R.E. stories as a conduit. This has been mentioned earlier and is stated again because of the importance of building the likeability factor.

According to another national survey, business owners and corporate executives were asked to rate what they valued most in a new employee. They said dependability/reliability = 35 %; honesty = 27%; good attitude = 19%; and competence = 19%. The results of this survey were clear: Corporate America rates personal competencies, habits, and traits, far more importantly than hard skills. It does not matter what level of employee you are. Personal competencies and intellectual capacity are what you should be selling.

If you think about the word "dependability," you might tempted to conclude that it is weak to sell at high corporate levels. However, if you consider that dependability includes initiation of action on problems, accurate interpretation of a customer's concerns, or providing effective leadership, then it has strength. If you can get these types of thoughts across during an interview, then you are really showing that dependability is one of your key strengths.

The building of your likeability factor is critical. To do this successfully, you must take a skill, such as teamwork, and determine what makes up teamwork. For instance, teamwork takes listening, communicating, participative management, informing, management of individual goals, collaboration, the ability to influence and persuade, the maturity to confront others when needed, and using guidance wisely, just to mention a few characteristics.

So when you say teamwork is a skill and

strength for you, you need to discuss that skill in the terms suggested above. There is an example coming up. When you communicate in this way, you impact your likeability factor. All of the competencies you wish to sell should be broken down in this way, as the components will give you the ammunition to deliver an effective message.

The SHARE structure is critical to your interview success.

h-37

SHARE STRUCTURE

The S.H.A.R.E. structure is critical.

This structure allows your listener to hear what the challenge/opportunity was, how it was assessed, decisions made, actions taken, outcomes/ results achieved, and what personal behaviors/competencies were in use to get the work done. To communicate in an anecdotal fashion like this will take some practice and studying on your part. Use of the S.H.A.R.E. structure is a powerful tool when handled correctly. The S.H.A.R.E structure provides you with the opportunity to have a bullet point mindset and helps to avoid forgetfulness. Let's look through a sample interview answer using the SHARE structure on teamwork:

The Question:

It has been said that one of the best ways to manage people is to teach them to manage themselves. Tell me about a time when you contributed to team's ability to direct itself?

S-situation/problem:

When I joined my last company, I inherited a team that was considered talented and experienced but was seen as not pulling together.

H-hindrance/challenge:

During my experience with a number of challenging teams, I recognized that one of the keys to bring a team together was dealing with goal congruence, which is the overlap between individual goals and group objectives.

A-actions:

My first action was to let the team know the importance of matching individual goals to the overall department objectives. This understanding was accomplished through individual meetings in which I focused on each member's interests and strengths. Then, as a group, I discussed the overall objectives and pointed out how their personal interests and strengths would impact the team. I call this "leader facilitation," because it influenced their thinking. Also, I focused on confronting any negative attitudes that surfaced. Last, and very importantly, I encouraged each member to challenge any of my thoughts or decisions impacting the team. That really brought the team together.

R-results:

Those continuing actions resulted in the team not only meeting the department's goal of increasing sales annually by $1 million, but also gained an additional $335,000. It also has led to early problem solving as the team felt free to come to me on any issue.

E-evaluation:

I have learned to develop a high level of perceptivity in my team activities as it is important for me to recognize verbal and non verbal behavior, which has allowed me to identify potential problems quickly. It also has impact with my customers. Participating with the staff to mange themselves through having the knowledge of personal goals and how these are meet though group activity, is a huge key in bringing the group together. My participative management style consistently has produced effective teams. What was really nice is that other mangers started coming to me to see what I was doing with my team. Does this type of style fit at XYZ?

Competencies Shown:

Participative management, confronting attitudes, communication, listening, early problem solving, shows task and people concern, able to create common goals, all of which resulting in high morale and group commitment to goals and objectives.

Now go back and look at the message that was delivered. You have said that you are successful with teams; you are good at listening; communicating and thinking; you are good at developing pictures of the integration of individual goals with overall goals; you are the type of person who is willing to look at yourself through the eyes of another; you have an open mind for learning, you have said you are perceptive and good with customers; you have said that you resolve problems before they become big; and most times avoid challenges; you recognize opportunities; you get the best out of folks by teaching them to manage themselves by developing the connection of individual goals and department goals; and you bring value to other mangers and to the corporation.

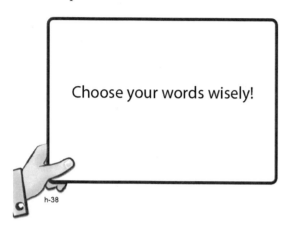

Choose your words wisely!

h-38

Wow! That is a mouth full, and it carries a lot of impact.

Job interviews are often about an individual's cultural fit and can be determined by the language you use, which makes up part of your likeability factor, along with your behaviors. The words you use to present yourself offer a big clue to who you are. "Speech is a mirror of the soul; as a man speaks, so is he." (Publius Syrus).

In addition, many times an interviewee will say things or use words that can open the door to further inquiry, and I have seen these inquiries go in directions that the interviewee would rather not be going. You can control the direction of the interview by controlling your messages through your choice of words as well as the volume of your content! Your S.H.A.R.E. is the structure. Don't open negative doors.

Great interviewing is about preparation

and listening. Regardless of your overall job skills and accomplishments, you cannot give a winning performance and you most likely will not get the offer without reflecting your behaviors during the interview.

It has been quoted that "Culture in a company, is the sum of the beliefs and values that shape the norms of behavior and dictate the way things get done." A company's culture is not based on ideas on how the business should be run, but on how employees interact. A common question of clients involves how to determine a company's culture. You could be the very best fit for a position, from a job skill and knowledge point of view, but if the company's culture does not fit you, your values and beliefs, there is little doubt that you will become unhappy, because you will not be in an atmosphere or in the right fit for you.

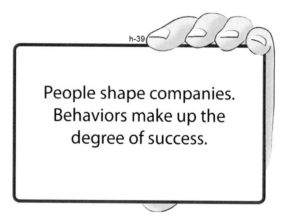

h-39

People shape companies. Behaviors make up the degree of success.

It would be illogical not to seek a situation where we can be in an atmosphere that allows us to perform and be excited about going to work each day. Best fit is as important as the job. This excitement is not only made up of being able to use your job skills, but more importantly the opportunity to use your key behaviors, traits, and habits. Just reading to this point should begin to raise your consciousness of the need to be aware of who you are, and what you use to get work done in terms of your behaviors, traits, habits, and values. It is your behaviors, traits, habits, and values that you must match to the prospective company, the position, and to your boss.

Let's say you are dealing with a company that has the goal of building positive relationships with customers. If that is the case, then you want to see people facilitating that goal. How do you discover that? Think about the questions you will ask that might include: "Give me an example of how customer complaints are handled?" "Describe how or what your sales people do to find ways to satisfy the customer." "What is the level of community involvement of the company and of the sales personnel?" "How would you describe your company's culture?" "Describe the elements that make up your company's culture?" "In terms of an individual's traits and value, what would you like to see in an applicant, or what do you look for in employees?" "Would you discuss the decision-making practices of the company?" "What kind of forum is available for presenting new ideas?" Any of these types of questions could open the door to in-depth discussions about a company's culture.

What do you need in order to get a handle on a prospective company's culture? The hardest thing might be for you to get a handle on yourself in terms of your behaviors, traits, habits, and beliefs. Your knowledge, your own characteristics will drive the questions that you will ask during your interview. Secondly, your research of the prospective company via the Net, annual reports, from recruiters, from your network, sup-

pliers, the Chamber of Commerce, etc., will help you develop a picture of what you will want to determine about a company's culture during the interview. Third, as you go into the interview, observe all things around you.

> What you see or sense about the corporate environment may help you come up with questions, or can open the door to a cultural discussion in the interview.

Also, during the interview, how does the interviewer talk and sound? What level of excitement is that person, or any person you meet, demonstrating? Even the way in which they ask you questions is an indicator: Is the process crisp and sharp? Do they seem to know their company? You would be surprised at how many folks do not know their company's annual report. How they answer your questions is a very big clue: Are they searching for an answer? Are they well informed? Do they make sense? Can they really talk company values and beliefs? Watching their eyes and mannerisms are indicators that can offer clues for you to evaluate. Bottom line, ask yourself if you would like to have dinner with, or be a friend to the person with whom you are speaking.

Cultures are, in large part, an outgrowth of leadership styles and preferences. However, nothing you ask will help unless you know yourself, your beliefs, your habits, and your traits against which someone's answers can be compared. If you cannot see the desired characteristics demonstrated around you during an interview, you might want to ask yourself the questions, "Do I really want to be here?"

From a practical standpoint, as you

prepare for a competency-based interview, you should do the following:

1. Review your resume, word by word. Think about each word and think about the experiences that you would use when asked about any word or phrase in the resume. Also, as one goes into an interview, typically there will be a job description, and that should be examined word for word. Think about what every word means, think about the why of the words, how they relate to you, and how are you going to talk about the words, each of them as they come up in an interview.

2. Develop and attach to each of your S.H.A.R.E. stories the behaviors or traits applied, which will allow you to demonstrate the use of your key behaviors and traits.

3. Make sure you have factored in your personal traits/competencies into your work experiences. A good place to put them is in the Evaluation piece of the S.H.A.R.E. story. If you keep them in a focused area, your interviewer, hopefully, will clearly hear the message.

4. Last but not least, to prepare for an interview one needs to think about ANY possible inquiry and that means "ANY" type of inquiry. Let your imagination run. Think about the work you do, what is required to know and to use, and the skills and knowledge required. Think about why you are good at what you do. Think of your motivators, about how you impact or how you affect the people around you, and about how you build relationships. Once you have a clear picture of all of that, then you are in a good position

to use your behaviors / competencies to sell your likeability factor.

You would be surprised what can happen, and what can be said during the stress of an interview. You should have no fear of the unknown, because an unknown can only exist if you are not prepared, and have not practiced enough, and have not thought about yourself. I am of the opinion that there is no way for you to get into an interview without knowing: • what you will be talking about • what every word on your resume means (or other marketing material) • what makes you tick in terms of behaviors, traits, habits and values • and without having done research about the prospective company and knowing how you are going to discuss the value you bring to that company. There is no such thing as too much research.

One other point: on many resumes, the words manager and leaders are used often. I have received various responses when asking questions about the qualities of managers and leaders that have often caused me to wonder how well an interviewee knew himself or herself. Am I more of a manager or more of a leader? Or am I some of both depending on the situation? Most likely, those of us in the senior corporate setting are probably some of both, and we know when and how to use one or the other.

In a study by Paul Birch in 1999, he revealed that an effective leader creates and sustains competitive advantage though attainment of cost leadership, revenue leadership, time leadership, and market value leadership. A leader is characterized by the fact that they achieve! If leadership is about influencing, you need to know that there is no right way, nor is there only one way to influence others. Absolutely everything is a factor when influencing people. The components are: interpersonal skills, communication, presentation, and assertiveness techniques. I am sure you have heard this, but the saying is, "Managers see the trees, and leaders see the forest."

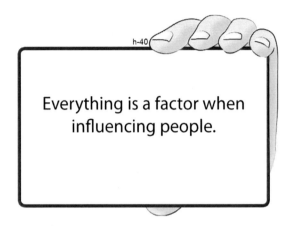

Everything is a factor when influencing people.

In any behavioral interview, or any interview for that matter, keep things specific and simple. Expect to be asked about anything you say orally and in writing. Look at questions and responses as being potentially sequential rather than as standalone inquiries. Realize that responses will be looked at in their total net effect and not only as individual answers. There is an important decision to be made while interviewing, and that is to determine the focus or subject of the question. Clarify each question as needed to be sure what is being sought by the question. You might ask, for example: Your question seems to focus on [specific topic vs. general], is that correct?" Or, I am not sure what you mean by [key word or phrase]; would you clarify that for me?

INTERVIEW ANALYSIS EXAMPLES

Are you ready to test yourself? Below, I've included a few questions and answer analysis statements from a new book that establishes

a measurement rating system we suggest be used by companies to evaluate the behavioral competencies of those being interviewed. It is a simple and easy to use rating system. The actual rating scale is not shown here. This effort is being jointly authored by Ron Venckus and me.

Here is what the other side of the table will be asking you and what they are looking for from you. There are over 50 such behavioral competencies that are identified and analyzed but I thought I would share one or two with you in this book. Your job now is to *form your own answers for each of the questions listed below*. The competency is defined, and then it is followed by questions related to that specific competency, and those are followed by the Interpretative Guide. Do not look at the Interpretative Guide until you have answered the questions. Good Luck!

COMMUNICATIONS:

Ability to present information clearly in variety of business situations with the results of creating a positive influence and persuading others.

COMMUNICATION QUESTIONS:

a. The word communications means different things to different people at different times. I would imagine that at your level, there are situations that occur when it is important that you speak your mind truthfully. Tell me about a specific situation when you had to tell superiors objective facts that they did not want to hear. I would like to know what led up to the discussion, and what the outcome was.

b. Listening is a key element for being an effective communicator. Discuss a specific circumstance that demonstrates how your listening skills had a positive result.

c. How would you rate yourself in public speaking? And if I was sitting in your audience during one of your presentations, what would I see?

d. This job will require you to spend a good deal of time writing. Tell me about your writing experiences that you feel will contribute to your ability to do this job, and describe a specific situation in which your ability to write clearly and succinctly had the desired effect.

e. I am sure you have made many management presentations. If I was watching you, what would I see, and tell me about an incident when you wish you could take back something you said?

INTERPRETIVE GUIDE: Communications

Did the applicant show an ability to present information in difficult and positive situations? Were they positive in their presentation, show a level of comfort in their presentation, express an easy ability to choose the correct words, use clear and articulate language, keep a positive facial expression, and show genuine interest in their approach? Did they show excellent organization of their thoughts, the ability to understand the messages of others, and skill to develop a mutual understanding of other's thoughts? Was leadership shown by talking about being interested in other ideas, and the ability to work with others?

Listening and feedback are critical elements of communication. Was information presented in a clear manner, and was technical information explained properly so it could easily be understood? Did they seem excited about what they were saying? Did they encourage staff to state thoughts? Were they informing in a timely manner? Bottom line is assessing the approach-ability level of the applicant, that they show good listening, rapport building, patience with others, and willingness to spend extra time to learn about others.

ADAPTABILITY:

Ability to readily fit and react to changed circumstances or challenges, maintain effectiveness during changes, and adjust to new work structures, processes, requirements, and cultures.

INTERVIEW QUESTIONS: Adapability

a. Tell me about a situation in which you had to adjust to changes over which you had no control. What were your thoughts, and what behaviors allowed you to handle it effectively?

b. Describe a time when you had to modify your plans at the very start of a task or project following new information. Be specific on what the new information was, and how you had to modify your efforts.

c. As your look at yourself, what changes have you seen in yourself over the years, and what kinds of organizational changes do you find difficult to deal with.

INTERPRETIVE GUIDE: Adapability

Did the applicant show the ability to maintain effectiveness and enthusiasm when faced with major changes, and an ability to adjust to new structures easily? Did the applicant show an open mindedness when dealing with comparing different points of view, and come to appropriate conclusions? Was the applicant able to show a variety of reactions to changed circumstances, seeing problems as opportunities, and thus being open minded? Was going with the flow demonstrated, thus, being resilient and easy going, and cool under pressure, and one who could demonstrate that they could be counted on in adversarial situations, showing resilience? Was the ability shown to not think in fixed patterns? Humans are creatures of habit, and thinking can stay in rigid patterns. Overall, did the applicant demonstrate being able to work in a dynamic environment?

LEADERSHIP:

Ability to influence and persuade the thinking and actions of others towards meeting organizational objectives, along with projecting confidence in difficult situations.

LEADERSHIP QUESTIONS:

a. We are looking for someone who has the ability to persuade and influence our senior management. Discuss a situation in which you were able to cause senior management to re-think a particular decision?

b. Being able to change another person's attitude is both a skill and a responsibility. Tell me about a time when you were successful in this area, what payoffs accrued to you, the other person, and the organization?

c. What do you consider the most challenging aspects of leadership when entering a new situation, and how do you plan to handle them?

d. Describe a situation where you had to deal with a person who was not initially responsive to your guidance.

INTERPRETIVE GUIDE: Leadership

Leadership is a complex subject; however, common leadership factors are the ability to influence, handle disputes, be assertive, focus on the right things, recognize problems early on, persuade people to do tasks that they may not want to do, be looked up to, model key behaviors, challenge the status quo, build a network of followers, and generate loyalty. Was the applicant able to show being effective in motivating others to follow through on commitments towards stated goals? Was there evidence of being able to identify projects that were not progressing well?

Leadership ingredients: intelligence, ambition, understanding, cooperation, initiative, providing a clear vision, can energize change, can motivate people, can work through conflicts, has an open mind, tactfulness, being responsible, positive attitude, insightful judgment, patience, cheerfulness, kindness, integrity, and common sense. Leaders do the right things; Managers do things the right way. Was an impression created of respecting employees? Bottom line, was leadership demonstrating a belief in others and of empowering others, presenting information in a positive and in a negative situation, and articulating a passion for success?

CONCLUSION

Finally, in the interview, be relaxed, be a good listener, and remember that good interviewing involves building a relationship that leads to trust, that leads to disclosures (theirs), that leads to SHARE stories (yours), that builds value, and that leads to a reason for them to buy you as opposed to your competition.

Sources used to structure the interview sections in our new book are: Why Shouldn't We Hire You? The Career Architect; Lominger: Quintessential Careers; Behavioral Technologies; Drake Beam Morin, Behavioral Interviews: American Express, Behavioral Interviews: Intel, Management Group, Behavioral Approach and Interpretation of Behavioral Interviews; Principles of Effective Personal Marketing by Bill Temple who is in charge of the Executive Career Management team at Stewart, Cooper & Coon.

The more prepared you are, the better you communicate.

h-41

Chapter 10
<<< The Power of Words

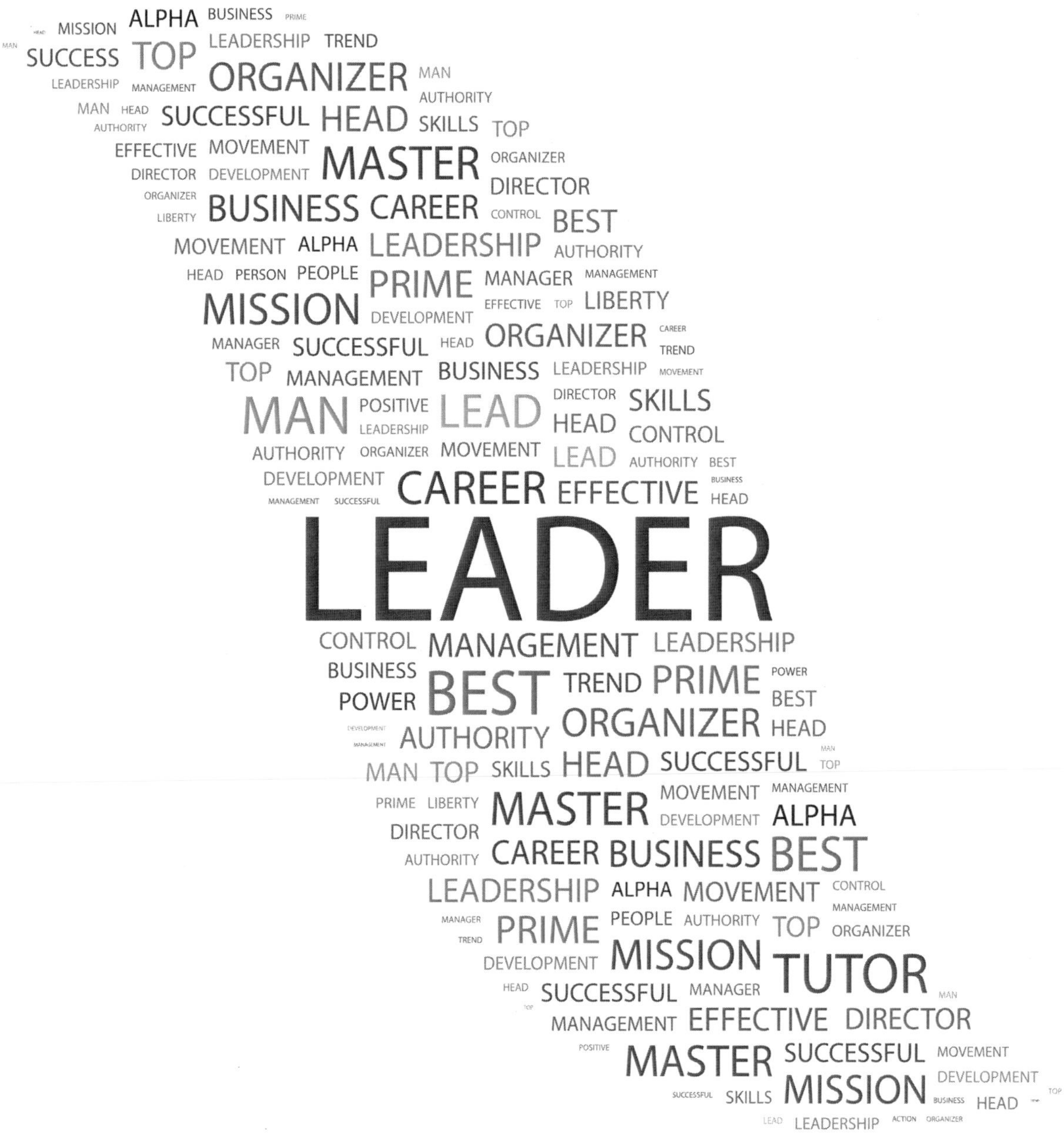

Language impacts how you are perceived, how others react and how you get hired!

Bill Temple

Many years ago my parents-in-law gave me a book: Use the Right Word, by S.I. Hayakawa. In their dedication of the book to me, Mom Wright wrote, "To Bill from Mom and Dad (however, I never felt you needed a book to find 'the right word.')" While that is a wonderful sentiment, I have in any number of occasions in my life, sought for, and failed to find, the "right word" to use to comfort, praise, uplift, inspire, educate, or simply inform others.

Despite my inability to always hit the verbal mark for people, I have come to appreciate how important words are as we try to communicate with others. I realize how a simple shift in how words are used can make a huge difference in gaining the desired results we look for from others.

In the process of landing a job, words have the power to make or break you. Therefore, using the right words becomes critical to your success. In the sections to follow, we are going to explore how interpersonal communication works, how to motivate and help others to assist you in your job search, and how to use some basic communications tools that can improve the outcome of your communication, both in inter-

viewing and in networking communications.

COMMUNICATION THEORY

To understand the impact of language in interpersonal communications, let's first look at how words fit in to communication as a whole.

If you and I are in the same room talking with one another, there are three channels of communication that make up the signal going on between us:

- Content – the data being conveyed, i.e., the words themselves
- Word packaging – the way the words are spoken, i.e., inflection, volume, tone, intensity, etc.
- Non-verbals (body language) – including eye contact, body posture, clothing, location, etc.

These three channels make up 100% of the interpersonal communications signal. If you were to break down the signal into its component parts, what percentage would you apply to the importance of words alone? What percentage to word packaging? And how big a percentage would apply to non-verbals?

After asking this question to thousands of students and clients, the following response ranges are most common:

Content:	20-50%
Packaging:	30-60%
Non-verbals:	20-50%

The actual values, however, are as follows:

Content:	~8%
Packaging:	~30%

Non-verbals: ~60+%

This comes as a big shock to people who love to talk! There are exceptions, of course. People speaking about technical subjects have words that are clearly defined. An Ohm is an Ohm, a Volt is a Volt; bits and bytes are bits and bytes. Words in scientific, technical or other highly specific context areas carry much greater value to the communication because of their degree of specificity; they cannot be defined multiple ways. The other instance in which words have greater relative value is when they are part of a story, because in their delivery, they stimulate memories in the other person that become the non-verbal portion of the communication.

Even though words carry very little weight in the overall value of our communication, they still are important, and not to be taken lightly.

POWER TO COMMUNICATE VALUE

If I tell you about the fast food restaurant that my family visited under the balmy twilight and inspiring sunset of early summer, and about the double cheeseburger, fries and shakes that we all enjoyed, aren't you already picturing the scene in your mind? Yet the restaurant you're picturing is not the one I am picturing, nor the food, nor the family, nor the balmy twilight or the sunset!

Words stimulate responses: sensory (sight, sound, smell, taste, touch) recall from our individual memories, emotional, empathetic or sympathetic responses, fight or flight impulses, "gut feelings," and so on. Each person on the planet, all 7+ billion of them, will image things differently.

How they respond to you, and how they feel about you, and their reaction may be the key to whether you get hired – or not!

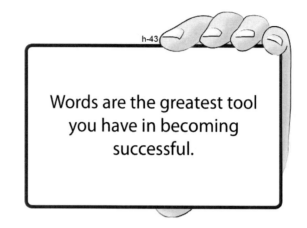

Words are the greatest tool you have in becoming successful.

If I tell you that I am in IT (Information Technology), you might first think of me as a person who can fix your hard drive, or correct a bug in your software. What happens if I tell you that as an IT leader, I "integrate technology into business solutions?" Changes your impression of what I do a great deal, doesn't it? I sound like someone that understands the application of technology to a business environment. I know how to use technology to make better business decisions and drive profitability. I lead others in the carrying out of the process. If the first "impression" was a $100K job, the second impression could be a $150+K job. Quite a shift, based on the use of a few words to describe what I do.

Just as an example, here are some word changes that might make the difference between $100K and $150+K in your pocket:
- Project Management versus
  Complex Program Implementation
- Training and Development versus

  Global Team Development / Deployment

- Budgeting and Forecasting versus Maximizing Financial Performance / ROI

One of the best ways to improve your language skills (word power) is to read job description from the types of positions to which you aspire. Use the words and phrases that most resonate with you in your written and oral communications and you might be very surprised at the results!

POWER TO INFLUENCE

Both in interviews and in the networking process, the words you use will have a major impact on outcomes. There is excellent material in this book about the interviewing process. What I want to address here is how words can dramatically <u>improve the networking process.</u>

Be careful though: you don't want to say ANYTHING that is not defensible by way of example (SHARE® story). If you don't really know what the words mean or have not really used or done what the words suggest, don't use them.

First, here is how most networking conversations start, if not word by word, for sure by intention:

Hi, Bob. How are you doing? Hey, you probably know that I'm looking for a job and I wondered if you know anyone that might have an opening for an IT guy? No? OK. Well, if you hear of anything, let me know, OK? Thanks, Bob!

The chances that Bob might know of a position at that moment are virtually 0%;

the odds that he might actually run across an opening are probably only slightly better. If you were Bob, and you knew that I was coming to you with a question like that, would you be thrilled to see me?

By nature, we like to help people if we have the time, the resources, and the inclination. Rarely have I met people that would not want to help a person in a job search if they could, but the odds are stacked against that help because of the way the request was presented – because of the words used!

Let's say that I come to Bob, and this is my new communication:

Hi, Bob! How are you doing? Say, Bob. I need your advice on something. As you know, I'm a senior-level IT executive with a focus on technology integration, and performance improvement. I put together a target list of companies* chosen because they are in fast changing business environments and my experience in consolidations, mergers and reorganizations is likely to be of value to them at some point. That is my opinion, of course, so I'm trying to generate conversations with people who either work for the industries or companies, or who might know someone that does to determine if my assumptions are correct. I don't want to chase after these targets if I am not going to be a good fit there.

Please understand, Bob, I don't want you finding me a job. I can do that myself. You might, however, come across people with whom I should connect because of their knowledge and experience in these industries, or because they are well connected with people that might. I do not expect them to know of any openings. Their advice and insights might be very valuable, however, in getting me in front of people that do have needs that are not being met.

In the event you think of anyone that I should talk to, would you keep me in mind, and I'll stay in touch with you? [* Target list is a 1-page word document on your letterhead that has 3-5 industry groups, a number of companies listed under each group with not more than 35-50 companies total]

What is that chance Bob will say, "Yes" to this request? Probably close to 100%. First, Bob cannot NOT keep me in mind, as I have provided him with what I call a "baseline" (what I am, where I'm going, and WHY it makes sense).

Second, notice that I did not ask Bob to do anything other than keep me in mind. I asked him if I could stay in touch with him, and why would he say, "No" to that? From that moment on, I have added Bob to my human antenna, his subconscious acting like a little digital recorder, ready to recall me when stimulated by an outside event.

> The subconscious will hang on to this information, even if Bob's cognitive mind "forgets" our conversation 30 minutes later.

The net result is that by changing the words that I used, I made Bob a participant in my search process without his having to do anything other than be himself: enjoy his family, go

to church, play golf, take trips, go to his Lions Club meeting, etc. I have given him the clear understanding that the job is mine to get. I have the football, and I have to score the touchdown. I have to get bruised and battle-worn, not him. He, on the other hand, is free to throw in plays from the sidelines any time, and he might come across people who are also willing to be spectators to the event who, in turn, provide information that will ultimately get me where I want to go. We live in a volunteer country: we like to help; we just need to be in control of when and how.

To follow through on the situation I described, Bob has gone to a meeting of one of the organizations to which he belongs. In the course of a conversation, something said triggers a recall of my name: "Bing!" This is someone Bill should talk to. Out of the blue, there it is! A connection. The problem is that within an hour (or less), Bob has forgotten about me and gone on to other things. How do I get the connection if Bob does not pass it on?

I said that I would stay in touch with Bob, remember? The next week, as a regular part of my communications, I touch base with Bob NOT to ask if he has done anything for me, but to inquire about him, or to let him know how a conversation turned out that he might be interested in, or about a mutual friend I bumped into. Whatever the reasons, it is a "passive" communication in that I am not requiring nor expecting anything back (or if I am, it has nothing to do with my job search). My email shows up in Bob's email and "Bing!" he remembers the connection he wanted to tell me about, and he passes it along to me. If I had not stayed in touch, I might never have received the blessing from Bob's thoughtfulness.

I don't know of any psychology test to back this next statement up. I think you would probably agree from common sense alone:

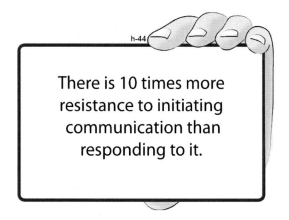

There is 10 times more resistance to initiating communication than responding to it.

If I left it up to Bob, he would have so many other priorities that even with the best of intentions, he may not get his suggestion back to me. But if I show up in his email, all he has to do is reply and send. Done!

Follow up is critical. Not every day; perhaps not every week. But if you do not initiate the "touching base" process, you will miss critical information that could shorten your search dramatically!

COMMUNICATIONS TOOLS: A.I.R.©

We all like to feel important. When someone seeks out our advice, we feel valued, appreciated, and somehow more in control of the communications. One of the most effective communications models is built on that premise. I call it "A.I.R.©" and acronym that stands for Advice, Information, and Referral. While the context here is in job search, you will find this concept applicable to any communication where you are trying to get buy in and help from others.

Advice: We all like to give it. Most of us, however, don't like to ask for it. Yet asking for advice generates some amazing transformations. By making the other person more important than yourself, that person is more likely to SHARE© information that you need to know. By asking for advice, you have become the servant; the other person the master. You are down at the bottom of the hill; they are on the top. From a military perspective, the top of the hill is the most defensible position. When you allow someone to take that role in the conversation, he/she will feel less threatened, and will often, therefore, be more open and communicative. Information, like water, will flow down to you. All you have to do is ask the questions, which reveal little, while the answers you get will reveal a lot!

Information: Your job in preparation for an interview is to know as much as you can before you walk in the door about the company, the position, and the person with whom you will be interviewing. From this information, you will identify your SHARE© stories that can support your ability to meet the present and future needs of the individual and the company.

Once you have the information you need, and you are in the interview, LISTEN! By taking the stance that you are there for Advice, you are making the interviewer's information more important than your own. Your information is only valuable IF it demonstrates how your past experience translates into his or her future. The exchange of information under this model will be more detailed, more substantive, and will lead more easily to an affirmation of your value that leads to an offer.

Referral: Every conversation must lead to an outcome. If you leave the building without a clear sense of what the next should be, you have missed the point of the process. In a job interview situation, the referral is the confirmation that you are still in the game by asking what the next step is. There are two ways to do this:

First, you can use the "positive assumptive" close. You have completed your discussion, you have recapped the key competencies, skills, behaviors that THEY have confirmed that they want, and you end your recap with the statement / question: "I'm very excited about this opportunity. From our discussion, it looks like my background is a great match for the position. What is that next step, and with whom should I stay in

> More powerful is the "reverse close": Same summation, different question: "This looks like a great match of my background to your needs, and I'm very excited about the opportunity. Is there anything, however, that you see that would keep me from moving forward in the process?"

touch?"

The value of this second "close" is that you can often surface issues that can keep you from getting a job; things that might be gross misunderstandings. Here is an example:

Mack interviewed six people on his way to trying to land a consulting position with a major international consulting firm. In every instance, he used the structured interview process that you will be learning in this book. In each of the six interviews he used the positive assumptive close, "Looks like a

great match! What's the next step?" and was referred on to the next person in the process. Then came interview number seven.

The seventh and last interview was with the Managing General Partner who had total authority over whether Mack got hired or not. The interview went exactly as the others had, except that when Mack went to close the interview, as he told me later, it came out more like a reverse close. He said, "It looks like a terrific match. Would you agree?"

Within a split second, Mack knew he was in trouble. The MGP paused and said to Mack, "I think you have terrific qualification, and are really a great guy, Mack, but I need someone with a lot of B2B experience in this position."

Mack nearly fell off his chair. His last 11 years had been spent doing B2B work with AT&T at the most senior levels. The MGP apparently had not read Mack's resume. The MGP assumed that since Mack didn't bring it up, Mack must not have it. Mack assumed that since the MGP did not bring it up, he already knew about Mack's background.

To Mack's credit, he jumped on that misunderstanding immediately and took the MGP through a mini interview covering his AT&T days. After about 15 minutes of further discussion, Mack asked if the MGP had any further misgivings about Mack's B2B experience. The MGP said no, and thanked Mack for the clarification. To lighten the mood, Mack leaned back, looked at the MGP and said with a smile, "I'm almost afraid to ask this question, but is there ANYTHING ELSE that might keep me from this position?"

The MGP said no. Mack is now a consultant with that company!

In the networking process, the A.I.R.© model is a terrific communication strategy. Since there is no job, you want those around you to be positive participants in the process with you. By getting their advice about how things work in their worlds, understanding how their companies/industries function in light of the work you do, and obtaining their thoughts / advice on others with whom you should be communicating (personal referrals, recruiters they might know about, or organizations that might be important to explore), you are building connections that will pay huge dividends both in landing the job and doing the job!

TRIANGLE THEORY (From The Principles of Effective Marketing©)

The concept of "triangulation" in interpersonal communications has multiple applications within the personal marketing arena, as well as in dealing with life in general. Most of us use it on a day-to-day basis without really knowing it, or fully understanding its value.

Triangulation becomes a far more critical element, however, when we are trying to conduct successful Information Meetings and job interviews. The triangulation process allows participants to view their needs and your solutions as unifying elements rather than as obstacles created by a "you have the job, I want the job" attitude that often accompanies a job search.

Do you remember your basic geometry? Below is a straight line. At one end is the employer, at the other end is you, seeking a position represented by the black dot in the middle.

What is the degree of arc between E and Y?

Answer: 180º

You and the employer are at opposites, by definition. Getting an offer can become an intellectual tug-of-war between what you want and what they think they want (which, by the way, may not be what they really need!).

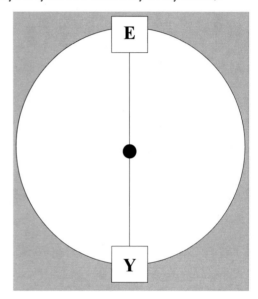

How many degrees are represented by the total of the angles of a triangle?

Right! 180º.

When you make the objective, a job, the third point of the triangle, this means that the sum of the angles between you and the employer

In psychological terms, you and the potential employer are no longer at opposites... you are both focused at the third point in the triangle: their corporate or individual goals and objectives. Therefore, the conversation is no longer about "a job"; it is about how you can help them reach their goals when and if the opportunity arises!

must be less than 180°.

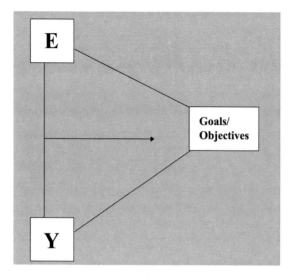

Shifting focus requires an understanding of where you want the listener to be.

h-45

In networking/informational meetings, the **Triangle Theory** is about taking an immediate need – your getting a position – and communicating it as a future objective. By using the disclaimer, **"I do not expect you to have a position that fits with my qualifications",** you take the immediate pressure off of the potential employer. You are conducting an Information Meeting to see where the possibilities lie. You have changed the tone of the interview to, "if you had a position at some point, how might I apply my knowledge and abilities to provide economic value to you, or a company like yours?"

In the case of a job interview, the Triangle Theory, or the use of triangulation, changes the communication from a sales pitch – your **Product** in terms of their position description (i.e., **what** you do and why they should buy it) – to how they do what they do. Would you be interviewing with the company if they did not think you were basically qualified? Probably not. So **what** you do should not be the issue, should it?

Yet that is the nature of most job interviews, and the results are often less than favorable for either side. To help the company make a better decision, and to help identify the best opportunities for you, it behooves you to interview them. Not about the "job," per se, but about **how** the position supports the overall goals and objectives of the hiring manager, the department, the division, and/or the company. To do so requires that you think like a consultant, evaluating the situation in front of you to discover what the **real** issues are so that you can demonstrate from prior experience (SHARE© stories) that you can find the appropriate solutions for those issues.

When you use triangulation, **what** you do becomes a given. It is a part of the **Baseline** that you have provided the potential employer. As a result, the focus shifts from what you do to **how** they do what they do, **who** makes it happen, **when** it will happen, and **where** you can be of greatest value!

In other words, go in to the interview with the attitude **that you already have the job!** Your communication strategy then becomes a question of determining where to start to meet the present and future needs of the employer... and in the process, you are far more likely to demonstrate your value to the hiring managers than your competition.

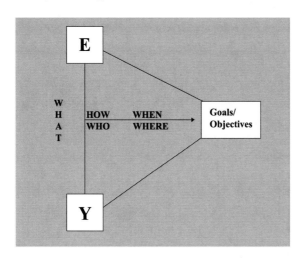

The Triangle Theory is the translation of your past experiences into the employer's future opportunities. To accomplish this you...

■ Create the Baseline,

■ Identify the company's/individual's short-term goals/objectives

■ Bridge the "psychological gap"

■ Follow up

CREATING THE BASELINE

A Baseline consists of two points: first, **what you do** (your 1-minute commercial); second **how what you do fits within the potential employer's business.**

Your **Product** identity should be simple, well focused, to the point, and should incorporate those attributes and functional skills that seem logical for the **Positioning** you are trying to develop with the potential employer. As mentioned above, by creating a Baseline for your con-

versation, **what** you do becomes a "given," and often will not come up again unless you bring it up in the form of a SHARE© story that substantiates your value in terms of a specific set of functions that are important to the potential employer (your "**PE**" for future reference).

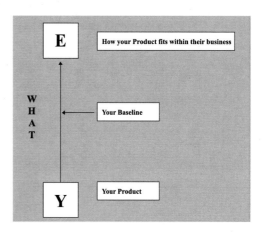

IDENTIFY THE COMPANY'S/ INDIVIDUAL'S SHORT-TERM GOALS/OBJECTIVES

What are the company's goals and objectives? Where does the PE want to be in 6-12 months? (Use the model questions presented earlier, along with more specific questions related

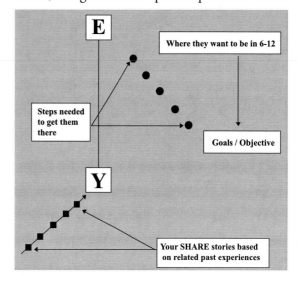

to your functional value, and how such functions are to be used to establish the steps necessary to accomplish the stated objectives.) Based on your preparation you should have a fairly good idea of where they might like to be, and of the steps necessary to get there. These steps **will be the same as you would likely have to take** were you working in the company in a capacity defined by your **Positioning**.

If you understand the steps that will likely be necessary, then you should also be able to identify those SHARE© stories most appropriate for the situation. Not all stories will match up exactly, but your preplanning for the most logical stories will allow you to be a better listener.

When you provide a few well chosen stories, your past experiences seem to fit well with their future requirements. The PE has a greater opportunity to picture you as a part of that future, since in your SHARE© stories you did not dwell on where you did it, when you did it, what your title was, or how much you got paid to do it!

The result is that you seem to be a good fit with the PE's company! There may not be a position yet, but the more you can "Bridge the Gap" between your past and their future, the more you will appear to line up with their situation and the more tangible you will seem to be as a part of their solution!

BRIDGE THE PSYCHOLOGICAL GAP

Each SHARE© story brings you closer... and closer... and closer... to a point where the distance between you and the employer seems to be almost irrelevant! By then it is quite possible that the PE has psychologically "bought" your

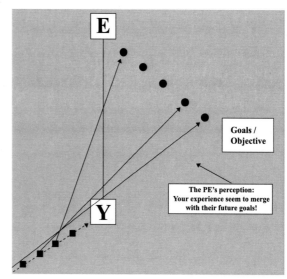

Product (or at least the benefits your **Product** provides). You have changed the situation from **if** he/she would hire you to a question of simply **when!**

One of the ways you might move the "when" a little closer to the present is to introduce your Target List of companies. If the PE has a high level of interest but a position does not currently exist, ask him/her for referrals by presenting your Target List and saying something like:

"I really am interested in working for a company like yours, when and if an opportunity should arise. If it is all right with you, I'd like to stay in touch from time to time to see what might develop.

"In the meantime, I have to continue my search, of course. To help with that process, I have prepared a list of companies and industries that interest me, and where I think my abilities might have a good fit. I wonder if you might take a look and see if any names come to mind of people who either work for one of these companies or within one of these indus-

tries, or, because of their connections might know someone that does.

"I don't expect anyone you suggest be aware of a specific position that might fit with my qualifications, naturally. But you never know... they might know someone that does! Any suggestions?"

In the course of conducting a really positive Information Meeting in which you apply the Triangle Theory, you can build a lot of value. When you then ask for referrals you are using a tactic that is probably the most powerful closing technique known to sales professionals: **The**

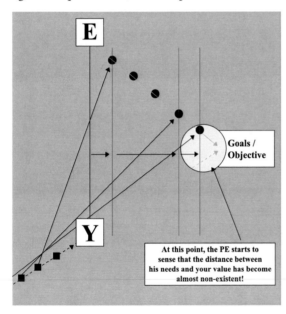

E

Y

Goals / Objective

At this point, the PE starts to sense that the distance between his needs and your value has become almost non-existent!

Takeaway!

You have experienced its use, I'm sure. You find a car you like, but are not quite ready to buy, so the salesperson says, "Sure, take your time... oh, I should let you know that a couple is coming in later today to look at it, and from what I understand, they will probably make an offer. Since it's the only one we have I thought

you should know."

That is a Takeaway. If you have any real desire to buy the car you will be even more motivated to decide now rather than later because you don't want to loose what you have psychologically purchased. The salesperson realizes that after you leave the showroom, the longer you are away from the car the less likely you are to buy.

By asking for referrals you are subtly doing the same thing. The PE would really like to have you, but no position exists. As you start to remove your **Product** from their consideration, their interest level goes up, and sometimes – not all the time – the employer will decide to find a way to hire you, even if no defined position exists. **Warning**: the desire to turn decision into reality is inversely proportionate to the time it takes to do so.

> Ultimately, the ability to get someone to "buy" your product will be the combination of multiple factors, some over which you have no control, some over which you have a lot of control. Words are incredibly important, so use them sparingly, and use them wisely.

IN CLOSING:

In communications there is what is known as a "rhetorical triangle." This triangle is comprised of the sender of the message, the message, and the audience. You are the sender. But you have no value unless you are sending the right message. The message, in turn, is of no consequence unless it is important to the right audience. Every audience you speak to will have different perceptions and expectations of the job you wish to fill. Try to anticipate what would be important to the HR director, or the CEO, or the CIO, or the key stakeholders, or to your future employees, and adjust your communications accordingly. Be perceived as someone who is truly there to serve their needs, to increase their value such that they have a reason to pay you to do it!

Good hunting!

Bill Temple

Chapter 11
<<< Negotiating Strategies
That Work

"Don't Leave Money on The Table"

They want to pay you what they want and not a penny more. You want them to pay you what you think you are worth and not a penny less. The difference is the reality of the situation and how you address this variance determines how successful you will be in negotiating your package increase.

In light of what you know about yourself, the company making the offer, the differences between what you want and what you need and the "ideals" you've described in earlier exercises, you must now evaluate and balance one against another until the offer works or is rejected. They are doing the same thing. Your win-win scenario is achieved by developing a close match that is agreeable to both of you.

> High Stakes Poker – "Know when to hold 'em and know when to fold 'em, know when to walk away and know when to run" … from the Kenny Roger's song, "The Gambler."

h-poker

A consultant I once employed used to tell clients that "negotiating a salary is much like playing high stakes poker. There are good hands and bad hands, just as there are good offers and bad offers. The expert poker player knows how to handle both." This is very true, isn't it?

As you went through your interview process, you collected information of all kinds. Now you should organize this information so you can form a negotiation strategy. The _Potential Package Items_ form found in the Workbook, Unit 4, will assist you in sorting out what is really important to you and what is not. Print several out and have them handy in your portfolio binder to use during your interview process.

Before you begin to negotiate, go through the list and prioritize what you want for yourself. If you have a search partner, they too must go through the list and prioritize what they feel is important. The two lists combined are the backbone of your strategic position.

Exercise 11.1 - Potential Package Items

Each job is different and this will change the importance ranking for your Potential Package Items. Repeat the exercise for each job. www.RAH2010.com

On the Stewart, Cooper & Coon, Inc. (www.stewartcoopercoon.com) website, in the resources section of the sitemap, I have listed a number of research sites, some of which can be used to determine salary and package information. This is important because you want to know going in whether or not your expectations are even in the ballpark. Some companies post these on their sites.

The purpose of this research is to support your SHARE stories so that the prospective employer will feel embarrassed to offer you a salary at the beginning level or lower end of the salary range. Bill Temple says: "Until an offer is made, there is nothing to negotiate; and, just about everything is negotiable!"

SETTING THE SALARY RANGE

At some point, someone has to put a dollar amount on the table. Consequently, when the money question comes up the second time, you should ask if the company has any kind of salary range in mind. If they tell you, great! The sad truth is, that even if you do what I've told you in the preceding paragraphs, there is a better than 50-50 chance you still might have to answer the question about money.

If you are forced into this position, keep these important points in mind:

- The hiring company really doesn't care "what you need." Do not say I _need_ $90,000 or whatever your target salary might be. Rather, answer that, with what you currently know about the job and its responsibilities, you believe that the salary range for the position should be $90,000 to $120,000. Follow up by asking if this is the salary range that the company has in mind.

- Let's assume that the salary range that you have selected is too high. The company has a $80,000 to 95,000 salary range in mind. Because you have attached the salary range only to the position, you can get yourself out of trouble. Start by saying that you want to make sure that you have understood the responsibilities of the job.

  Repeat those responsibilities back to the Hiring Authority. Your hope is that, by hearing the responsibilities repeated, the Hiring Authority would realize that the salary he/she has placed on the position is too low and will meet your salary range.

- On very rare occasions, the salary range that you have selected is too low. A quick

way out of this fix is to say that the dollar figure you gave was base salary, not total compensation.

- The higher the position, the longer the interviewing process and salary negotiations will take. Don't be impatient. The rewards are there for those individuals savvy enough to continually add value to themselves in each interview, and for those who strategically plan each interview.

ACTUAL JOB OFFER

There is really no way to predict when a job offer will be forthcoming. When one does, however, there are certain protocols that should be followed:

No matter what the offer (even if it is the pits), graciously thank the person for thinking enough of you and your skills to want you to join their team.

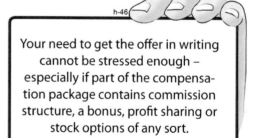

Your need to get the offer in writing cannot be stressed enough – especially if part of the compensation package contains commission structure, a bonus, profit sharing or stock options of any sort.

Ask for the offer in writing. Almost all large companies do this as standard operating procedure. But small companies may not. If the company does not, you should offer to jot down the points of the offer just to make sure that everyone is on the same page. Read your notes to the hiring authority and ask if there is anything you might have overlooked from your discussions.

Provide your notes to the company and get their agreement on all points before proceeding. This means writing a formal letter thanking them and recapping your notes from the meeting and asking for a written response concurring with your notes. If they are not willing to do this then either they are poor managers, crooks, or you are not the candidate of choice and they will likely blow you off anyway.

Make sure that you understand each point of the offer. Make sure you know how the commission, bonus or stock options are to be determined. An excellent way of testing your understanding of the offer is to try and explain each point to another person. If you can't do it, you don't understand it!

Once you have the offer in writing and have a mutual agreement that all the pertinent points are included, ask for a few days to review the offer. There is really no rule of thumb about how long you should consider an offer. Unless there are extenuating circumstances, such as other pending offers, keep it under a week.

ANALYZING A JOB OFFER

There is more to a meaningful job than just money. To make sure that you make a logical decision, take the time to answer the following questions about the new position. After doing so, not only will you know if the company is right for you, but you will also have a clearer picture of how strongly to further negotiate your contract.

Take a look at the preferences you have selected using the exercises throughout this book. As a quick reference point, some of the most common ones are listed below.

Exercise 11.2 - Analyzing a Job Offer

Use this exercise to analyze your job offer.
www.RAH2010.com

Additionally, you will also know what items in a compensation package are truly important.

Various types of surveys have been conducted over the years that may be of interest when you consider job offers. These surveys vary slightly in results but are fairly consistent in their data. These benefits are considered to be the most effective in helping to retain employees:

RANK/BENEFIT

1 Health care

2 401 (k) or 403 (b)

3 Flexible work schedules

4 Training-cost reimbursement

5 Pensions

6 Relocation-cost reimbursement

7 Non-cash recognition programs

8 Casual dress

9 On-site parking

10 Early eligibility for benefits

These are the most common benefits employers offer:

PREFERENCES/BENEFIT

Health care

401 (k) or 403 (b)

On-site parking

Training-cost reimbursement

Casual dress

Relocation cost reimbursement

Non-cash recognition programs

Flexible work schedule

Pensions

Severance packages

Stock options

Outplacement services

Child-care assistance

Elder-care assistance

THE "PERFECT" JOB OFFER

Now, let's assume that after all of your careful analysis, you find that the job is ideal for you and fits all of your objectives. Should you negotiate just for the sake of negotiation? Probably not, except if you believe that the company expects you to make a counter-offer.

Think back over the information you gathered when you were diligently researching the company and the people you met during the interviewing process. Is the company known for being aggressive? Does the company have status within its particular industry? Are the people you met with competitive?

If the answer is "yes" to each of these questions, you should prepare a counter-offer. In this instance, don't be afraid of losing the deal. Pick some of your more expendable "bargaining chips" for use in your counter-offer. For

instance, ask for an additional week of vacation.

These expendable chips are great for this purpose because you really don't care if you lose them. Yet, they are construed as being important by the other side. In other words, using these expendable bargaining chips make you appear to be negotiating.

Now, let's look at an offer given by a company that does not appear to want much negotiation or is in a non-aggressive industry. Do not pull the company out of its comfort zone. They may just decide that you are too much of a firebrand. Save your aggressiveness for the job at hand. In other words, play your counter-offer off the personality of the hiring authority and the aggressiveness of the company or business sector.

THE "NOT SO PERFECT" JOB OFFER

Step 1: Let's face it. Since we do not live in Utopia, chances are the job offer will not be perfect. Rather than slipping into a deep depression, go back to the job analysis form above, and concentrate on all of your "no" answers. Make a list of them in ascending order of importance.

Step 2: Beside each of them write what you ideally want as well as your "walk-away position." Come up with plausible reasons for each. Then decide how many you'd like to "win" in order to accept the position.

Congratulations! You now have your counter-offer and the strategy to be used.

DELIVERING THE COUNTER-OFFER

The ideal way to deliver a counter-offer is face-to-face. Start out by telling the Hiring

Authority, not the HR clerk, that you are pleased that she/he wants you to join his/her team. Follow-up by saying that, from your perspective, you and the company have a deal but there are a couple of points that need adjusting.

Most people are more comfortable starting with the least important counter-offer item on their list. Go for your ideal, present your case and see what happens. You will learn a lot about your future with the company and your potential boss with this first item.

You will see how your new "potential" boss reacts to negotiating with an employee, and you will learn how comfortable you are negotiating with your new boss. If they dig in their heels over a fairly minor issue, and cannot offer a valid reason for holding firm, this is probably not a good fit for either of you.

Don't walk away simply because your new boss hangs tough on the first issue. Try the second counter-offer item on your list, using the same strategy. You might say to her/him: *We might want to come back to this point later, but let's move on to another matter of importance to me.*

This one might go your way. A good rule of thumb is that, if you have failed to renegotiate three items in a row, you have probably reached the limit of how far the job offer can be negotiated.

When you reach this limit, or when you have renegotiated all the points that you can renegotiate, you then have a choice to make regarding accepting the position. Sounds simple enough, especially with all the facts and clues you have gathered from your negotiations.

Frequently, however, the ultimate decision is still a difficult one. When you can't make a decision regarding the acceptance of the job, simply ask yourself if the position being considered will add to or detract from your career objectives and your future resume.

Always plan for the next job or career advancement, and make your decision accordingly.

ACCEPTING A NEW JOB OUT OF DESPERATION

Often economics are the driving force behind accepting a job offer. If this is the case, don't despair. Take the position with the intent of continuing your job search or picking it up again after a pre-established period of time.

Does this sound like a complete lack of loyalty to your new employer? Not really. Continuing to look for a better position does not mean that you are going to skip out on your new boss. It merely means that you are striving to manage your career to the fullest and that, should a new position become available, you will evaluate your current position versus the new one using the *Job Evaluation* Form above or the following form.

Exercise 11.3 Job Advantages and Disadvantages

www.RAH2010.com

FIGURING YOUR TOTAL COMPENSATION

Earlier, you learned the difference between total compensation and base salary. In order to figure your total compensation use this work-sheet

Exercise 11.4 Total Compensation

www.RAH2010.com

In summary, here are some additional tips:

1. How badly does this job need to be filled? Find out what you are worth to the employer and how badly (or not) they need to fill this position with a qualified candidate. This gives you more negotiating power.

2. Be prepared with salary options. Come up with three salary figures for yourself: the low-ball (not on your life) offer, an offer that would make you smile, and one that would make you jump up and down and call all of your friends. Shoot for a salary between your middle figure and your high figure.

3. Remember that the employer has a budget. Understand that most employers have a range in mind (budgeted for the position) and will actually start at the low end of that budget to give themselves some negotiating room. This does not mean they will try to low-ball the position and pay less than they think the position is worth. This is usually not in their best interest since they are looking for qualified candidates.

4. Know your absolute bottom line. Know what your minimum salary range must be to support the life you want to live. Although it is not advisable to bring this up in the interview, you will need to know what your absolute bottom figure is.

5. Employers like negotiating. Remember that potential employers often look on negotiating for salary favorably. It reinforces the idea that they've made the right decision in offering you the position.

It lets them feel confident that, because you can keep your best interests in mind, you can probably look after the best interests of the company as well.

6. Do your comparative salary research. Know the going rate or fair market value for your position. Be prepared to discuss these figures once salary negotiating has come up. Have a salary range in mind. You can find help on salary issues at www.myjobdoctor. com/resources.

7. Understand your geographical area's strengths and weaknesses. When tracking down your worth, make sure you look at similar positions at similar companies in your geographical area. Salary ranges vary dramatically across the nation and even from rural to urban areas.

8. Be prepared to explain your salary history. If your previous salary has been at a high rate, be prepared to freely let the employer know what you have been making in a previous position, (i.e., a written salary history).

9. Anticipate the employer's objections. Anticipate that the employer will have objections for the salary range you want, (e.g., they can't afford more; don't think you're worth more, etc.). Know in advance how you will overcome them.

10. Make your salary discussion a friendly experience. Assume amiability when discussing salary, not conflict or controversy. You

should make the employer feel that you are on the same side and working together to find a compensation package that would satisfy everyone's needs. Anticipate a win-win situation.

11. Remain calm and poised. Once the offer has been made, and appears too low, remain quiet as though you were pondering the offer. This will imply your dissatisfaction with the offer, and the uncomfortable silence may prompt the interviewer to improve the offer on his/her own.

12. Be creative. If the company just can't afford a higher salary, try asking for other benefits: a company car or allowances, bonuses, 3-6 month performance raises, stock options, profit sharing, vacation days, or temporary housing.

13. Be flexible. Consider working fewer hours, on a consulting basis, four days a week.

14. Consider other options and perks. Sometimes companies offer one-time cash bonuses, or "hiring bonuses," to help entice undecided candidates. Try to find out how the company feels about this issue. Don't expect to receive one if you are unemployed because you have less value than if they need to entice you away from a competitor.

15. Count on the future. Remember that, even if you aren't able to increase the salary (because of a fixed company cap - not because these tips weren't helpful), the employer will feel reinforced from your negotiations - as though he got a good deal. This will play better for you when raises are taken into account in the future.

Be prepared to walk away if necessary. You can always walk away from the negotiating table if you just aren't getting into your minimum range.

16. Consider future values. You may be worth more than they can afford today, but not in the near future. Consider adjusting performance bonuses, deferred. Compensation plans, on even equity as a way to recapture some lost "present value."

SUMMARY

Ok, you now have the career you want, in a wonderful location, making the money you feel comfortable with, in possession of benefits satisfactory to meet your present and future needs, and in an industry with future potential for growth. Now you think you are finished. WRONG! Chapter 13, *Post Employment Rules*, identifies important requirements you must heed in your new career.

Potential Package Items   Exercise 11.1

The "Probable Dream"	Must Have	Want To Have	Dream On
Salary			
Profit Sharing			
Benefits			
Medical Plan			
Travel Reimbursed			
Location			
Continuing Education			
Work Environment			
Work Hours			
Vacation			
Moving Expenses			
Stock Options			
Vehicle Allowance			
Pension Plan			
Life Insurance			
Tax Assistance			
Child Care			
Severance Pay			
Athletic Club Membership			
Other			

Analyzing a Job Offer   Exercise 11.2

There is more to a meaningful job than just money. To make sure that you make a logical decision, take the time to answer the following questions about the new position. After doing this, not only will you know if the company is right for you, but you will also have a clearer picture of how strongly to further negotiate your pending contract.

The Job

	Yes	No
1. Will I get along well with my boss?		
2. Will I have more than one boss?		
3. Do I clearly understand the nature of the work?		
4. Do I know specifically what I will be doing?		
5. Are my responsibilities reflected in my job title?		
6. Is the position interesting and challenging?		
7. Can I make final decisions affecting my work?		
8. Will I get along with coworkers?		
9. Will I need more training?		
10. Will the company pay for it?		
11. Will overtime be necessary?		
12. Will travel create problems?		
13. Will I need to relocate?		
14. Will the company pay for relocation?		
15. Is there reasonable job security?		
16. Will I be proud to tell my friends what I do?		

Positioning:

17. Could this job result in a significant promotion?		
18. Will this job broaden / increase my background?		
19. Can this job be a springboard to something better?		
20. Does this job expose me to other opportunities?		
21. Will I be visible to decision-makers?		
22. How frequent are my performance reviews?		

The Company:

23. Is the organization too large / rigid for my personality?		
24. Is the organization too small to offer room for advancement or impressive credentials for a future resume?		
25. Is a written personnel handbook available?		
26. Is the company growing faster than its competitors?		
27. Is the company's financial position healthy?		
28. Is there a high turnover of personnel?		
29. Is the company's location convenient?		
30. Is the commuting time acceptable?		
31. Is the physical setting acceptable?		
32. If I relocate, will I like the lifestyle of the new location?		
33. Does the firm have a reputation for treating its employees fairly?		
34. Is the organization in a growth industry?		

Analyzing a Job Offer

Financial Rewards:

	Yes	No
35. Is the salary competitive?		
36. If not, is it possible to get an early review and increase?		
37. Do I clearly understand the method of payment?		
38. Are raises based on merit, length of service, exams?		
39. Is there health insurance?		
40. Dental insurance?		
41. Vision insurance?		
42. Life insurance?		
43. Retirement plan?		
44. Paid membership dues?		
45. Bonus?		
46. Profit sharing?		
47. Car allowance?		
48. Are there an adequate number of vacation days?		
49. Are there an adequate number of paid holidays?		
50. Are there an adequate number of sick days?		
51. Maternity leave?		
52. Company car?		
53. Clothing allowance?		
54. Expense account?		
55. Employer paid tuition?		
56. Travel to conferences, conventions?		
57. Subscriptions to professional and trade journals?		
58. Stock purchase plan?		

Job Advantages and Disadvantages

Aspect of Job	Advantage	Disadvantage
Salary		
Profit sharing plan		
Benefits		
Medical plan		
Travel required		
Location		
Continuing education		
Work environment		
Job satisfaction		
Work hours		
Vacation		
Moving expenses		
Stock options		
Vehicle allowance		
Pension plan		
Life insurance		
Tax assistance		
Child care		
Severance pay		
Athletic club membership		
Other		

Total Compensation Worksheet

Compensation	Yearly Amount
Base Salary	
Benefits	
Bonuses	
Commissions	
Stock Options	
Anticipated Raises	
Memberships	
Employee Discounts	
Car / Allowances	
Other	
TOTAL COMPENSATION	

Chapter 12
<<< Leveraging New Media

INTRODUCTION

Originally, you had your resume and your professional network. Generally, those were two separate entities: a piece of paper with your professional work history, education and accomplishments, and your network included connections that you have made over time likely alphabetized in a rolodex on your desk. However, times have changed.

Over the course of the last five years, a job search has transformed from handing out your resume to your established network, to demonstrating your abilities to the world, and connecting with individuals that can help you the most. This is all thanks to the recent new media boom. It was first thought that the ever-evolving new media boom was somewhat of an annoyance; clutter in your internet browser that was getting in the way of you accomplishing your goals. However, it rapidly evolved into an industry that in itself has revolutionized the recruiting industry, as well as the job search as a whole.

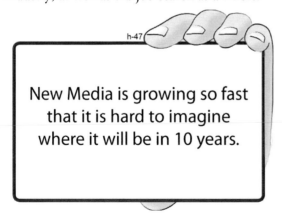

New Media is growing so fast that it is hard to imagine where it will be in 10 years.

New media is a term that encompasses a variety of technology and resources that make up an industry. And, depending on the technology there are right and wrong ways to leverage that technology to your benefit. In this chapter, we will highlight key aspects of the three most powerful social networks, LinkedIn, Facebook and Twitter, and show you how to use each to expand your network and solidify your brand.

LINKED IN

The section on LinkedIn will be the most detailed and lengthy section in this chapter, as it is by far the most powerful online network for working professionals. Currently there are more than 70 million members in 200 countries, including executives from each company on Forbes' Fortune 500 list.

THE BASICS

■ **Achieve 100% profile completeness.** The more complete your profile is, the greater the chance you stand of appearing higher in searches. It is impossible to achieve a complete profile without including a profile photo, filling in information in each section, and receiving three recommendations.

Hi, Fred

➜ Forward your profile to a connection

➜ Edit Contact Settings

➜ Edit Public Profile Settings

➜ Create your profile in another language

100% profile completeness

■ **A LinkedIn profile is not a resume.** It should showcase the full spectrum of your abilities, how you can add value, specialties and areas of expertise.

■ **Your profile must be rich in keywords.** A profile on a social network is not just for the reader, but for the search engine as well.

■ **Three isn't one preferred voice in a profile.** Even leading experts on LinkedIn vary on whether to use resume language or first-person. The goal is to have a consistent feel from section-to-section.

■ **Regularly update your status.** This can enhance both the marketing of your service, as well as let others know you are still around. Your status updates will remain on all of your connections' homepage until cleared out by more recent information. A constant flow of status updates guarantees a constant presence in front of your connections.

■ **Each section of a LinkedIn profile has a character limit.** As this isn't a resume and space is not an issue, use as many of the allotted characters as possible. Again, we want to make your profile rich in content.

■ **Make your profile 100% visible to the public,** regardless of whether or not they are a con-

nection. The whole purpose of LinkedIn is for prospective employers and business professionals to be able to get a look at who you are; with a private profile that won't happen.

■ **Contact Settings:** Make sure you select all contact settings, as this will increase your chances of showing up in a search. If someone searches for an "Expertise Request," and you do not have that option selected, it limits the number of people who are able to view your profile.

HEADLINE (120 character limit)

The goal of the headline section is to define "who" you are. You will reach 120 characters before you know it, so try to include your most valuable information, including current job title, industries or product lines and information that puts you at an advantage.

Example 1:
John Smith

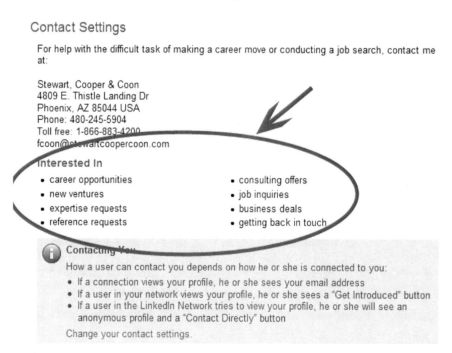

VP of Business Development
Seasoned executive capable of building
and leading teams to maximize company
profitability. (117 characters)

Example 2:
Jane Smith
Chief Marketing Officer
Traditional Media | E-Marketing | Corporate
Branding | Market Penetration | New Product
Launch (117 characters)

SUMMARY (2000 character limit)

The goal of the Summary section of your LinkedIn profile is to strategically position yourself in the reader's eye. This section, as opposed to other sections in the LinkedIn profile, should be written for the reader. Include short paragraphs, bullet points, specific accomplishments and other impressive information.

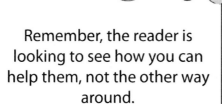

Remember, the reader is looking to see how you can help them, not the other way around.

***Note:** LinkedIn does not enable the user to include symbols such as bullets. Additionally, there is not an automatic spell check feature built into LinkedIn. So, it is best to write all of your profile information in Word, format to your liking, check for spelling, and then copy and paste into your LinkedIn profile.

Below, is a LinkedIn profile for Fred Coon. Use this as an example, including sub-sections shown as indented sections below.

Example (1961 characters):

CONTACT INFO:
www.stewartcoopercoon.com/contactus
• I provide high quality services to clients by precisely matching executives' career experiences, skills and goals with employment marketplace needs.
• At Stewart Cooper & Coon, we help executives achieve their career goals. I have advised thousands of executives on their job search campaigns, providing advice and career-related services to over 75,000 clients, throughout the U.S. and Canada. http://www.stewartcoopercoon.com.
• I am a Licensed Employment Agent, a Nationally Certified Job and Career Transition Coach, a Behavioral Consultant and a Certified DISC Administrator.

AUTHOR
• I authored the national best-selling career book titled, Ready Aim Hired (www.readyaimhired. com).
• I have two more books coming: one on behavioral interviewing and the other on civilian transition for commissioned officers.

PUBLIC SPEAKER
• 2010 Intl. Council of Shopping Centers - Workshop Presenter
• Phoenix - East Valley Career Conference
• 25th ICDC Conference Workshop Presenter
• 21st ICDC Conference Workshop Presenter
• Quoted in Wall Street Journal and other newspapers
• On TV as "The Job Doctor"

I can help you or your company ~
Stewart, Cooper & Coon - four operating divisions;
1. The Executive Placement division
2. The Recruiting division
3. The Outplacement division
4. The Pre-Boarding division
For more information please visit our site at: http://www.stewartcoopercoon.com/index

Why I am here on LinkedIn:
√ TO NETWORK
√ TO MARKET
√ TO RECRUIT
√ TO SET THE STANDARD FOR EXCELL-ENCE in the development of innovative, strategic and tactical career coaching methods to executives and others engaged in job search or career change.
√ TO BUILD a company that is nationally recognized as the best in the career services industry.
√ TO OFFER others resources they may not have exposure to.
√ TO HELP others with the difficult task of making a career move or conducting a job search.

SPECIALTIES (500 character limit)

The Specialties section of your LinkedIn profile is where you can list your areas of expertise that might seem out of place in other sections. This is a section that is written primarily for a keyword search. However, whenever you write you can't forget about the reader. Simply listing a string of words might work for computers, but a reader needs to be engaged. This can be achieved simply by strategically organizing the words in the paragraph, and combining them carefully

with industry-specific achievements or honors.
Example (498 characters):

Business development, corporate development, business manager, acquisition | recruit, recruiter, recruiting, staffing, human resources, HR | career marketing, career management, career coaching, career development, executive resume, resumes, webfolio, web portfolio, web profile | sales, marketing, sales management | consulting | website designer, website development, website management, web marketing strategies

■ Quoted in the The New York Times and The Washington Post as a leading career expert.

EXPERIENCE (1988 character limit per position):

The goal of the Experience section of your LinkedIn profile is to write keyword-rich content. The majority of the content should be accomplishment-focused, but also take into account your roles and responsibilities. In this section, you are not as constricted by a character limit and, like a resume, constricted by space on the page. Use this as an opportunity to showcase roles and responsibilities, as well as specific accomplishments at each job. Below are some tips to maximize this section.

■ Include all positions and companies, as you never know who you might connect with. Additionally, this paints a picture of not only what you have done, but what you are capable of doing. With that said, do you need to include your position as a waiter 25 years ago? If you are now mid-level accountant, the answer is likely no. Use your best judgment.

■ Use a combination of paragraphs and bullet

points, by doing this you can dictate where you want the reader's eyes to go on the page.

EDUCATION

This section is not just for the colleges or universities that you attended. This is a place that you can also include additional credentials, seminars, academic honors, awards and other educational-related qualifications and accomplishments. The more of these you include, the more you showcase your abilities, AND the more you connect with others who have attended the same seminars, trainings, hold the same certifications, etc.

Example:

John Smith

The University of Arizona

BA in English

Member

National Association of Resume Writers / Career Coaches

Member

Career Directors International

RECOMMENDATIONS

It is essential that you receive recommendations through LinkedIn. Not only for the fact that you will not have a complete profile without them, but because it shows that people have first-hand experience with you in a professional setting, and they are putting their reputation on the line by recommending you. Below are some key facts about LinkedIn recommendations.

■ You MUST have at least three recommendations on LinkedIn, otherwise your profile will not be considered "complete." Complete profiles are weighted higher in search

results, so it is essential that you have a complete profile.

■ Strive to attain recommendations from 10%

Recommendations are essential to proper positioning.

h-49

of your connections. LinkedIn experts agree that this is the optimal ratio for this section. So, if you have 90 connections on LinkedIn, you should have a minimum of 9 recommendations.

■ Try to have a recommendation for each position held. This demonstrates a consistent pattern of success from job-to-job.

GROUPS AND ASSOCIATIONS

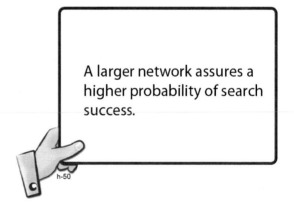

A larger network assures a higher probability of search success.

h-50

This is by far the most crucial section of your LinkedIn profile as it pertains to expanding your network. The more LinkedIn groups you join, the more professionals you are able to directly connect with. When adding a

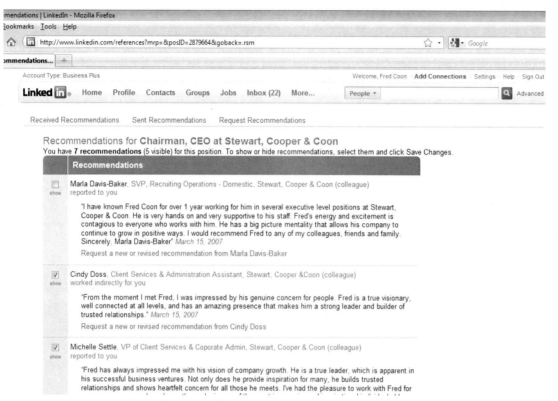

connection, you must indicate how you know that individual. If you share a group with that individual, you are able to use that as the "point-of-contact" and extend a connection request.

■ Join groups that demonstrate professional, industry and personal involvement and contribution.

■ Be ACTIVE in each group that you join. This could mean posting links to interesting and related articles, starting conversations in the discussions forum or introducing yourself to other members in the group.

■ Join as many groups as possible. You are allowed by LinkedIn to be a member of 50 groups at any given time, and with more than 100,000 groups to choose from, maxing out your groups should not be difficult.

Twitter is so important to your marketing strategy.

h-51

HONORS AND AWARDS

This is a section where you can highlight any distinguishing recognition that you have received over the course of your career. This can range from any articles you have published, listing any publications in which you have been quoted or any expertise that you have that wouldn't fit

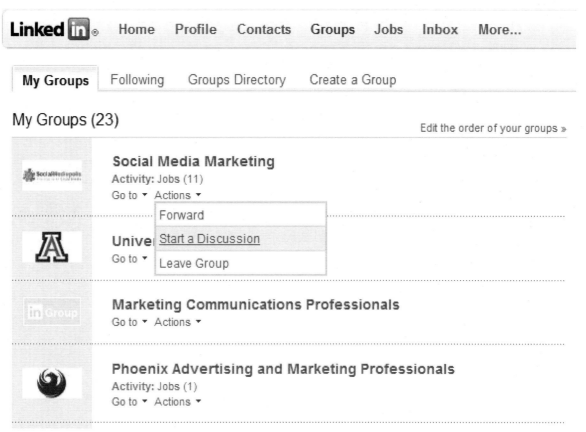

into other sections of your profile. This is just one more area where you can demonstrate how you will add value to an organization, and why someone should join your network.

LinkedIn-related questions (arbita.net)

Q: When building one's social network, should I focus on people who know me well for my first-degree connections?

A: No. If you worked at the same company with someone but not with them, maybe bumped into each other occasionally, they should be made first degree connections. Same for people you went to school with, and maybe had a class in common. You don't have to be buddies with someone to make them first degree. They have something in common (membership in an association, etc.).

First-degree should extend to them as well.

Q: When building one's social network (e.g., on LinkedIn), should my emphasis be to add as many well-connected people as possible, even though I hardly know them and they know nothing about me?

A: Yes and no. It's fine to add the super-connectors who accept connections from anyone (these so-called "Open Networkers" are people who have an icon of a ring of small blue circles next to their name and/or display their email address on their profiles). You can find these people in many ways, such as at TopLinked. If you want to add people in your particular industry, etc., then first reach out with a short get-to-know you communication (not a connection request).

Q: Is professional credibility or having something substantive in common crucial when asking for introductions?

A: Having worked at the same company, attended the same school, member of the same association, or have any other common interest, is sufficient to initiate an introduction. But if you want to be introduced to someone, choose the person who you think knows you best, would be more likely to do you a favor, and/or would give the most meaningful introduction. LinkedIn lets you pick the person among those with a path to your target to forward the introduction through.

Q: After I use LinkedIn's Outlook contacts import, it shows hundreds of names of my contacts using LinkedIn. Should I send a mass-invitation through LinkedIn to connect?

A: No, because if some of those contacts are old and the recipient clicks the "I don't know this person" button on the connection request, you get a strike against you. Certain restrictions on your account begin after five strikes. This can be remedied, but it's safer to send a mass-email via regular email with a link to your profile, requesting they click it and connect or give their permission for you to make the connection.

Q: How can you filter for Open Networkers when searching?

A: On the Advanced Search form, search only open network members (the checkbox beside the circle of colored blue and orange dots).

Q: Once you find someone via social networks that you want to approach for a job, is it best to just send a direct message and see if they will talk with you?

A: Yes, but first try to learn something about the person by looking at their profiles, their past blogposts, etc., much as you would prefer to research your recipient when sending a resume so the cover letter isn't generic. How you approach matters: Be succinct, think about what would intrigue the recipient, and lead with that. Don't indicate a job hunting need in the first communication. Focus on how you can help them (not your job-search), a common point of interest (same industry niche, location, alma mater, etc.) and just a web link leading to more detail about you

LinkedIn Groups

Q: Why should I create a group on LinkedIn?

A: First, it allows you to see the name and email address of everyone who asks to join your group, so you could save that contact information for future outreach. Second, you can help shape the group's focus by inviting people in your area of interest. As the group grows, you create a network that helps you both to find work and to enhance your career and others' even afterwards. You create goodwill that pays you back in unforeseen ways. For many more reasons, see Shally Stackerl's blog. The link is included at the end of this chapter.

Q: How do I create a group on LinkedIn?

A: Go to LinkedIn Groups Directory search and

see if another similar group exists. (If another such group is large and active, you may or may not want to create your own.) Click the Create a Group button and follow the free steps.

Q: What is the most important factor to the success of a group on LinkedIn?

A: The level of participation. If it's not seeded with posts early on, and builds in activity, it will wither and die. So don't just get people to join. Encourage them to post news, updates, jobs, respond to discussions, etc.

Q: Once you find someone via social networks that you want to approach for a job, is it best to just send a direct message and see if they will talk with you?

A: Yes, but first try to learn something about the person by looking at their profiles, their past blogposts, etc., much as you would prefer to research your recipient when sending a resume so the cover letter isn't generic. How you approach matters: Be succinct, think about what would intrigue the recipient, and lead with that. Don't indicate a job hunting need in the first communication. Focus on how you can help them (not your job-search), a common point of interest (same industry niche, location, alma mater, etc.) and just a web link leading to more detail about you.

FACEBOOK

Facebook has gone through substantial changes since its inception in 2004. Originally just for use by college students, it rapidly expanded to include city, state and organizational networks. However, over the past few years, Facebook has exploded into not only the largest social network in the world, but into the driving force behind change in the new media industry,

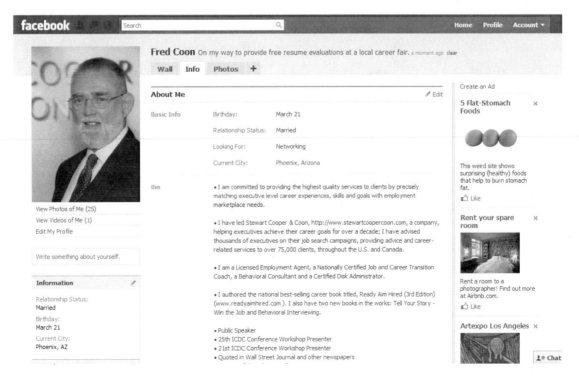

setting the pace for all future improvements and enhancements.

As previously stated, Facebook has undergone considerable changes, primarily around catering to its expanded demographic. As it is no longer just for the age group of 18-25, an entire new string of capabilities are opened up for users, including being able to market yourself, a product, business or even just solidify your network in both a personal and professional sense.

FIND A GOOD MIX

What sets Facebook apart from other social networking sites such as Twitter and LinkedIn is Facebook is a place where you can merge the professional "you" with the personal "you." Unlike LinkedIn, Facebook affords you the opportunity to include multiple photos, a personal bio, favorite quotations and things like interests. This is where you can demonstrate "who" you are, as opposed to what you can do.

Additionally, if you use Facebook solely for personal use, do not accept friend requests from professional contacts. If this occurs, simply reply with a message stating that you manage your professional network on LinkedIn, and include a link to your profile, as well as an invitation to join your professional network.

The key is to find a good mix between personal and professional. A good way to achieve this is to think of a profile that you would be comfortable showing to your boss, and that the same time a profile that your family wouldn't feel "lost" in business terminology.

CONTENT

As with any webpage or social network, you have to be cognizant of what you are putting onto the web. It is commonplace to see or hear of an individual that was turned down for a job due to content that was found on his or her social network. Note: Just because Facebook is

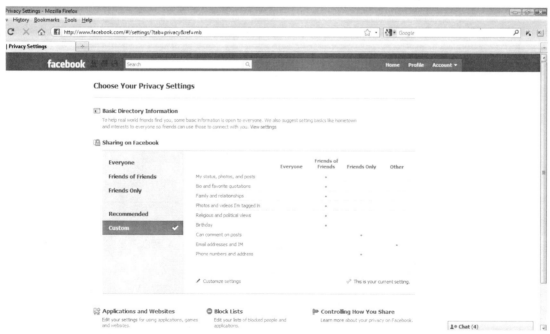

primarily for personal use, does not mean that you can post information that might hinder your job search or reputation.

On Facebook, set your default privacy settings to where only accepted friends can view your personal information. From there, you can edit specifics, including which of your "friends" you want to view all content, and which you would just like to have as a connection.

While it might be fun to connect with old college friends and reminisce about "that one party," it isn't wise to leave those conversations up on your wall for the rest of your connections, and potentially the world to see. Just as you would with any conversation, if there is certain information that you don't want broadcast to a broad audience, hold that conversation via a personal message, sparing you and the other party possible embarrassment, or worse.

PRIVACY

One of the most common gaffes with Facebook is people thinking their profile is private, and only your accepted friends can view its content. This is NOT the case. Facebook has detailed privacy settings that you can adjust to fit your profile. You can have certain people as accepted friends, but make those same individuals only able to view certain, basic information.

GROUPS AND PAGES

Facebook puts a cap of 200 groups that you can join as a member. Unlike LinkedIn, you do not have to be as selective when joining a group, as the majority are fun and recreational. Additionally, Facebook also has pages that you can become a "Fan" of, and those pages will show up in your profile.

You can also create groups and Fan Pages for products, services, events, businesses or even people, and depending on your specific career, this can be a tremendous marketing tactic.

STATUS UPDATES

One of the key features of Facebook is status updates. You can update your status to include anything from where you ate lunch to an informative article that you read. If you are unemployed and searching for a new career, you can use your Facebook status update as a marketing tactic. As with LinkedIn, you should regularly update your status, as it will show up on your connections' News Feed. However, remember to keep your status updates targeted toward your ultimate goal, whether that be finding a new job or establishing yourself as an expert in your field.

TWITTER

As one of the most popular social networks in the world, Twitter offers users the ability to say what is on their mind in quick, 140-character bursts known as "tweets." Twitter has developed quite a divide among the population; some feel that it is childish and could never help in a job search. However, others feel that is one of the most powerful career and marketing tools to hit the market in the last 10 years, and they might be right.

In fact, the majority of users on Twitter don't even realize its full potential. Twitter is a tremendous marketing tool that needs to be strategically used for more than just a job search. Because let's face it, you can only make so many variations of a "looking for a position in the XYZ industry." This section includes a few reasons

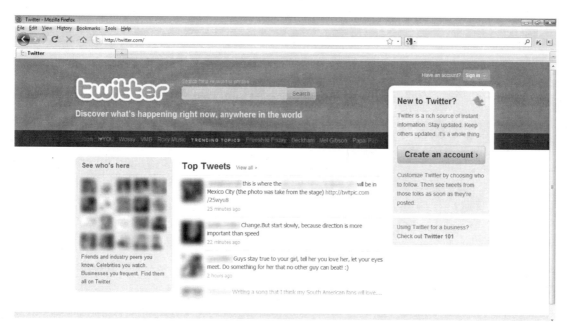

why and how you can use Twitter to solidify a brand.

EXECUTIVE PRESENCE

If you are a company, it is extremely beneficial to have your executives remain "readily available" in the public's eye. So if you are an executive, it makes sense that you will do everything you can to get in front of the public, right? Since it isn't every day that you are front of a camera, Twitter is the perfect opportunity to step in the spotlight.

CONTINUING ENGAGEMENT

If you are like most people, you don't have enough time to keep up with your own personal webpage or blog. You already have to maintain and post regular contributions to your other social networks, and combine that with your work and home life, where will you find the time? That is the good thing about Twitter.

The more you become engaged, expand your network and contribute to your field, the more you are SEEN as an expert. On Twitter, you can follow an unlimited amount of people, and in turn can have an unlimited number of followers.

Since each post, or "tweet", can be only a maximum of 140 characters, it is easy to make regular contributions to your Twitter account, without feeling a nagging need to make constant and lengthy additions to the profile.

BECOME AN EXPERT

The good thing about the new media boom is that you no longer need to be "published" to be seen as an expert in your field.

Therefore, connect with as many industry leaders as you can, and find ways to encourage others to follow you.

ENGAGE RECRUITERS

Social networking has changed the face of recruiting. Recruiters are using sites such as Twitter and LinkedIn more and more often to find the right candidate. If you do a simple internet search, you can find networks for recruiters, as well as lists of the top recruiters on Twitter. Once you have that information, and once your profile is complete, don't hesitate to follow and engage recruiters. That is what sets social networking, and Twitter, apart from other media; it is acceptable to engage others in conversation, especially when it revolves around their line of work.

CREATE YOUR BRAND

Ask 100 Twitter experts about what is the most important part of your Twitter profile and nearly all of them will say creating your brand. More importantly, you need to effectively communicate it. There are many ways to create a brand, but the most effective way of doing so is by bringing consistency throughout all of your social networks. It doesn't do you any good to have one underlying message on your LinkedIn profile and a completely separate message on your Facebook or Twitter profiles.

PROPERLY BUILD YOUR PROFILE

Building a Twitter profile is not nearly as complex or detailed as say a LinkedIn or Facebook profile. However, it still needs to be optimized. Twitter offers a "dual name" feature, where you can list your username, as well as your Twitter name.

Example:
Twitter Name: FredCoonSCC
Username: @FredCoon

Also, make sure you make your Twitter Bio as powerful as possible, by filling it with a high-impact statement. There is a 160 character limit, so make sure you "wow" anyone who reads

it.

CONCLUSION

Hopefully this chapter has given you some insight into how to capitalize on new media. If you can take one thing away from this chapter, other than how to effectively leverage LinkedIn, Facebook and Twitter for to impact your career, it is that you must remain engaged.

Simply optimizing your profiles and joining select networks will not get you where you need to go. You must remain engaged in those networks and be a regular contributor to your industry. Make the right connections, join new social networks and groups, and always keep yourself aware of changes in new media, as you never know how it will benefit your career.

NOTE: Information for this chapter was gathered from research, as well as seminars and blog posts from:

Wendy Enelow
        http://www.wendyenelow.com/
Louise Kursmark
        http://yourbestimpression.com/blog/
Susan Ireland
        http://joblounge.blogspot.com/
Shally Stackerl
        http://aces.arbita.net/blog/shally
        *The Q&A sections of this chapter are attributed directly to Shally's blog.

Chapter 13
<<< Post Employment Rules

"Good Enough Never Is"

If you don't take anything away from this book, pocket the following tidbit of wisdom. *Neglect your references and helpers and you are committing future career suicide.* Do you remember how hard it was to develop this newly found network? Why would you spend all this time, money and energy putting it together and then just dump it?

OK, you have finished all the required tasks and you have your job. Putting this book on your bookshelf is one of the greatest mistakes you will ever make unless you do the things listed below.

This chapter is mainly a quick list of the do's you need to implement for future success. It addresses network obligations, certain performance task guidelines and general tips for career success.

The first order of business is to ensure your long-range future with your new company by clarifying management expectations for your individual performance and implementing the following rules.

1) The very first thing you do before you report to work, or no later than the first month of work in your new job, is to rewrite your resume! The only thing you can't fill out fully is the quantifiable accomplishments section. Please give them excellent performance and constantly update your resume as you climb each step of your career mountain. These you may add each quarter.

2) We are all human. All humans have buyer's remorse. If you turned down a "seemingly great" job offer, you'll probably wish you hadn't done so. If you accepted a "seemingly great" job and now, in retrospect, you start over-analyzing it and wish you hadn't, don't. Indulging yourself in this is wasting two precious luxuries, time and energy. Live with your decision and stay in your new position for at least 3-5 years.

3) Write thank-you and update letters to *everyone* with whom you came into contact during your search within the first month. This is so easy to say, and so boring to do, but it is essential in maintaining your future referral base. Listen people, everyone needs to be told that their efforts, no matter how small, helped someone. Who do you know who doesn't like to feel good about themselves? It's very boring, but do it!

4) Every three or four months, take 25% of your referral and contact list, and write them an update on your progress at your new company that they helped or encouraged you to find. Use the *Ready Aim Hired Activity Tracking System*™ to keep track of your activity in this area. This is one of the critical things you must do to make your next move easier. Not planning on a next move? Ha Ha, whom do you think you're fooling?

5) Before you report to your new job, take one hour and review interview notes, gleaning from them what you are expected to do in your job function.

6) Look at your new boss's answers to your questions about the job, the company, the people and any other relevant information.

7) On the first day at work, go ahead and schedule a meeting with your new manager. Things shift in the hiring process, and you need to know where you stand and what

might have changed. One of my clients reported, and his manager had been assigned to manage another department. Luckily the new manager was nice, but it could have been a disaster.

8) In your meeting with the manager, re-confirm all performance goals, expectations, and time schedules. These change, too. What are your immediate assignments? What is the priority for these duties in the mind of your immediate supervisor or manager?

9) Utilize a schedule and planning system to properly manage your time and efforts.

10) Secure a Palm system, a Franklin or Day-Timer schedule management system and use it!

11) Lay out your priorities from the previous day. Don't lose sight of them by getting bogged down in day-to-day minutia.

12) Figure out who the movers and shakers are, and get to know them. It is amazing what you can find out about your boss and others in the company by listening instead of talking about yourself.

13) Be friendly, courteous, but never familiar. This is a cardinal sin, and it will come back and bite you where you don't want it to.

14) Figure out who the strongest secretary or administrative person is, and get to know them. They will help guide you through the minefields everyone experiences early on in a new position.

15) Figure out the logistics of how the company operates. This means expenses, travel and reimbursement, etc. Those folks in bookkeeping and payables can be a great asset,

pardon the pun, if you simply do things their way from the beginning.

16) At the end of the first, second, fourth, and eighth weeks of employment, schedule a meeting with your manager, and discuss how you are doing, and get feedback from their observations. Their observations are important, but so are those of their peers. Managers do talk to one another, and you will need to secure all relevant input.

17) Remember that control of information is power. Build your power base early on in this company. Whatever you are told, write it down, and keep it in your files. Also, act on the information and improve. Do you remember the phrase, GOOD ENOUGH, NEVER IS?

18) Don't get sloppy and forget to dress well every day.

19) Always be enthusiastic.

20) Volunteer only for projects you know you can tackle with success and ONLY AFTER MANAGING SEVERAL ASSIGNED TASKS TO SUCCESSFUL COMPLETION.

21) Get your numbers. In other words, keep track of the numbers you generate so you'll have them for your new resume.

22) Don't whine, win.

23) Develop an action plan for your career. 1-year, 3-years, 5-years out and review it annually. Please involve your search partner.

24) Don't talk about fellow workers with anyone. Not anytime, NOT EVER! The level of trust your fellow workers hold you in will act as a booster to both your career growth

and promotability.

25) Eat healthy, exercise and appear to be in good physical shape. Appearances count!

26) Before you make any decisions about anything, take quick stock of the upside and the downside of everything you do. People's feelings count, but so do results. You are measured on both.

27) Study the "successful" people in the company and figure out what they did to get that way. Emulate that behavior, and get better results than they did.

28) Keep copies of every piece of written documentation and electronic information that deals with anything relevant to your performance goals or that could impact your performance.

29) ALWAYS GIVE CREDIT TO OTHERS. IN FACT, TRY NOT TO CLAIM ANYTHING FOR YOURSELF. I promise you that the more you practice this, the more credit you will receive.

30) Become an expert on something. Be a company resource. Have others seek out your advice. Advice giving is tantamount to influence and influence is power.

31) Whenever possible, take the initiative. This is one of the best ways to distinguish yourself and your capabilities. Only do so with your manager's approval. Otherwise, you appear to be too interested in his/her job, and you only set yourself up to fail or get canned.

32) Never quit a project. See all projects through to full conclusion.

33) Go back to school and continue to receive re-training, certification and any other form of continuing education that will enhance your credibility and usefulness to the company. Don't make the mistake so many make and put this off until you wind up at age 45 with no MBA, or other advanced degree, and find yourself competing with much younger people who can educationally out-gun you and who will work for less.

34) Join and participate in as many professional organizations as you can. What better source of references and networking. Establish and maintain your network! Do, or die!

There are many other rules I could give you but these will hold you in good stead. Implement them. Don't get lazy and forget them or your full career potential will never be realized and you will look back saying I shoulda, coulda, woulda, hadda, oughta, instead of, I did!

Chapter 14

<<< Thoughts About the 50+ Job Seeker

The following scenarios are a few I have worked through with my clients as a career coach and recruiter. There are too many different situations to list them all, but most people in their 50's, at one time or another in their careers, have fallen into one of these.

There is no one solution or answer to solve the search problems inherent in each scenario. There is no magic wand to wave to re-direct circumstance or correct bad judgment or poor decision-making that might have led to these situations. All you can do is plan better in the future, act upon the plan and do the best you can to push ahead.

There is a new statistic that may give some comfort to those over 50. Up until this year, hiring managers and recruiters were stating that those over 50 were "difficult" employments to achieve. Now, that survey number has moved to age 52. I believe it will continue to rise as baby boomers age.

This means there are more qualified job seekers in the market as competitors. Moreover, companies are continuing to recognize the increasing "retirement age" segment of the population and the "baby boomers" who are returning to the marketplace. As more and more companies recognize the value of the "virtual" worker, this bodes well for those who are fifty.

DO YOU FALL INTO ONE OF THESE SCENARIOS?

Scenario #1: You are 50+, your credentials are a little out of date, and your salary is a little too high for comparable positions in the same market because you've been at your company a long time.

Now, for the first time in a long time, you find yourself either unemployed or about to be, for whatever reason.

Scenario #2: You are 50+, been with the company for a number of years, are rocking along fat, dumb and happy, and someone upstairs makes a decision to move the plant and not move you.

Scenario #3: You are 50+, you've been with the company forever and the scuttlebutt is that company is in financial trouble. There is talk of closing and maybe a filing for bankruptcy. You really don't know what to do.

Scenario #4: At age 40-something, you acted on your hormones, decided to take a career risk, were lured by the potential rewards of a dot.com, self-employment or other venture situation, and then, after being employed there for nearly two years while simultaneously working a 24-7 schedule have learned that the cash burn-rate is too high, and people around you are being laid off. You feel your time might be any day. It now will appear on your resume that you have made a serious tactical error in judgment, reflecting badly on your critical thinking abilities.

Scenario #5: You are somewhere in your mid-life crisis, wondering what to do with the rest of your life, frustrated by your apparent lack of career progress, unhappy about choices you've made and want a change. In some cases the operative word is escape. Either way, you want to make a major move and change careers altogether.

Scenario #6: You are making excellent money, have a good benefits package, are respected in the company, but somewhere in the back of your mind you have this feeling that you need to be doing something else or want more money or something else in life.

Scenario #7: You jumped corporate ship, and decided to be a consultant. Now, your market has dried up for some inexplicable reason, and you find yourself not meeting your own income or career expectations. Your cash flow is poor, and you aren't making enough to satisfy you or those depending upon you for income excellence.

In my role as a certified career coach and recruiter, I have worked with each of these client scenarios, and many others as well.

If you find yourself unemployed, through no fault of your own, and feel unfairly treated, my first recommendation is to allow yourself a week to pout and act foolish, blaming everyone else for your situation.

Sometimes, wallowing in one's own self-pity can feel really good. It's not really healthy, but it happens in life so we might as well recognize it for what it is and deal with it. Any more than two weeks of this self-indulgent, whiny, negative-oriented, self-directed therapy is a waste of precious time.

Don't spend time looking for sympathetic allies. They will smile, pat you on the back and confirm how unjustly and unfairly you've been treated. Remember, they can't hire you. They can only make you feel good, so don't waste your time.

When you spill your guts to them, you eliminate them from the potential referral list, and place yourself in double jeopardy. First, their sympathy will obfuscate reality and subsequently delay implementing your action plan, and second, you will have burned a potentially valuable referral or job acquisition resource.

Don't make the mistake of taking your serence package and going on a vacation. Oh, all right, maybe a week or two in order to clear your head, but more than this will start you on a path of career and economic suicide. You may think you are ok financially. When you run out of money however, because your expenses exceed your cash flow, then you will begin to realize that self-indulgence, in the form of an extended vacation, was foolish.

I can't tell you the number of times my executive clients look at me proudly in the eye and tell me that they have taken the last 2-6 months off to clear their heads and now they are refreshed and ready to go back to work. My follow-on question is always, *how long can you hold out before you run out of savings and available cash resources?* They usually tell me anywhere from 3-6 months.

If they have just left a position supporting a salary of $75,000, and using the U. S. Department of Labor statistics on search timing as a predictor in this regard, they will be in the financial hole 45 days before becoming employed and it will be 60-75 days before they see any money from their first pay check. Do yourself a favor and don't indulge yourself or play too long in la-la land.

There are a few tactics you may employ to deal with the issues of being 50+ and looking for work. Some of these might offend you or seem controversial and, therefore, you may choose to take a more traditional route. Your vanity may not permit you to implement some of them.

1. If you have been recently unemployed, or are about to be, cut your expenses immediately! The search will take longer because of your age. Work at the search job a minimum of 8 and no more than 10 hours each day. It will be a long haul, so don't burn out halfway through and wind up looking bad at your interviews.

2. Don't put more than 15 years experience on your resume. The objective is to get in front of someone, then sell yourself. If you don't get there, no matter how good you are, you won't be afforded that opportunity.

3. Prepare both functional and chronological resumes, or a combination of both.

4. Engage in heavy-duty company research, and determine their corporate makeup in your targeted area. If the workforce is aged 26, then you probably won't have success there. On the other hand, if the workforce at that company is approaching 40+, you are in pretty good shape.

5. Men, please remove all beards and other facial hair, especially if the color is gray. The clean-shaven look will make you appear younger and less set in your ways. Remember, at 50+,

you are seen as older and less flexible. Why contribute further to this myth? Remember, you never get a second chance to make a first impression!

6. Diet and remove the middle age spread, as well. Exercise. It will make you appear more vital and alert. Good for skin tone too.

7. Women, please exercise, remove excess weight, and consult your hairdresser as to how to make yourself look younger and go for it!

8. Color your hair to lessen or remove the gray.

9. Go back to school and enroll in a program of your choice. Whether it is an MBA or other program, this is important. First, you will be seen as flexible and not locked into older ways of doing things. Someone I once knew said, "My going to school makes me look like I'm going someplace." How right he was.

Second, when you negotiate and you are being asked to move to another city, you have one more thing in your negotiation arsenal to work with that is of perceived value.

Either way, move or not, ask them to pay for your education because you will be more valuable to the company when you complete your training or education. This is an excellent tool in your arsenal.

You, at 50+, face added discrimination barriers. But they are not insurmountable. You are employable. It will just take longer, that's all. Therefore you should accept the challenge, implement the RAH System and go to work getting work.

Here is the last client scenario. Hope you like it, and I include it because **there is always hope!** *Scenario # Unknown:* My client was 68 years old, wanted to work because he felt he had many years of valuable service left in him to give to a company, and was told he was too old. Before you get up in arms, no one told him directly he was too old, but he came away from the meetings and interviews feeling this way. It took him three months to land a job, and he is now happily employed at the student services department of a major university, going to work each and every day, and giving it his 110%. They like him too.

Every day, you make decisions that affect your destiny. In this way, you are personally in control of many of your outcomes. So, go out there and make it happen! The Ready Aim Hired System™ will help you get there.

My staff and I are also prepared to help you. Visit us at www..stewartcoopercoon.com.

Activity Tracking System

Target Company Tracking   ATS 1.0

Company Name	Location
Address	Num of Employees
	Daily Commute
Web Address	Annual Sales Units of

Contacts

	Name	Organization	Phone
Address		Position	Cell
		Email	Fax

	Name	Organization	Phone
Address		Position	Cell
		Email	Fax

	Name	Organization	Phone
Address		Position	Cell
		Email	Fax

Contact Record

Date of First Contact [   ]

Date	Who	From/To	

Positions Available

Job Title	Salary Range	Location

Networking Chart

ATS 2.0

1	

101	

102	

103	

2	

104	

105	

106	

3	

107	

108	

109	

4	

110	

111	

112	

5	

113	

114	

115	

401	
402	
403	

404	
405	
406	

407	
408	
409	

410	
411	
412	

413	
414	
415	

416	
417	
418	

419	
420	
421	

422	
423	
424	

425	
426	
427	

428	
429	
430	

431	
432	
433	

434	
435	
436	

437	
438	
439	

440	
441	
442	

443	
444	
445	

Weekly Events   ATS 3.0 | Week |
                                                                     | |
                                                                     | Date |

1 Interviews

	Sun	Mon	Tues	Wed	Thurs	Fri	Sat		Total
Interviews attended									
New interviews scheduled									

2 Recruiters

	Sun	Mon	Tues	Wed	Thurs	Fri	Sat		Total
New recruiters									
Letters/Resumes sent									

3 Network Contacts

	Sun	Mon	Tues	Wed	Thurs	Fri	Sat		Total
New network contacts									
Letters sent									
Phone calls made									

4 Targeted Companies

	Sun	Mon	Tues	Wed	Thurs	Fri	Sat		Total
New companies identified									
Companies researched									
Letters/Resumes sent									

5 Networking Associations

	Sun	Mon	Tues	Wed	Thurs	Fri	Sat		Total
New associations identified									
Meetings Attended									
Letters sent									

Total Events | Total |
                    | |

Week in Review   ATS 4.0

What did you accomplish this week?

Sunday	Thursday
Monday	Friday
Tuesday	Saturday
Wednesday	

Event Tracking

A Network Contacts

	S	M	T	W	T	F	S	Total
New network contacts								
Letters sent								
Phone calls made								

B Targeted Companies

	S	M	T	W	T	F	S	Total
New companies identified								
Companies researched								
Letters/Resumes sent								

C Recruiters

	S	M	T	W	T	F	S	Total
New recruiters								
Letters/Resumes sent								

D Interviews

	S	M	T	W	T	F	S	Total
Interviews attended								
New interviews scheduled								

Your goal is to have 50 events every week.   Total Events

INDEX

INDEX

INDEX

INDEX